Postwar British Politics in Perspective

David Marsh
Jim Buller
Colin Hay
Jim Johnston
Peter Kerr
Stuart McAnulla
Matthew Watson

Polity Press

Copyright © David Marsh, Jim Buller, Colin Hay, Jim Johnston, Peter Kerr, Stuart McAnulla and Matthew Watson 1999

The right of David Marsh, Jim Buller, Colin Hay, Jim Johnston, Peter Kerr, Stuart McAnulla and Matthew Watson to be identified as authors of this work has been asserted in accordance with the Copyright, Designs and Patents Act 1988

First published in 1999 by Polity Press in association with Blackwell Publishers Ltd

Editorial office:
Polity Press
65 Bridge Street
Cambridge CB2 1UR, UK

Marketing and production:
Blackwell Publishers Ltd
108 Cowley Road
Oxford OX4 1JF, UK

Published in the USA by
Blackwell Publishers Inc.
Commerce Place
350 Main Street
Malden, MA 02148, USA

A catalogue record for this book is available from the British Library.

Library of Congress Cataloging-in-Publication Data
Marsh, David, 1946–
   Postwar British politics in perspective / David Marsh . . . [et al.].
      p.   cm.
   Includes bibliographical references and index.
   ISBN 0–7456–2029–9 (alk. paper).—ISBN 0–7456–2030–2 (pbk.   : alk. paper)
   1. Great Britain—Politics and government—1945–   2. World War, 1939–1945—Great Britain—Influence.   I. Title.
DA589.7.M37   1999
320.941′09′045—dc21
                                                              98–47771
                                                                   CIP

Typeset in 10 on 12pt Times Roman
by Wearset, Boldon, Tyne and Wear.
Printed in Great Britain by TJ International, Padstow, Cornwall.

This book is printed on acid-free paper.

Contents

About the Authors

All the authors are members of the Department of Political Science and International Studies at the University of Birmingham.

Jim Buller is a lecturer in politics. He is author of *National Statecraft and European Integration: The Conservative Government 1979–97* (Cassells, 1998). He has also written a number of chapters and articles on British foreign policy and British relations with the European Union.

Colin Hay is a lecturer in politics. He was a visiting fellow in the Department of Political Science at MIT during the academic year 1997–8. He is also a research affiliate at Harvard University. He is the author of *Re-Stating Social and Political Change* (Open University Press, 1996), which was awarded the British Sociological Association's Philip Abrams Memorial Prize, and *Labouring Under False Pretences?* (Manchester University Press, 1999).

Jim Johnston is a researcher in political theory, political economy and postwar British politics. The main focus of his research is Britain's relative economic decline and the extent to which postwar governments failed to address inherent structural problems within the economy. His published work includes a chapter on Marxism and social class and a paper criticizing much of the literature on Britain's economic decline.

Peter Kerr is a researcher in the political history of postwar Britain, with particular reference to the political processes of postwar reconstruction, the postwar consensus and the politics of both the Thatcher and Major governments.

David Marsh is Professor of Politics and Head of Department. He is the author of a wide variety of books and articles, mainly in the fields of British politics and political sociology. He is editor of the *British Journal of Politics and International Relations*.

Stuart McAnulla is researching political change under the Thatcher and Major governments, with a case-study focus on schooling policy. Other research interests include social and political theory, particularly in relation to postmodernism, post-Marxism and critical realism. He has published on political change under the Thatcher and Major governments.

Matthew Watson is researching the political effects of economic ideas, the political discourse and the economic reality of globalization, the political economy of inward investment and the macroeconomic policy of the new Labour government. His publications to date are concentrated within these areas.

Acknowledgements

The authors and publishers gratefully acknowledge permission to reprint copyright material in this book as follows: Table 1.4, reprinted by permission of Oxford University Press. Table 7.1, reprinted by permission of United Nations Publications; the United Nations Conference on Trade and Development is the author of the original material. Office for National Statistics material by permission of the Office for National Statistics, © Crown copyright. The introductory quotation in chapter 3 from 'Winnie-the-Pooh' by A. A. Milne, 1926, reprinted by permission of Methuen Children's Books (a division of Egmont Children's Books).

Introduction

Explaining Change in the Postwar Period

In our view much of the work which attempts to explain political change in the postwar period is superficial and atheoretical. In addition, some of the work which looks at particular parts of this period is ahistorical, failing to put the period under analysis in a proper theoretical perspective. What is more, even the better work too often makes broad generalizations and lacks detail. Our aim here is to remedy some of these deficiencies by presenting a theoretically informed, but empirically grounded, analysis of the whole postwar period.

Of course, it is possible to construct a number of different classifications of the literature on the postwar period. So, for example, we could distinguish between Marxist and non-Marxist accounts, between accounts by historians and those by sociologists or political scientists or between agency-centred and structure-centred accounts. Such distinctions might have heuristic utility, but would lack sophistication. In our view the literature is too diverse for any simple classification. Rather, we identify seven elements which need to be incorporated into any satisfactory account:

- it should have a strong historical perspective, being theoretically informed but empirically grounded;
- it needs a sophisticated, rather than a simplistic, conception of change;
- it should recognize the importance of political, economic and ideological factors in any explanation of change, rather than exclusively emphasizing one of them;
- it needs to be underpinned by a stated and developed epistemological position;

- it must utilize a dialectical approach to structure and agency, rather than giving priority to either;
- it must acknowledge that the relationship between the material and the ideational is crucial and, again, dialectical;
- it must recognize that any explanation has to take account of the inter- national as well as the domestic context within which change occurs.

Our aim in this chapter is to establish the importance of these questions while indicating the weakness of most existing accounts in addressing them. We will not offer definitive answers to any of these questions; indeed, given our epistemological position, that is impossible. However, we contend that by addressing them directly we are moving the debate forward. More specifically, the distinctiveness of our own account will begin to emerge in the context of this review.

A strong historical perspective: theoretically informed, but empirically grounded

Much of the literature which looks at particular parts of the postwar period lacks a sophisticated historical dimension. At the same time, a lot of it is atheoretical or, perhaps more accurately, operates with an implicit, rather than an explicit, theoretical position. So, a number of accounts (Barnett 1986; Kavanagh 1990) effectively tell a story of the postwar period; the material is not located and interpreted within a stated theoretical framework. What is more, the interpretation of the past is often shaped by present political concerns which are not made explicit. Our own analysis is also politically informed, but we are clear about the epistemological and theoretical position which underpins our approach. Finally, some accounts make heroic generalizations which are insufficiently grounded in empirical work. The literature on the postwar consensus provides clear examples of these three weaknesses.

Too much detail: where's the theory?

The postwar consensus literature is diverse and is dealt with at much greater length in chapter 3. However, much of the work by historians, while detailed, lacks a developed, or at least explicit, theoretical posi- tion. So, the postwar consensus is not located within a general theory of political change and both descriptions and explanations of it are *ad hoc*. In this way, for example, there is no agreement as to who shared in the consensus, with different authors identifying party supporters, White- hall bureaucrats, the leaders of the two political parties, or a political elite which included not only party leaders and senior bureaucrats, but also the leaders of the major incorporated interest groups. Similarly, there is no agreement as to when the consensus ended, with different authors suggesting seven dates: 1960, 1964, 1967, 1970, 1973, 1975 and 1979.

Reinterpreting the past in terms of the present

At the same time, historians' interest in the postwar consensus has fluctuated in a way which has been influenced more by political events than by theoretical concerns. While the concept had something in common with 'Butskellism', a word invented by *The Economist* in February 1954 to highlight the policy convergence between the two major parties, it is normally Paul Addison's *The Road to 1945*, published in 1975, which is credited with the origin of this particular term. Ironically, just as Addison was coining the term, interest in the idea of continuity and consensus declined, particularly among political scientists. Indeed, in the late 1970s a number of authors (see especially Finer 1975; also Brittan 1975; King 1975) were obsessed with the ideas that the two-party system, far from being a pillar of the postwar consensus, was a major cause of Britain's relative economic decline. Here, the emphasis was upon both the ideological differences between the two major parties and the view that, in order to appeal to the electorate in a competitive two-party system, parties had to offer distinctive policies. Overall, the argument was that the British system produced adversarial politics; policies were constantly changing and this meant that industry had to operate within an uncertain, constantly changing, environment.

This is not the place to assess this argument. However, the key point is clear. This analysis is almost diametrically opposed to the postwar consensus analysis. One analysis stresses continuity and consensus, while the other emphasizes discontinuity and dissensus. Yet, they purport to describe the same period. Even more significantly, in the period immediately prior to 1979 the adversarial politics argument, particularly if it is related to the broader argument of over-governance (see Brittan 1975; King 1975), had more resonance for many, if not most, political scientists, if not political historians.

More importantly, as Seldon argues:

The consensus debate was little visited in the academic literature for some years after the mid-1970s. The arrival of Mrs Thatcher as Prime Minister, and her seeming attack on many aspects of the post-war

consensus, altered that. Dennis Kavanagh was the first to give the debate
its new high profile airing. (Seldon 1994a: 502)

In fact, Kavanagh's first piece on the postwar consensus was published
in 1985. He, along with others, emphasized that Mrs Thatcher was
transforming the features of the consensus, an interpretation that
seemed to be validated by Mrs Thatcher's own claims. As a result, there
was renewed discussion of the postwar consensus, but the vast bulk of
the conclusions drawn about this era have been made in the light of the
Thatcher period. As Kerr (1995) puts it, 'our assumptions about both
Thatcherism and the pre-1979 era have, to a large extent, been mutually
constructed'.

There are two key problems with this analysis. First, as Pimlott
(1988) points out, we are in danger of reading history backwards. It is
the view of the present, rather than any broader theoretical perspective,
which drives the interpretation of the past of many historians and political scientists. Second, as Tiratsoo contends: 'the result ... is a situation
where ideological distortion distilled from prejudice and hindsight all
too often masquerades as real [*sic*] historical analysis' (1991: 1). He goes
on to add: 'Re-assessments of the past have, of course, been especially
prevalent on the political Right, since a key belief amongst Thatcherites
has been that a decisive break with the alleged post-war consensus
founded by Attlee is vital for Britain's future' (1991: 6).

Too much heroic generalization

Until recently, much of the work on the postwar consensus, particularly,
although not exclusively, among political scientists, has dealt in heroic
generalization rather than detailed analysis. Many of the assertions in
the literature are not based upon primary research but rather report
other secondary sources. As Marlow (1995) points out, in post-
modernist terms, the literature on the consensus suffers from 'intertextuality'; the concept becomes defined through its repetitive use within a
variety of texts. Thus, Marlow argues that the idea of consensus has
achieved its legitimacy via a process of sustained use by a large number
of authors rather than as a result of any sustained empirical investigation.

In fact, more detailed analysis throws doubt on the idea of consensus. As Pimlott (1998: 12) puts it: 'consensus is a mirage, an illusion that
rapidly fades the closer one gets to it'. Seldon develops this point, in
part as a criticism of political scientists:

consensus might appear to have existed ... when looked at from a very broad perspective. But when viewed from close to the ground, or the documents (the archives), the reality was very different. To an extent, the difference typifies the different approaches of historians, who tend to see trees, and political scientists who prefer to see the whole wood. (1994a: 503)

In large part, this is because political scientists, like Kavanagh, use the PWC as a way of illuminating the present not the past; they want to be able to sketch a broad, but relatively clear and simple picture, against which to compare the present. Detailed analysis would present a more accurate, if almost inevitably less clear, picture.

Overall, we need detailed empirical analysis, but we must acknowledge that it is our theoretical position which shapes our definition of the problem (for example, who was involved in the postwar consensus and when it ended), our choice of empirical material and our interpretation of it.

Of course, there are many types of theory and we need to make clear how we approach our theoretical task. Our aim is not to produce a parsimonious explanatory / predictive model of the sort beloved by rational choice theorists. There is much to commend such an approach – we are certainly in favour of parsimony if it is not bought at the price of explanatory power, However, rational choice theory (or, indeed, behaviouralism more broadly) relies on simplifying assumptions which tend to exclude precisely the question of change which is our central concern. Indeed, rational choice models, like the neo-classical economics on which they are based, assume equilibrium. It is unsurprising, then, that they are of limited utility when it comes to explaining crisis, change or disequilibrium. Change, or at least the processes of change, are very complex; in order to understand them adequately, our assumptions must be suitably complex and realistic. Unfortunately, this reduces the utility of theoretical modelling. Hence, in our analysis, the role of theory is very different from that adopted by rational choice theorists. We are not attempting to construct a model, to make predictions or to generate and test hypotheses. Rather, in our view, theory informs enquiry, suggests questions, and problematizes taken-for-granted assumptions. In that sense, this book is a reflection of our conception of critical political enquiry.

A multidimensional approach

It is common when attempting to explain political change to focus on economic, political or ideological factors. More specifically, many authors stress the importance of one set of explanatory variables and downplay the role of others. A brief consideration of the literatures on economic decline, dealt with at more length in chapter 2, and Thatcherism, considered in more detail in chapter 8, will amply illustrate this point.

Of course, there are almost as many explanations of Britain's economic decline as there are people writing about it. Nevertheless, these explanations do tend to give priority to one set of explanatory variables, either economic or political or ideological, and downplay, while not ignoring, the importance of the others.

The explanations which stress economic factors take one of two forms. Authors broadly located in the Marxist tradition suggest that Britain was the weakest of the developed capitalist states, partly because of the international orientation of its financial sector and the concomitant weakness of links between banking and industrial capital, and partly because its union movement was more successful in defending employees' interests than its counterparts elsewhere. As a result, domestic investment, productivity and growth were too low, while wages, inflation and outward investment were too high. The New Right explanation is also strongly economistic and, indeed, shares some common ground with the Marxist position; although, of course, their policy recommendations are diametrically opposed. New Right authors also stress low productivity and growth and high wages and inflation. However, while the Marxists see these developments as an inevitable result of capitalism, New Right theorists believe that the constraints which exist on the effective operation of the market are the culprits. So, to such theorists, too much government intervention, and the resulting high levels of public expenditure, and too powerful trade unions, granted too many rights by a weak state, acted as crucial constraints on the operation of the market.

The political explanations also take one of two forms, although they are related. First, some New Right authors argue that the social democratic consensus, with its commitment to high levels of state expenditure, a developed welfare state and strong trade-union rights, led to increased state intervention in the market on which it acted as a major constraint. Second, many suggested that the political system itself was a major cause of decline. They argued that the competitive two-party system encouraged adversarial politics. This had two consequences. The parties competed for votes by offering more programmes to the voters and more programmes meant more government expenditure. At the same time, in order to distinguish themselves, each opposition party rejected the policy proposals of the government and tended to reverse them when in government. This led to policy discontinuity and failed to provide a stable political environment within which business could operate and flourish.

Authors such as Weiner (1981) argue that Britain's relative economic decline could be explained in terms of the country's peculiar political culture; essentially, an explanation which stresses ideological factors. It is argued that the culture of the British ruling elite never accepted, let alone adopted, the values of the industrial bourgeoisie; that Britain retained an anti-industrial political culture. In this view, the values of the British aristocracy were dominant in the political elite and this was reflected in the international orientation of British capitalism, the weak links between industrial and banking capital, and the related dominance of financial interests, and the elitist education system, with key jobs in the political class dominated by public school and Oxbridge-educated men. This dominance stifled investment in domestic industry, encouraged many of the best brains to go into the City and the professions rather than industry and meant that those who took the political decisions were isolated from the world of industry, let alone the world inhabited by the majority.

Similarly, in the literature on Thatcherism, many authors overemphasize one set of explanatory variables, usually the personality and style of Mrs Thatcher, New Right ideology or the search for political and electoral advantage, less often economic crisis; these are unidimensional explanations (see Marsh 1995).

The largest number of unidimensional explanations of Thatcherism emphasize the importance of Mrs Thatcher's personality or political style (see Riddell 1983; Young and Sloman 1986; Finer 1987: 140; Kavanagh 1987: 248–9; Minogue and Biddiss 1987; Jenkins 1988; King 1988: 57). The argument here is obviously that politics changed because of the intervention of Mrs Thatcher – a woman with strong decisive opinions who was willing, and able, to force change on often reluctant colleagues. Thus, to authors who emphasize the political causes of Thatcherism, the key aspect of the political context was a widespread belief that Britain in the postwar period, and particularly in the late 1970s, had suffered from over-government and weak government. This provided the political space into which Mrs Thatcher, herself a strong, decisive personality, expanded. However, a number of these authors argue that it was New Right thinking which provided the sense of direction, the route-map which the strong decisive leader followed (see Kavanagh 1987: 11; Beynon 1989: 170–1). Here, political and ideological explanations are linked.

While most authors who stress the importance of political factors pay particular attention to the role of Mrs Thatcher, there is also considerable emphasis on the electoral imperative which it is argued pushed the Conservatives into a break with the postwar consensus (see, for example, Krieger 1986; Crewe 1988). However, Jim Bulpitt (1986) offers the most interesting version of this position and the most politicist explanation of Thatcherism. Bulpitt argues that parties are most concerned to win elections, and, in order to do so, they search for a successful statecraft based upon effective part management, a winning electoral strategy, predominance in elite debate about political problems, and a governing competence, especially concerning policy implementation (ibid.: 21–2). Bulpitt does not find a great deal of consistency in terms of ideology, ideas or policies in the 1979–83 Thatcher government. He does see a search for 'a governing competence, through a reconstruction of ... traditional central autonomy' (ibid.: 34). For example, the great virtue of monetarism was that it could be presented as economic theory but used as a policy framework which enabled certain decisions to be taken out of politics and which gave politicians autonomy from other groups (ibid.: 32–3). More crudely, monetarism meant no incomes policy and no deals with unions. 'Arm's length, anti-corporatist government' gave the centre a degree of autonomy (ibid.: 33). In this view, then, the policy style of Mrs Thatcher, and at least some of the policies pursued by her government (perhaps particularly industrial relations policy), were designed to cultivate an image of governing competence in order to win elections.

As indicated, some authors who develop political explanations of Thatcherism still emphasize the importance of New Right ideology as the glue which held Thatcherism together. However, other authors see Thatcherite changes as more directly driven by a commitment to New Right thinking, So, for example, Joel Wolfe (1991) suggests that the conversion of key opinion-formers to support for a neo-liberal ideology provided the motive for institutional and policy change, particularly, although not exclusively, in the area of privatization. However, Wolfe overemphasizes the coherence of Thatcherite policies and, particularly, fails to examine the relationship between privatization policy, the deepening economic crisis and the political and electoral judgements of the Conservative government.

In essence, most economic explanations view Thatcherism as a response to economic crisis. The majority of this material is Marxist and offers a strong determinist explanation of Thatcherism and Thatcherite policies; Thatcherism existed to serve the interests of the dominant section of capital – that is, the City and large transnational companies (see Nairn 1981; Atkins 1986). In the vein, Coates (1989) sees industrial relations policy as a key element in the government's response to a deepening economic crisis. In this view, the crisis of capitalism, given the fundamental incompatibility of the interests of capital and labour, led to the collapse of corporatist strategies, the pursuit of market solutions and, in particular, the attack on trade unions. To Coates (ibid.: 118), New Right ideology, and its attack on trade unions as a crucial constraint on the operation of the market, was a toll used by a government intent on shifting the balance between class forces in the interests of capital.

Of course, many authors acknowledge the importance of more than one set of factors. However, most of these analyses are additive, not integrated. So, for example, New Right theorists examining economic decline often link the economic and political explanations, arguing that a key reason for too much state intervention in the economy was the persistence of the postwar social democratic consensus. Similarly, as we saw, a number of explanations of Thatcherism link the political role of Mrs Thatcher with the influence of the rise of New Right ideology. Here, there is little attempt to examine the articulation between the explanatory variables. Of course, there are some more integrated explanations. Of these, the most impressive is Andrew Gamble's (1988) more nuanced interpretation of Thatcherism, which, while essentially politicist, acknowledges both that economic crisis provided the context in which Thatcherism emerged and that New Right ideology was a key tool used in the Thatcherite project. Nevertheless, there is generally little attempt to integrate these different factors and most explanations are partial, in both senses of the word. Any attempt to explain change in the postwar period must acknowledge the importance of the three sets of factors and consider the articulation between them.

A sophisticated conception of change

Much of the literature on the postwar period operates with a simplistic notion of change. Some authors emphasize transformation. So, it is common, for example, to see 1945 itself as marking a watershed. In this view, the Attlee government is seen as fundamentally transforming the contours of the economy, with the introduction of nationalization, the growth of the state, welfare provision and civil society and with more rights for workers. Similarly, many authors see 1979 as another turning point. Here, Thatcherism is seen as rejecting the postwar consensus established by the Attlee government and instead emphasizing the market and privatization, cuts in welfare provision as part of broader cuts in public expenditure and a reduction in worker and, especially, trade-union rights.

In contrast, other authors take issue with these arguments and play down transformation. So, some authors contend that the Keynesian welfare state, which is most often seen as the great radical achievement of the Attlee government, was not particularly Keynesian, redistributive or social democratic (see Miliband 1970; Coates 1980; Tomlinson 1981; 1984; Rollings 1988; Newton 1991; Taylor, I. 1991). Similarly, a number of authors have questioned the transformative character of the Thatcher years, suggesting that some of the changes predated 1979, involved as much rhetoric as reality and were nothing like as radical when implemented as when proposed (see especially Marsh and Rhodes 1992, 1995).

In effect, the main purpose of this latter literature is to question orthodox accounts, often because the authors are wary of the way in which this literature has been used to underpin the current dominant view that there is no alternative to the market, lower public expenditure, a curtailed welfare state and reduced workers' rights. However, while it is useful to question orthodoxies, a full analysis requires a more sophisticated treatment of stability and change.

Actually, three separate points need to be made here. First, it is clear that there are degrees of change; the absence of transformation does not mean that important things have not changed. It is important not to write off the notion that the election of Attlee and Thatcher marked significant discontinuities in the postwar years, just because a number of authors have overemphasized the change by talking of transformation.

Second, the question of the amount of change over time needs to be separated from the question of when change occurred. This point is most easily made by a consideration of the literature on Thatcherism. Most people agree that many features of the economic, political and social world are different in 1997 than they were in 1979; indeed, it would be perverse not to do so. However, there is considerable difference between those who think this change was evolutionary and those who think the evolution was punctuated; that is, that there were key events which marked a major leap forward in the evolutionary process. These positions are reflected among the authors of this volume. Kerr, McAnulla and Marsh have argued that the radicalization of Thatcherism occurred in the third term of the Thatcher government and in the Major years. Here, the emphasis is on the fact that the eighteen years the Conservatives had in power gave them ample opportunity to engage in policy change, much of which was informed by a process of trial and error. Hay, in contrast, contends that the 'Winter of Discontent' marked a crisis point which transformed a lot of the values held by the political classes. It led to a questioning of the role of the unions, the proper relationship between the state and interest groups, and the relationship between state and market. This provided the space for the Thatcherite project. We cannot adjudicate between these positions here; indeed, this is not a question this book will resolve. The key point, however, is that it is a question that must be raised and it is a much more sophisticated question about change than that normally raised in the literature.

Third, we need to ask: change in what? Most authors are in danger of talking past one another. So, if we again take the literature on Thatcherism as illustrative, we can see that while Marsh and Rhodes (1992) and, to an extent, Kerr, McAnulla and Marsh (1997) are discussing change in Thatcherite policies, Hay, following Hall and others, is mainly concerned with change at the ideational level. Of course, this raises questions as to the relationship between the material and the ideational, which we shall return to later. Here, we merely wish to make three related points: there can be more or less change at the policy or ideational level; change may occur at different times at the different levels; and the relationship between the two is not simple and unidirectional.

Let's question positivism

Most of the literature on the postwar period does not operate with a stated epistemological position – that is, with a position on the status of knowledge. This is a major problem because an epistemological position is not optional, it is inevitable; it is not like a pullover, more like a skin. Indeed, although most authors do not acknowledge their epistemological position, they operate with an implicit one. In a way, this leads to the worst of all worlds, as analysts operate with a position which they do not acknowledge and which they cannot understand or defend. In our view, it is essential that authors render explicit their implicit epistemological positions, and that is our intention here.

Much of the literature is implicitly positivist. The core of positivism is fairly straightforward:

- the world exists independently of our knowledge of it – in this, positivism is at odds with relativism and at one with realism;
- the social scientist can establish regular relationships between social phenomena, using theory to generate hypotheses which can be tested, and falsified, by direct observation;
- unlike the realist, for the positivist there are no deep structures which cannot be observed;
- positivism also assumes that there is no dichotomy between appearance and reality; that the world is real and not meditated by our senses or socially constructed.

The positivism in much of the literature is reflected in two main ways. First, most authors adopt a positivist methodology, So, they attempt to falsify (or give support to the idea of) the existence of the postwar consensus, or of the Thatcherite transformation of this supposed consensus, by examining direct empirical evidence. For example, in testing the consensus argument, a positivist would, amongst other things, look at the level of agreement about policies between members of the political elite in the 1940s, 1950s and 1960s. Similarly, in looking at the Thatcherite transformation argument, the positivist might look at the extent of change in policies in the post-1979 period. The point is that, to the positivist, the extent of the postwar consensus or Thatcherite transformation can only be assessed in terms of analysing such direct evidence. The positivist would not accept an argument that consensus or transformation could occur at a deeper structural level or that relationships between those deep structures and political outcomes may not all be directly observable. Second, most of the literature emphasizes agency in its explanation of outcomes; so, for example, a great deal of emphasis is put on the role of Mrs Thatcher when accounting for the rise of Thatcherism. We will return to this issue at more length in the next section. Here, the main point is that this emphasis on agency, which is more directly observable, rather than structure, which is less directly observable, is generally underpinned by positivist methodology.

As against positivism, in this book we wish to argue both that structures, although not always directly observable, have an influence on outcomes and that the world is socially constructed, to the extent that ideational factors, which are constrained but not determined by the material world, have a crucial effect on outcomes. To make this point clearer, we need to look briefly at the other major epistemological positions, first relativism, which we acknowledge the force of, but ultimately reject, and then realism, which is the position we adopt.

Like positivism, the core of relativism is fairly straightforward:

- unlike the positivist or the realist, the relativist's world does not exist independently of our knowledge of it;
- as such, the world is socially, or discursively, constructed, a view that, with significant differences, it shares with realism but which is totally at odds with positivism;
- unlike the positivist or the realist, there is no extra-discursive social sphere, no 'real' social world beyond discourse;
- this means that social phenomena do not exist independently of our interpretation of them and it is this interpretation / understanding of them which affects outcomes;

- for this reason, it is the interpretation of these social phenomena which is crucial;
- however, meanings can only be established and understood within discourses;
- objective analysis is therefore impossible – knowledge is discursively laden.

This view is thus diametrically opposed to positivism. It denies the possibility of objective social science, or objective historical analysis, and privileges discourse. So, from this view, for example, Thatcherism was a discourse (see Hall 1979; Laclau and Mouffe 1985; Howarth 1995). Its features could only be interpreted from within that discourse. Thus, to Hall, Thatcherism cannot be viewed as a response to economic crisis or the political interests of the ruling class. Rather, we need to 'examine how economic crisis and political processes are discursively constructed and "lived out" ideologically and discursively by people in society' (Howarth 1995: 125). This involves, for example, establishing how two, seemingly contradictory, sets of ideas, the 'strong state' and the 'free economy', were fused into one discourse: Thatcherism. The strength of this position is that it acknowledges the importance of discursive construction, emphasizing that ideas, or, in the terminology used here, a hegemonic discourse, affects political outcomes. However, in our view, its weakness is its failure to recognize that there are limits to the possibility of discursive construction, or rather, more accurately, that while any discursive construction is possible, some are unlikely to have resonance because they run counter to material realities – we wish to hold on to the idea that there is a real, material world out there which is independent of our knowledge of it. However, that real world is mediated by our discursive construction of it and those discursive constructions, or what we choose to call the ideational level, have real material effects.

This means that we are realists; more specifically, critical realists. The core of realism is as follows:

- realists, like positivists and against relativists, argue that the world exists independently of our knowledge of it;
- to the realist, unlike the positivist, there are deep structures which cannot be directly observed;
- realists, unlike relativists but like positivists, argue that there is necessity in the world – objects / structures do have causal powers, so we can make casual statements;
- while social phenomena exist independently of our interpretation, or discursive construction, of them, nevertheless that discursive construction affects outcomes;
- for this reason, structures do not determine outcomes, rather they constrain

and facilitate; social science involves the study of reflexive agents who are capable of constructing, deconstructing and reconstructing structures.

Our view, then, is that the discursive construction of real phenomena has a crucial effect on political outcomes, but that the nature of the real phenomena constrains and / or facilitates that construction. So, if we take the putative phenomenon of globalization as an example, and it is one that has become increasingly important in British politics over the past two decades, we can see both that there are real processes going on and also that it is the discursive construction of those processes that has shaped policy. There has been an increase in the internationalization of trade and the flexibility of capital and there has been a globalization of American culture and an increase in the ease of global communication and the role of the global media. Of course, there are significant arguments about the extent of that globalization, but there is little doubt that some has occurred. At the same time, however, the way that globalization impacts upon national policy-making is mediated by its discursive construction by economists, the business community and politicians particularly. In the British case, for example, as we shall see at more length in chapter 6, the extent of globalization, using the usual economic measures, is not as great as the dominant rhetoric about globalization suggests. Yet it is rhetoric, rather than the reality, that has shaped government economic policy over the last decade.

The epistemological position one utilizes underpins most aspects of one's work. In this case it certainly affects the approach to the next two issues: the views taken on the relationship between structure and agency and the relationship between the material and the ideational. Nevertheless, both issues are sufficiently important to receive brief attention.

Beyond structure and agency

The structure / agency debate is one of the most crucial within social science. However, there is a tendency throughout the social sciences for authors to favour structural or agency explanations. The literature on British postwar politics reflects this tendency. Again, the literature on Thatcherism amply illustrates the point. So, a large amount of material explains change in this period to a large extent in terms of the role of Mrs Thatcher. She was a strong, decisive leader with a definite ideological position and some strongly held policy preferences. As such, she broke the mould of British politics, moving Britain away from the postwar consensus towards a market-dominated economy, less state intervention and more self-reliance. In a sense, this view was well summed up in the two epithets beloved of Mrs Thatcher and many analysts, particularly in her first two terms: The Lady's Not for Turning and There Is No Alternative. In contrast, other analysts give priority to structural factors. For example, many argue that Thatcherism was a response to economic crisis; that the move towards privatization and the market represented an attempt to restore capitalist profitability after the failure of Keynesianism and corporatist policies.

This is not the place to analyse such contentions, which are dealt with in more depth in chapter 8. However, such explanations suffer from the fact that they take a simplistic approach to the relationship between structure and agency. As we suggested earlier, our own position follows naturally from our epistemological position, In our view, the relationship between structure and agency is dialectical. Agents are, in a sense, 'bearers' of structural positions, but they interpret those structures. At the same time, structures are not unchanging; they change in part because of the strategic decisions of the agents operating within the structure. Certainly, outcomes cannot be explained solely by reference to structures; they are the result of the actions of strategically calculating agents. However, those agents are located within a political and broader social-structure context. Significantly, agents do not control that structured context. At the same time, they do interpret that context and it is as mediated through that interpretation that the structural context affects the strategic calculation of the actors.

This dialectical view has significant implications for the interpretation of the postwar period; it argues against partiality in both senses of the word. First, it emphasizes that any analysis must consider change over a considerable period of time, as a dialectical approach necessitates a longitudinal analysis; it cannot take a partial snapshot of one brief period. So, any analysis of Thatcherism which fails to trace how it emerged over time cannot assess the interaction between structural factors, such as the nature of economic relations, and agency factors, for example the role of Mrs Thatcher. Second it emphasizes that we need to examine the interaction between economic, political and ideological factors, which returns us to a point made earlier: we cannot undertake a partial or unidimensional analysis.

Don't neglect the ideational

There are approaches to the postwar period which emphasize material factors, while others stress ideational factors. The relative economic decline literature amply illustrates this point. As we saw earlier, a number of authors see decline as an inevitable result of capitalist crisis;

of the tendency for the rate of profit to fall under capitalism. Here, the material relations lead to decline and are not affected by any ideational representation of that crisis. In contrast, others see decline as a response to the peculiarities of the British culture; the cultural construction of the British elite involved, among other things, a devaluing of the competitive ethic which affected economic performance. Of course, some other authors would see the effect of the two sets of factors as additive; that is, decline resulted from a combination of material and ideational factors. In contrast, we would see outcomes as a result of an interactive, or again dialectical, relationship between the two. The material world does have an effect, but it is mediated through the ideational construction and both that ideational construction and the outcome affect the material world. So, there may be an economic crisis, which we can establish by reference to broadly agreed economic indicators. However, such a crisis only has an affect on economic policy to the extent that it is perceived as being a crisis by key political and economic actors and in a way that reflects the nature of that discursive construction. What is more, that discursive construction will have an influence on the crisis, as measured by these indicators. For example, investors may disappear as the result of a decline in business confidence. In addition, the decisions taken by economic policy-makers will probably also affect the crisis. Overall, then, the outcome reflects the ideational construction of the material and that outcome, in turn, affects the material level, which is then discursively constructed, etc., etc.

Don't forget the international dimension

Rose argues: 'The tradition of writing about British ... politics is to assert uniqueness through *false particularisation*. Every institution, individual and event is described with nominal differences implying the absence of generic qualities' (1991: 450). This is a problem with a great deal of the literature under discussion here. Again, the Thatcherism literature is typical. A considerable number of authors subscribe to the 'Thatcher exceptionalism thesis' (for a review of the literature which accepts the thesis, see Douglas 1989). The argument is that Mrs Thatcher represented a break with the past, she was exceptional in national and international terms and she was the main reason for change. We have already dealt with the first point, although it is worth mentioning that this view offers another strong reason why we need to look at the postwar period as a whole, otherwise any claim that the

Thatcher period represented a major break with the past cannot be sustained. The second point is rather different. Many authors claim that Britain post-1979 was different without introducing any comparative analysis. More specifically, they do not establish that there was a Thatcher effect, that the reason for any changes which occurred in Britain post-1979 was the election of Mrs Thatcher as a strong decisive leader with a clear agenda. In order to do this one would ideally need a systematic inter-country comparison. Such a comparison would immediately throw doubts on the exceptionalism thesis. So, to take just one example, the most radical anti-trade-union legislation introduced in the 1980s in Europe was not in Britain but in Spain, which had a socialist government; it might be argued that both were driven in the same direction by a desire to attract mobile multi-national companies. At a minimum, one needs to examine how international factors impinged upon British policy-makers and the extent to which these international pressures produced similar outcomes in different states. We do not undertake a systematic comparative analysis here because we do not have the space or the knowledge. However, we do acknowledge the importance of these international factors and recognize that they interact with national factors in complex ways. In particular, we examine the effects of the European Union in chapter 5 and of globalization in chapter 6.

Conclusion

We have outlined the key theoretical issues and positions which underpin this book. More specifically, in this book we shall:

- utilize a strong historical perspective which is theoretically informed but empirically grounded;
- utilize a sophisticated, rather than a simplistic, conception of change – our aim is to adopt an evolutionary approach to change, but to remain agnostic on the extent to which this evolution is punctuated;
- recognize the importance of a multidimensional approach, acknowledging the important role of political, economic and ideological factors in any explanation of change, and develop an analysis which integrates these explanations rather than seeing them merely as additive;
- underpin our analysis with a critical realist epistemological position;
- utilize a dialectical approach to structure and agency rather than giving priority to either;
- acknowledge that the relationship between the material and the ideational is crucial and, again, dialectical;

- recognize that any explanation has both to take account of the international and the domestic context within which change occurs and to focus on the interaction between them.

The structure of the book

In order to focus on these issues and questions, this book is divided into two parts. Part I examines key themes and part II looks at key narratives of British postwar political development. In chapter 1, Hay focuses upon the question of continuity and discontinuity in the postwar period, emphasizing the uneven nature of political change over this time frame. Here, the focus is upon the process of change itself. In chapter 2, Johnston critically assesses accounts of Britain's relative economic decline, stressing the need for an explanation which moves beyond either cultural or economic determinism. He argues that much of the existing literature on this period is characterized by a tendency towards structuralism, consequently downplaying the significance of political actors. In line with the core claims of this volume, he advances a more dialectical understanding of the relationship between political actors and the structured contexts in which they found themselves over this period. In chapter 3, Kerr examines the literature on the so-called postwar consensus and suggests that much of it is atheoretical and ahistorical. He proposes that we reject the notion of consensus for a more nuanced and evolutionary conception of convergence and divergence over the postwar years. In chapter 4, Hay turns to the role which crisis has played in postwar British political development. He rethinks the notion of crisis itself, highlighting the significance of narratives of crisis for the process of political development. This is illustrated with respect to the widely identified crisis of the British state and economy in the mid- to late 1970s. The final two chapters in this section are concerned with the processes through which external factors have helped (as, indeed, they continue to help) to condition domestic politics. In chapter 5, Buller explores Britain's relations with the European Union, offering a reading which emphasizes questions of 'statecraft' and the difficulties of maintaining sovereignty in an era of growing interdependence. Watson concludes this section with an analysis of the impact of globalization upon the domestic political economy. He focuses in particular on globalization as both a material economic tendency and also a discursive-political project, concentrating specifically on the dialectical relationship between ideas held about globalization and the very processes such ideas purport to describe.

In part II, the focus shifts from key conceptual and theoretical issues involved in the analysis of postwar British political development to the key narratives used to account for and explain change during this period. Our focus on the Attlee years, the Thatcher administration and the post-Thatcher period by no means exhausts all possible interpretations of the crucial moments in the political history of postwar Britain. It reflects instead the principal concerns of the existing literature and the central periods of controversy. The Attlee years, covered by Johnson in chapter 7, and the Thatcher period, covered by Kerr and Marsh in chapter 8, are chosen because they are most widely identified within existing accounts as moments of radical and fairly rapid change. Given that focus of this book is upon explaining change, a detailed consideration of these periods is clearly essential. The final substantive chapter by McAnulla then turns to the most recent, post-Thatcher period. He argues that the radicalism of the Major and Blair governments is often downplayed since both tend to be compared to an exaggerated reading of the transformative character of the Thatcher governments. Instead, he offers an alternative perspective, sensitive both to material and ideational factors, which stresses the radicalization of the Thatcherite agenda under Major. He concludes by assessing the likely trajectory of the British state and economy under a Blair administration.

Part I

Key Themes of Postwar British Political Development

1

Continuity and Discontinuity in British Political Development

> All social reality is pure dynamics, a flow of change of various speed, intensity, rhythm and tempo.
>
> Sztompka 1993: 9

There are few questions more controversial and fundamental to the political analysis of postwar Britain than the extent, pace and timing of political change in this period. Do the structures, practices, conventions and the institutional contours of the 'political' in postwar Britain exhibit clear and distinctive characteristics that set them apart from other national capitalisms and / or other periods of political development? Has this institutional and behavioural architecture remained essentially static and unchanging throughout the postwar period, or has it been the subject of significant change? Can the change that has occurred best be characterized as evolution – of iterative or incremental adaptation – or as transformation – of periods of relative stasis punctuated periodically by ruptural moments of institutional destruction and creation? These are the concerns of this book and the focus of this chapter.

Arguably, the notion of 'change' is one of the most basic and funda- mental concepts of political analysis. For if politics is above all con- cerned with power (its distribution, exercise and consequences) and power is above all about the ability or capacity 'to make a difference' (the ability to shape or transform the context in which actors find them- selves),[1] then politics and political analysis are essentially concerned with change – with those who get to shape it, with the strategies they deploy in so doing, with its intended and unintended consequences, with its timing, pace and duration. Yet despite this, political scientists have given remarkably little attention to the interrogation, interpretation, evaluation and analysis of political change (or for that matter to the political consequences of social, cultural and economic change).

This omission, we suggest, reflects a persistent failure (with few, rare exceptions) to elucidate or to reflect theoretically on the mechanisms and processes of social and political change and an associated failure to develop a conceptual and theoretical armoury adequate to deal with the complexity of such phenomena. For despite the disarming simplicity of the question of change, even a brief reflection on the issues it raises reveals a minefield of conceptual, theoretical and analytical difficulties. This makes the analysis and interpretation of political change one of the more complex tasks that political scientists set themselves.

As we shall see, it is much easier to assume that the political structures, institutions, codes, conventions and norms that we can readily identify and detail exhibit some regularity over time than it is to describe or explain their reproduction and transformation. Sadly, the temptation to do precisely that has led many political scientists to conceive of their enterprise (whether explicitly or more often implicitly) as one of 'mapping' an essentially static terrain. The temptation is perhaps an understandable one, made all the more irresistible by the considerable purchase of positivist (and more broadly empiricist) tendencies within political science wherever this assumption is valid (or is held to be so). For it is in systems characterized by rapid change that the (simplifying) assumptions used to generate scientific models, propositions and testable hypotheses about the social and political environment are revealed to be most problematic. The most basic assumption of the natural sciences – arguably the assumption that makes most if not all natural science possible (and a very good assumption at that) – is that the rules of the game do not change with time. The laws of physics (or at least macro-physics), for instance, can be assumed to pertain in all situations – past, present or future. Each time an apple falls, its motion can be accounted for adequately (given a few starting conditions) by the application of Newtonian physics. Moreover, that just such an apple fell in just such a way to land on Newton's head can be assumed to have changed not the 'natural' and trans-historical laws of physics but only our understanding of them.[2] Natural scientists 'never have to deal with the effects of their understandings on the very rules of the game that form the subject matter of those understandings' (Hay 1997b: 8).

Sadly for those who study them, neither assumption is valid for social and political systems. The rules of social and political life (in so far as they can be identified) are themselves subject to constant reproduction, renewal and transformation (whether evolutionary or revolutionary) – they are, one might suggest, culturally, spatially and historically specific. This is simply not the case for the laws of gravity,[3] which can be assumed to be universal. Furthermore, in what Anthony Giddens rather cryptically refers to as the 'double hermeneutic', the ideas that we hold about the social and political world (whether as theorists, commentators or merely as social subjects) are part of that world and may profoundly shape it (Giddens 1984: 374). Quite simply, the nature of the 'economic' and indeed the 'political' is different after Keynes (however much his ideas may have been distorted and misinterpreted) in a way that the 'physical' and the 'natural' are not after Newton or Einstein (see, for instance, Hall, P. A. 1989; Rueschemeyer and Skocpol 1996). This raises an issue crucial for much of what is to follow, namely, the role of ideas in recasting the parameters of what is politically possible and economically feasible, and hence in mediating complex social and political change.

If this serves to highlight the limits of the extent to which the social and political sciences can usefully be modelled upon the natural sciences (which, after all, don't have to deal with active subjects continually recasting the very context in which they find themselves), then it is important to note that it merely scratches the surface of the iceberg that is the problem of change within political analysis. In the sections that follow, we delve a little deeper to reveal some of the conceptual, theoretical and analytical issues that we must grapple with if we are to assess, evaluate and above all explain the extent and timing of social and political change in postwar Britain.

Continuity, discontinuity, change and stability

It is perhaps appropriate to begin by introducing two key conceptual distinctions frequently deployed within the analysis of institutional change yet all too often conflated: that between change and stability, or dynamism and stasis, on the one hand, and that between continuity and discontinuity on the other. It is certainly tempting to use these conceptual pairings interchangeably (and in doing so to confuse them), but this temptation must be resisted if analytical precision is to be maintained.

Since the former is the more general we will deal with it first. To do so requires that we consider what it is that we mean when we refer to change. Like many frequently used and taken-for-granted lay concepts, 'change' is difficult to define. We all know it when we see or experience it and, since we do, we do not spend very much time worrying about its definition. For current purposes, change implies a contrast between states or moments of a common system, institution, relationship or entity – a difference between the structuring of relations *then* and the structuring of relations *now,* or more generally between the structuring of relations at t_n and the structuring of relations at t_{n+1}. Yet, as Hermann Strasser and Susan Randall note, in order to identify change, 'the unit of analysis must preserve a minimum of identity' (1981: 16). This raises a crucial point. To speak of change is to imply some measure of continuity – it is, in short, to imply change *in* or *of something* and hence a common point or system of reference. The disintegration or termination of a system and its replacement by another is then not strictly an instance of change but one of substitution. Thus, if our system of reference is the feudal state, bourgeois revolutions represent not change but a substitution of the feudal state by the capitalist state; if our system of reference, on the other hand, is the state itself, then we can talk of institutional, ideational and behavioural change. To identify change over the time-frame t_n to t_{n+1} is then, ironically perhaps, to make the simultaneous claim that the system (s_1) exhibits some degree of continuity over this time-frame, a continuity, moreover, exhibited in the most essential qualities of the system (that which makes it s_1 and not s_2, say) such that it is indeed still the same system at t_{n+1} as it was at t_n.

Yet if change, despite being frequently conflated with discontinuity, does in fact imply a degree of continuity, it should not be regarded as synonymous with either. The distinction between continuity and discontinuity, though often mistaken for that between stability and change, in fact refers to *types* or *modalities* of change and, more specifically, to different temporalities of change. If we can then differentiate between issues relating to the extent of change on the one hand and those relating to the temporal characteristics of particular periods of change on the other, the distinction between continuity and discontinuity is concerned exclusively with the latter. Continuity implies that whatever change occurs is incremental, iterative, cumulative and unidirectional.[4] Furthermore, it implies that all moments in this gradual or evolutionary process are of equal significance and, hence, an even unfolding of events over time. By contrast, discontinuity implies rupture, transformation and an altering of trajectory (whether periodic, cyclical or random) – a process or processes of change punctuated by reversals, tipping points, turning points or other strategic moments of heightened significance. It implies an uneven conception of political time. Clearly, then, change is a necessary but not in itself sufficient condition of discontinuity.

Like the issues of change itself, whether we identify continuity or discontinuity will depend, essentially, on the system with respect to which we choose to assess such temporal characteristics of change. To return to our earlier example, if our system of reference is the feudal state, bourgeois revolutions will constitute a significant discontinuity (since arguably they destroy all that is distinctively feudal about such a regime). If, however, our system of reference is the state itself, we may tend to emphasize significant elements of continuity – the national form of the state, its continued monopoly over the means of violence, its patriarchal character, its centralized nature and so forth.

The above discussion, then, suggests three analytical questions that we might pose of any potential instance of change (whether institutional, behavioural or ideational): with respect to what system will we choose to evaluate change in this context? what is the extent of the change observed? and what are the temporal characteristics of such change – in effect, is the change characterized by continuity or discontinuity?

Continuity and discontinuity: the growth of the British state

The importance of these questions can be illustrated if we consider an issue very central to the concerns of this book – the growth of the state in the postwar period. A crude (and quantitative) measure of this is often taken from figures of public expenditure presented as a percentage of gross domestic product (GDP). If we examine such evidence over the postwar period, we see a relatively consistent trend increase (see figure 1.1). Although this accelerates somewhat in the 1960s and perhaps trails off in the 1980s and early 1990s, the picture is one of continuity. Yet it is important to note that this is continuity *in change* – whatever else it is, this is not a static situation. This should make us extremely wary of those accounts of the postwar period (of which there are many) that present such a stylized depiction of the so-called postwar consensus as to suggest an essentially static and invariant state apparatus unchanged throughout the postwar years (for a more elaborate critique of this literature see chapter 3 and Hay 1996c: ch. 4). The albeit crude quantitative evidence presented here would suggest that whatever else was happening during this period, the state was taking on greater responsibilities or at least was accounting for an ever larger proportion of the GDP.

Of course, such data in itself should not be seen as providing a refutation of the broader postwar consensus thesis. It is important to note that many proponents of such an account do not conceive of the postwar consensus as a static state settlement so much as an evolving regime of the state characterized by a set of dynamic political processes.

This latter view is entirely consistent with a trend increase in public
expenditure throughout the postwar period. What the evidence would
suggest, however, is that a process (or processes) either initiated during
the war years or inherited from the interwar period (without figures for
these years we have no evidence to adjudicate between these contending propositions) set in place or reaffirmed a tendency for increasing
public expenditure in the postwar period.

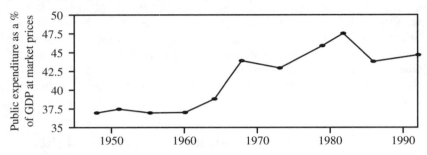

Figure 1.1   The growth of the state in postwar Britain, 1945–92
Source: HM Treasury (1993)

It is important at this point to note the limitations of such data.
Whilst quantitative evidence of this kind can provide useful insights
into the development of the state in the postwar period, it can tell us
very little about the specific processes of change at work. Continuity of
this quantitative kind can mask qualitative discontinuity in the sense
that a great variety of very different processes might sustain a continuous tendency for increasing public expenditure. The evidence presented
in figure 1.1 tells us nothing about the character or quality of the state's
interventions within civil society and the economy. Many authors would
suggest that this changed very significantly from the mid-1970s and that
although the overall level of public expenditure was little altered, the
form that such expenditure took and the rather different priorities of
the state after this period should lead one to identify a new regime of
the state emerging at about this time and continuing to evolve to the
present day (see, for instance, Clarke, S. 1988; Jessop et al. 1988; Overbeek 1990; Hay 1996c; see also chapter 4).

This picture of significant quantitative (if not qualitative) continuity
in the postwar period is placed in a rather different perspective if the
time-frame is extended to consider the whole of the twentieth century
(see figure 1.2). From one of continuity the picture now becomes one of
alternating periods of continuity punctuated periodically by intense
moments of discontinuity. In these rapid discontinuities, public expenditure first expands significantly (and almost instantaneously) and

subsequently falls markedly – but to a level greater than that produced by extrapolating from the previous trend. There are two such punctuating moments in the twentieth century, occurring between 1914 and 1918 and between 1939 and 1945. They correspond fairly clearly to periods of 'total war'.

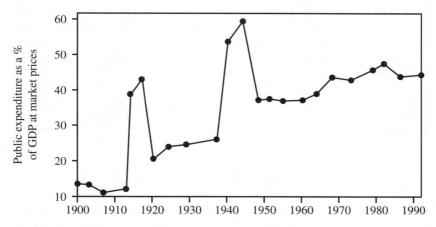

Figure 1.2 The growth of the British state, 1900–92
Source: HM Treasury (1993)

The crude quantitative evidence that previously supported a simple theory of the tendential growth of public expenditure now suggests a more complex process of change: of pre-, inter- and postwar continuity manifested in a tendency for public expenditure to rise (or, in the case of the period 1900–14, to fall); of a significant increase and subsequent fall in expenditure corresponding to the start and cessation of total war and of a trend increase in public expenditure in the postwar period, but from a significantly elevated base-line. This in turn suggests a 'ratchet theory' of state expansion and expenditure growth. During periods of total war, the state takes on greater responsibilities with a corresponding increase in its level of expenditure. Although many of these costs are specific to the prosecution of the war effort, a significant proportion of such expenditure (that, in particular, related to securing heightened levels of war mobilization amongst the working class) may prove difficult to shed in the initial postwar period, or subsequently. Accordingly, total war emerges within such an account as a significant accelerator or catalyst of state expansion, at least when measured in such quantitative terms (a point discussed at greater length in chapter 7; see also Marwick 1968; Cronin 1991; Hay 1996c: ch. 2).

The above discussion suggests that figure 1.1, by virtue of the rather narrow time-frame considered, in fact gives a somewhat distorted picture of the expansion of the state in the postwar period. For an analysis that concentrates exclusively upon the postwar years will fail to acknowledge the considerable impact of the war, arguably the most significant factor in accounting for change in the years that followed. War, and 'total war' in particular, might be seen as initiating new processes of social and political change and accelerating old ones, thus marking both a qualitative and quantitative break with the past which any adequate account of the postwar period must surely acknowledge. What this also indicates is that whether one observes continuity or discontinuity depends, crucially, upon the time-frame considered, demonstrating the need to consider not only the specific and immediate period of concern, but also the broader historical context within which it is situated.

The relativity of change

If continuity and discontinuity are to a large extent dependent upon the time-frame considered, then the same is equally so of the more general question of change. Change is essentially a relative concept. Whether specific phenomena are regarded as evidence of change or of stasis will depend on two key factors: the system with respect to which that change is assessed; and the time-frame or temporal perspective over which such change is considered. Piotr Sztompka's comment with which we began this chapter is here particularly apposite: 'all social reality is pure dynamics, a flow of change of various speed, intensity, rhythm and tempo' (1993: 9). The social and political world is a world of change and, moreover, a world of constant and incessant change, reminding us perhaps of Heraclitus' truism that one cannot step into the same river twice, as water has flowed in the meantime (1979). Yet some changes are clearly more significant than others. The analysis of social and political change is concerned above all with specifying the criteria by which significant change is to be assessed, selecting from the infinite scope and diversity of social dynamism and the 'white noise' of ceaseless change, key moments, cycles, paths and evolutionary trajectories.

Clearly, over the postwar period things have changed – economically, socially, politically and culturally. To live in Britain in the second half of the 1990s is to inhabit a very different conceptual, aspirational, behavioural and institutional environment from that of the late 1940s. Nonetheless, significant aspects of this experience, and perhaps even more so, significant aspects of the processes underpinning this experience, have been preserved, reinforced and maintained.

That there has been significant social and political change in postwar Britain is, then, in one sense undeniable. Yet whether such change is interpreted primarily in terms of continuity or discontinuity is clearly dependent upon the context and time-frame with respect to which that change is assessed. Analyses which focus on the pervasive patriarchal and / or capitalist character of the British state (and hence on general and pervasive systems and long spans of historical time) will tend to emphasize continuity (though often pointing to the changing form that capitalism and patriarchy take and their evolving relationship). Analyses which focus, more parochially, upon the rich texture of political practice (and hence on more ephemeral phenomena) will tend to identify significant discontinuities (though likewise alluding on occasions to certain enduring qualities of the 'British political tradition'). Clearly, then, when assessing the extent of political change in the postwar period, it is crucial that we specify explicitly the criteria by which the extent of change will be evaluated. Given that change has inevitably occurred, however, it is equally crucial that we resist the twin temptations either to 'flat-line' the postwar period by choosing criteria with respect to which change has been insignificant or inconsequential, or to choose criteria by which all change, however iterative, appears significant. While the accounts of 'British exceptionalism' which trace Britain's distinctive long-term trajectory of decline to its 'incomplete bourgeois revolution' and the peculiar institutional legacy of feudalism tend to yield to the former temptation,[5] much of the historiography of Britain's postwar reconstruction (in its tendency 'to miss the wood for the trees and the trees for the leaves') yields to the latter temptation.[6] The former strips us of any conceptual or theoretical resources with which to interrogate the processes of political evolution and transformation; the latter leaves us incapable of differentiating between significant processes and mechanisms of change and minor 'blips'. In this context it should be noted that all the authors of this volume, despite their different views about the evolutionary or punctuated nature of social and political change in postwar Britain, do nonetheless identify significant change over the period in question. The challenge this poses, a challenge taken up in the chapters which follow, is how best to understand, interpret and periodize this change.

The issue of time-horizon is perhaps particularly significant here and has important implications for the literature on postwar Britain. A number of accounts, many of them highly perceptive, seek to debunk the myths that have come to shroud the political history, political science and political sociology of the postwar period. In so doing, first, they dispel the notion of a radical and reforming Attlee government fundamentally transforming the contours of the economy, the state and civil society (Anderson 1992; Calder 1969); second, they challenge those accounts emphasizing a spirit of postwar harmony and consensus carried from the blitz into the postwar years (Blackwell and Seabrook 1988; Saville 1988; Fielding et al. 1995); third, they reveal that the widely identified Keynesian welfare state was, both in inspiration and in practice, not especially Keynesian, not especially redistributive, not especially socially democratic and not especially corporatist (Miliband 1970; Coates 1980; Tomlinson 1981, 1984; Rollings 1988; Newton 1991; Taylor, I. 1991); and, fourth, they detail, in an often quite meticulous manner, the extent to which the 'Thatcher effect' has been systematically overstated as political rhetoric has been taken at face value (Marsh and Rhodes 1992, 1995). In so doing they point to longer-term continuities, providing a powerful and important corrective to those accounts that tend to exaggerate the extent of change often by assuming too close a correspondence between the political rhetoric of the times and the harsh realities of political practice.

There is much in such accounts to commend. Indeed, a significant proportion of the text of this book is oriented to expanding and developing such perspectives. Yet arguably they, too, tend to exhibit a common and problematic tendency – to flat-line the postwar period, ironing out the changes identified within the orthodox accounts (however exaggerated they might be) to reveal a temporal map without contours. In so doing they seem to restrict themselves to an unhelpfully stark choice – to embrace full-heartedly the conventional orthodoxies which posit significant change in the postwar period on the one hand, or to reject altogether the notion of significant change in the postwar years on the other. Wary perhaps of the way in which 'strong' narratives of the postwar period have served as the foundation for contemporary mythology, they tend to content themselves with the largely negative task of debunking and demystification, offering in most cases no alternative periodization of this era (for rare exceptions, see Fielding et al. 1995; Tiratsoo 1991).

Two more general points can then perhaps be made. First, if we reject the dominant analyses and interpretations of change (of its extent, timing and significance) in this period – arguing that, for instance, they exaggerate the extent of a transition from liberal to Keynesian economics in the initial postwar period and of a return to liberal economics under Thatcher – then this does not entail logically that we need, or indeed should, subscribe to a view of no change. Preferable, perhaps, is to keep the question of change open, by suggesting at least in the first instance that change there probably was, but that it is captured inadequately by the conventional accounts. This is the approach that we adopt in this volume. Thus, with respect to economic policy and the 'Keynesian controversy', we suggest that the notion often conjured of a periodic alternation between liberal and Keynesian economics is simply too crude to capture the subtle complexities and uneven temporalities of change in economic policy-making over the last fifty years, but that this merely presents us with the challenge to find a more adequate and appropriate account of the significant changes that nonetheless did occur (for a sophisticated response to this challenge, see Hall, P. A. 1986a, 1993; see also the discussion in chapters 3 and 8).

At this point, it is perhaps also worth noting the significance of the often contested and contestable terms we use to describe change and, above all, to identify periods of relative continuity. Thus, much of the 'Keynesian controversy' revolves around the understanding and misunderstanding of the term 'Keynesian'. A number of authors, for instance, simply conflate and confuse Keynesianism (based on counter-cyclical demand management) with developmental statism (based on consistent supply-side intervention). Others, often those who wish to debunk the myth of a Keynesian revolution, and some of those responsible for the idea in the first place, adopt a textbook definition of Keynesianism. If understood in such rigid terms, the critics are surely right to challenge and demystify the notion of a Keynesian revolution in postwar Britain. However, many of the more sophisticated defenders of such an account of economic policy-making, an account that would emphasize the significance of Keynesian ideas, would reject such a restrictive understanding of the term. Arguably, they use the label as a convenient shorthand to describe the influence of ideas understood as Keynesian by those on whom they exerted such an influence (see, for instance, Clarke, P. 1988, Hall, P. A. 1989). Clearly, the latter use of the term need not imply, indeed may well exclude, the identification of such a textbook transition from liberal to Keynesian economics. It may well be, then, that many of the principal protagonists of this debate in fact disagree over little more than when Keynesianism is Keynesian. The moral is surely that we must be very clear and explicit about the terms we affix to phases, periods and moments of political time (for a further discussion of these issues, see chapter 3).

Moreover, and as the above discussion of terminology might also suggest, we should be very careful not to empty the notion of discontinuity (and hence the distinction between continuity and discontinuity) of all analytical purchase by reserving it for transitions so abrupt and monumental that they simply never occur in modern and complex political systems characterized by significant inertia. This temptation is perhaps particularly apparent in the literature on the Attlee and Thatcher governments, two administrations most often accorded the status of initiating a significant break with the past. Like the notion of a Keynesian revolution, the radicalism of the Attlee and Thatcher governments is often grossly exaggerated (for critiques of this literature, see chapters 7 and 8).[7] Unsurprisingly, in recent years a number of revisionist accounts have begun to emerge challenging the extent of the break with the past that these administrations represented, emphasizing the vast 'implementation gap' between radical rhetoric and pragmatic practice, and pointing to significant areas of continuity. Yet, important though such correctives are, we should again be wary of writing off the idea that the election of first Attlee and, subsequently, Thatcher did mark significant discontinuities in British political development on the basis of such an argument. It is worth reiterating that the judgement of continuity and discontinuity is a relative and not an absolute one. Thus, while very convincing narratives of the postwar period can certainly be offered that would identify no moments of discontinuity or of relatively abrupt change, there would seem to be some value in relativizing the notions of continuity and discontinuity over this period and asking, in comparative terms, whether some governments represent more of a discontinuity with the past, and are more radical in their ambitions and their ability to translate those ambitions into practice than others (over the time-frame considered).[8] Although it is a view not shared by all the authors of this volume, I would suggest that once couched in such terms, the election of the Attlee and Thatcher governments can be seen as marking significant moments of discontinuity in postwar British political development.

Interrogating institutional change: structure and agency

Thus far we have concerned ourselves with some of the principal analytical and conceptual issues which underpin any consideration of social and political change in postwar Britain, focusing in particular on the extent and temporality of change. In the remaining sections of this chapter we turn from the analytical to the theoretical, from the descriptive to the explanatory, in considering the problems of accounting for and explaining social and political change. In so doing we assess critically the ability of contending approaches to interrogate and identify the mechanisms and processes of social and political change. For this, we argue, is a characteristic failing of much of the literature on postwar

Britain and indeed a very significant proportion of the more general literature on institutional change. Although political scientists, political historians and political sociologists have shown an avid interest in detailing, charting and describing the often uneven contours of ideational, behavioural and institutional change, they have been far more reluctant, and, we would suggest, generally far less successful, to identify the processes and mechanisms of institutional change and hence in explaining political development. This, we argue, has much to do with the crucial question of structure and agency, of context and conduct and of the relationship between political actors or subjects on the one hand and the contexts within which they find themselves on the other (on which, see Giddens 1984; Archer 1995; Hay 1995b, 1997d; Dessler 1989). In what follows, we consider the importance of this question for the understanding of social and political change, before differentiating between contending accounts of political development in postwar Britain in terms of their treatment of the structure–agency relationship.

Structure, agency and change

Structure and agency are inextricably bound up and profoundly implicated in all instances of social and political change. Save for change resulting from purely natural or physical processes such as natural disasters, all social and political change is the product of human intervention, however mediated, however unintended its consequences. Indeed, even natural disasters only produce social and political consequences in so far as they result in a transformation of the conduct of human actors. Arguably, then, agency is common to all instances of social and political change. It is, accordingly, also an integral part of any adequate account and / or explanation of change. This should make us extremely wary of those analyses which contrive to explain change without reference to actors – by an appeal to structural, institutional or, worse still, functional 'logics'.

Yet if agency is common to all processes of social and political change, so too is context or structure. All action, not least that which might be seen as instigating social and political change, takes place and acquires significance within a structured terrain or context. Indeed, in so far as change occurs, it is in and through an interaction with that context. Change, then, is a product of the relationship between structure and agency, a consequence (however unintended) of human intervention within a structured environment (an environment of ideas, institutions, conventions and perceptions). Thus, perhaps equally problematic are accounts which accord little or no significance to structural or contextual factors (such as the distinctive inertia or dynamism of particular institutional environments or the relative entrenchment or openness of cultural conventions). For structures are in some sense the very condition of change and the very medium upon which it is inscribed.

Nonetheless, as we shall see, there are plenty of analyses that fail to give due attention to either structural or agential factors in accounting for change. Such accounts rely upon a misplaced dualism of structure and agency in which the two terms are held to be largely independent of one another and in which either one or the other is accorded a predominant (and in some instances an exclusive) explanatory role. A complex or dialectical relationship between the two is thus denied (on the dialectic of structure and agency, see Hay 1995b; cf. Bhaskar 1989: 74–7).

Although few analytical perspectives and theoretical approaches, far less specific analyses, are explicit about their treatment of the relationship of structure and agency, such conceptions are implicit in all explanations of political change and it is useful to subject them to critical scrutiny. If we do so, we discover a number of broadly agency-centred and a number of broadly structure-centred accounts of political development in postwar Britain. We consider each in turn.

Accounting for political development: agency-centred approaches

Agency-centred approaches to political development and change provide, in Alexander Wendt's useful terms, 'insider' accounts of social and political processes – accounts that the actors themselves might identify with, accounts couched principally in terms of immediate actors, factors, motives and intentions (Wendt 1987). They exhibit a characteristic tendency to lose sight of structural constraints and longer-term processes of change whilst tending towards voluntarism or intentionalism (the reduction of political explanation to the demonstration of motivation and intention to act). The clearest example of an agency-centred perspective to British political development is that of the archival political historian.

It is perhaps unremarkable that archival history – the reconstruction of historical events on the basis of often meticulous and detailed archival research using contemporary sources – should reveal itself to be an agency-centred discipline. For, to some extent, the very sources on which the historian must rely – memoirs, diaries, memos between political actors and so forth – serve to draw the analyst towards an account that will tend to privilege the immediate actors directly involved in historical events and indeed their own construction of events at the time. The result is an implicity instrumental view of the state where control over the apparatus of government, and indeed the intentions and motivations of those in control, is seen to hold the key to understanding political development (for a critique of this view see chapters 2 and 7). This instrumentalist framework, reflective as it is of the historiographic methodology, emerges more by default than out of conscious theoretical choice. For, in short, whilst archival data can be used to retrieve, reconstruct and reproduce elite political conflicts between and among politicians and civil servants, it cannot so easily be used to depict the constraints imposed by inherited state and economic structures, nor indeed public opinion. The result is a form of 'contextual parochialism' and a characteristic failure to consider the various constraints upon political agents which condition experiences, identities and strategic orientations.[9] If archival evidence is held to provide the privileged point of access to the past, it is hardly surprising that problematizing questions of context are often deemed inadmissible in the court of historiography. An instrumentalist and agency-centred account of the state and politics is thus strongly favoured.

Yet if this should make us somewhat sceptical of the periodizations of British political development sometimes presented by archival historians, then it certainly should not lead us to underemphasize the very considerable achievement of historians of this period and the very valuable (however partial) evidence they provide for more rounded accounts of social and political change. Historiography may not be a sufficient nor even a necessary condition of an adequate account of social and political change in postwar Britain, but it may nonetheless provide a very useful starting point if supplemented by more contextual or structural considerations.

Accounting for political development: structure-centred approaches

If agency-centred approaches to political development provide 'insider' accounts, then structure-centred approaches provide 'outsider' accounts – 'accounts which operate at some distance from actual human agents, preferring instead to contextualise actors within the structures that are understood to constrain them and that generally lie outside of their immediate perceptions' (Hay 1995b: 194). Within such a schema, structures are largely seen as constraining, and in some cases even determining of behaviour – independently of the intentions and motivations of political subjects. The latter are in turn seen as 'bearers' of structures over which they have little or no control and influence. Change, within structure-centred accounts, tends to be conceived of not in terms of intentional action, nor even the interaction between action and context, but in terms of the often inexorable unfolding of an inner structural, institutional or systemic logic.

If examples of agency-centred accounts continue to abound in the literature on British political development, crude structure-centred accounts are perhaps more difficult to find. Structuralism, which has become little more than a term of abuse since the 1970s, is now perhaps best regarded as a tendency towards which certain accounts are drawn, rather than a readily identifiable position in its own right. Nonetheless, structuralist tendencies do reveal themselves in a number of very prominent accounts of British political development in the postwar period. They tend to be associated with determinism, functionalism (the view that social and political processes can be accounted for in terms of the function they perform for a system or structure) and a relatively undifferentiated view of historical time. Here we consider just one, the thesis of British exceptionalism.

Perhaps the most obviously structuralist account of British political development, first formulated at a time when structuralism was still very much in the ascendancy, is the thesis of British exceptionalism associated with Perry Anderson and Tom Nairn in particular (Nairn 1976; Anderson 1992). The argument is elegant in its simplicity. Britain's seemingly inexorable trajectory of relative economic decline (a decline that has, if anything, accelerated in the postwar period) can be traced ultimately to the 'incomplete' nature of its bourgeois revolution. Lacking the creative destruction of a genuinely revolutionary upheaval, Britain's precocious capitalism inherited much of its institutional architecture and cultural distinctiveness from the feudal era. A fossilized traditionalism, the trappings of an aristocratic elite and many of the institutions of the *ancien régime* survived the transition to capitalism by and large intact. These peculiarities of primacy were to become what they remain today – fetters on continued economic development and capital accumulation.

In recent years the argument has received something of a revival, being presented in slightly different but still recognizable terms by Will Hutton (1996, 1997). Though Hutton softens the structuralism of the Anderson–Nairn thesis somewhat, placing a far greater emphasis upon political factors in the reproduction of Britain's trajectory of decline, the basic structuralist form of the argument remains essentially intact. To understand Britain's current predicament is to understand the peculiarity of British capitalism, a peculiarity and indeed an exceptionalism reflected in its arcane institutional structure, a legacy of the Glorious Revolution of 1688. While these institutions remain intact, Britain's determinism of decline seems assured. Within this schema, and despite Hutton's best intentions, little room is left for political factors or human agency (Hay 1997c). Moreover, the structure of the argument itself would seem to dictate that little of consequence occurs between the late seventeenth century and the present day, far less the postwar period, in which the legacy of the 1688 imperium is, presumably, merely reinforced and further entrenched. The irony of this, as Jim Johnston notes in chapter 2, is that Hutton and, before him, Anderson and Nairn all supplement their basically structuralist accounts with periodic lapses into instrumentalist and voluntarist positions. The contradictions of this are clear to see. Thus Hutton, for instance, seems to want his cake and to eat it, as he vehemently chastises the Thatcher governments for their hand in a trajectory of decline established, by his own account, in 1688 (on this vacillation between structuralism and voluntarism in the exceptionalism thesis, see chapter 2).

The exceptionalism thesis may serve usefully to remind us of the institutional distinctiveness and specificity of British capitalism, of the characteristic inertia of complex institutional environments and of the extent to which institutional factors circumscribe the realms of the politically possible and the economically feasible. Yet its tendency to absolve all political actors of responsibility for Britain's economic and political trajectory over the last three centuries and its associated flat-lining of the contours of institutional, behavioural and ideational change must be resisted. What is perhaps required is an account capable of resisting the twin temptations of structuralism on the one hand and an actor-centred intentionalism on the other.

Beyond structure versus agency: interrogating the process of change

If we are to move beyond the twin impasses of structuralism and intentionalism, we must first return to the question of the relationship between structure and agency itself. More specifically, we must seek to transcend the artificial and polarizing dualism of structure and agency that resolves itself into structuralist and internationalist tendencies in the first place. In so doing we can usefully draw upon and elaborate Bob Jessop's so-called *strategic-relational approach* (Jessop 1990; Hay 1995b: 199–202, 1997b, 1997d, 1997e; Hay and Jessop 1998).

Within this framework, political subjects are conceived of as reflexive and strategic actors inhabiting densely structured contexts which favour certain strategies as means to realize intentions over others. The context is, then, *strategically selective*, presenting an uneven playing field which advantages certain actors and strategies and disadvantages others. Within any complex social or political setting, strategic resources are unevenly distributed amongst actors (reflecting more or less enduring power structures); such resources in turn influence the ability of actors to realize their intentions and in so doing to transform (however iteratively) the context in which they find themselves.

Change thus arises out of the relationship between actors and the contexts they inhabit. Indeed, more specifically, change is seen as a product of the same-time interrelationship between strategic action and the strategic context within which it takes place and in the subsequent unfolding of its consequences – both intended and unintended. Strategic action may be singular, immediate and instantaneous, but its consequences may be multiple, deferred and drawn out over a long period of time.

The strategies that actors deploy, moreover, are informed by their perceptions and indeed misperceptions of the context in which they find themselves. These may in turn be revised over time, as actors monitor the consequences of their action and that of others and reorient their perceptions accordingly. This process is often referred to as social or strategic learning.

Although presented in relatively simple, abstract and general terms in the above paragraphs, such a schema can be applied relatively easily to the more complex, concrete and specific questions of political development in postwar Britain. It is precisely this task that we set ourselves in the chapters to follow. Yet it is perhaps useful at this stage to conclude by drawing out some of the implications of this approach for the rather more general questions of social and political change with which we have been concerned in this chapter. These can be grouped into three categories: the consequences of strategic action; the distribution of power and resources; and the role of perceptual, ideational or discursive factors.

First, the strategic-relational approach places considerable emphasis upon change as the consequence of action, though action constrained and conditioned by the structured context in which it occurs. Change is held to result from the relationship between strategically informed conduct on the one hand and a densely structured strategic terrain on the other. Yet since actors have, at best, a partial knowledge of the context within which they find themselves and in many cases hold perceptions which will later prove demonstrably false, the outcome of strategic action is in many instances unpredictable and contingent. Indeed, in an environment which is both densely structured and densely populated by strategic actors, the consequences of action over the long, medium and even short term will almost certainly prove conditional upon the conduct of others. This makes unintended consequences almost inevitable. Thus, in constructing narratives of institutional, ideational and behavioural change in postwar Britain we should be acutely aware both of the contingent nature of political development and the unintended consequences of strategic action, resisting the temptation to seek to offer *post hoc* rationalizations of all significant strategic interventions.

Second, in its emphasis upon the densely structured nature of the strategic environment, the strategic-relational approach should sensitize us to the uneven distribution of strategic opportunities and resources and to the way in which this in turn reflects more or less pervasive structures of power and social inequality. This is a central theme of this volume. Yet it is not to suggest that the relatively powerless and those not privileged strategically by the institutional contours of state, economy and society are impotent, nor that their actions are irrelevant to the determination of the trajectory of social and political change. What it does suggest, however, is that we consider the conditions under which particular social groups otherwise strategically disadvantaged by the institutional environment in which they find themselves may expand their strategic resources and come to reshape the strategic terrain they inhabit. It also suggests that the analysis of social and political change cannot be separated from the analysis of social and political power and, moreover, that relations of power, like other social structures, are themselves subject to constant evolution and transformation.

Finally, in its emphasis upon the necessarily partial and provisional knowledge with which all actors appropriate the strategic environment they inhabit, the strategic-relational approach accords a perhaps unusual degree of significance to ideational, perceptual and discursive factors (see in particular chapters 4, 6 and 9). More specifically, it suggests the need to consider the dominant paradigms and frames of reference through which actors understand the contexts in which they must act and the mechanisms and processes by which such paradigms emerge, become challenged and are ultimately replaced. It suggests, too, that such paradigms are not free-floating bodies of ideas but must bear a close (if perhaps never identical) relationship with the social and political realities they purport to describe. With respect to policy-making in particular, it suggests that the ability to transform the institutional context of state, economy and society may reside less in access to governmental power and more in the ability to make the case for a shift in the dominant paradigm informing policy. The political power of ideas and the political power of economic ideas in particular (Hall, P. A.

1989), though largely ignored within most conventional accounts, can scarcely be overemphasized.

Notes

1   See, for instance, Lukes 1974; Isaac 1987; Hay 1997a.
2   Of course to some extent Heisenberg's 'Uncertainty Principle' changes all this at least for the physics of small particles, suggesting that the velocity and position of an object (a sub-atomic particle, say) cannot both be known simultaneously. To measure one accurately is to impose limits on the accuracy with which the other can be measured. Yet even Heisenberg's principle, it should be noted, takes the form of a 'law' which is assumed to be immutable, infinitely generalizable and trans-historical.
3   This is not to suggest, of course, that the strength of gravitational fields does not vary (both over time and from system to system), but that the laws governing the gravitational field between two objects can safely be assumed to be immutable. It is this (useful) assumption that ultimately makes trans-Atlantic flight possible.
4   It should be noted that to identify continuity is not to imply that any change is taking place; neither is it necessarily to suggest that no change is occurring. The concept, unlike that of discontinuity, is neutral with respect to the identification of change.
5   See, for instance, Nairn 1976, 1993; Anderson 1992; Hutton 1996; for critiques, see Hay 1995a, 1997c.
6   Pimlott 1988; Middlemas 1986, 1990, 1991; for a critique, see Seldon 1994a; Hay 1996c: 45–7.
7   Kenneth Morgan, for instance, refers to the Attlee government as 'the British variant of socialism in one country' (Morgan 1984: 89).
8   In so doing it is obviously crucial to acknowledge that there is always likely to be a significant gap between what a government wishes to present as its aims and objectives, and what a government is ever likely to achieve. As well as an 'implementation gap', there is always likely to be a 'strategy gap' (see Hay 1996c: 152–3).
9   For a rare (indeed, perhaps unique) and quite explicit attempt to correct the characteristic 'contextual parochialism' that comes with archival immersion, see Tiratsoo 1991; Tiratsoo and Tomlinson 1993.

2

Britain's Economic Decline: Cultural Versus Structural Explanations

By the mid-1960s the notion of an effete British Establishment, utterly unable to compete in the international economy thanks to an educational system that was anti-industrial and virtually pre-modern, and a value system and ethos that revered the landed gentry and despised entrepreneurial effort, had become virtually ubiquitous in the informed popular mind.

Rubinstein 1990: 59

One of the major themes within British political discourse since the mid-1960s has been the nature and extent of Britain's economic decline. The gradual realization that the postwar economic boom camouflaged British industry's steadily declining share of global manufacturing output has led to a mini-industry in explanations of decline. This chapter is a contribution to this debate, and emphasizes some of the shortcomings within the existing literature.

First, I argue that we need a more specific definition of decline. Within the existing literature, there is a tendency to conflate the demise of Britain's manufacturing industry with general economic frailty. Second, it is important to develop a more intricate explanation of the trajectory of Britain's economic development. Most of the existing literature provides a deterministic analysis of decline. In contrast, I argue that we need to develop a more sophisticated and non-deterministic analysis of a highly complex and dynamic historical process. Finally, I argue for a multidimensional approach. Most existing accounts empha- size either *ideological* factors (an anti-industrial culture) or *economic* factors (early industrialization and the nature of industry–finance relations) as the main cause of decline. Here, I suggest that, in addition to these factors, we also need to account for the postwar *political* failure to rectify Britain's downward economic trajectory.

What do we mean by 'decline'?

It is important to emphasize that Britain's economic decline is not generic. Clearly, some sectors of the British economy have been more successful than others. Notable examples include the chemical and pharmaceuticals industry, in which Britain has boasted and continues to boast some of the world's leading companies (ICI, Zeneca, Glaxo, Beecham), the aerospace industry, where leading British firms include Rolls Royce, British Aerospace and Lucas Aerospace, and the food, drink and tobacco sector, in which Britain has a number of the world's largest companies (Coates and Hillard 1995: 15).

Most significantly, the City of London enjoys continued success as a leading international financial centre. As Radice argues: 'from the emergence of the Eurodollar market in the 1960s through to the abolition of exchange controls in 1979 and the "Big Bang" of deregulation in 1987, London has flourished as a centre for global finance' (1995: 244; see also Coakley and Harris 1992). Therefore, in explaining economic decline we need to account for sectoral differences in the performance of British companies.

If we recognize both the apparent success of many sectors of the British economy and the rapid rise in living standards which most people enjoyed during the postwar period, it seems quite odd to focus on economic decline. This leads to the obvious question: decline in relation to what or whom? Clearly, we need to view decline as a relative concept. It is important to develop both a spatial and temporal analysis of Britain's economic development which accounts for its own historical performance as well as the economic record of its main competitors.

While there is some disagreement among economic historians over the extent and timing of Britain's relative economic decline, it is generally accepted that, following the deep depression of the 1870s, both Britain's total output and the output per head grew more slowly in the subsequent forty years than they had done in the previous half century. As Marquand argues: 'Between 1873 and 1913, total output grew by about 1.8 per cent a year in Britain, compared with 2.8 per cent a year in Germany and 4.5 per cent a year in the United States' (1988: 116). Whereas globally industrial production grew fourfold between 1870 and 1913, in Britain it only doubled. In the same period Britain declined from being the 'workshop of the world' to only the third industrial power in the world behind the United States and Germany.

However, as table 2.1 demonstrates, an analysis of economic growth rates suggests that we need to be wary of viewing the historical trajectory of the British economy as an inexorable downward spiral. As we can see, Britain's annual average growth rate for the period between 1913 and 1950 is higher than that of France and comparable with those of both Germany and Italy. Whereas the depression of the interwar years meant that, in real terms, Britain's economic growth continued to be sluggish, in comparative terms the economic performance was much stronger than in the forty years prior to World War I. Further, in the more advanced industries, such as electrical manufacturing, motor manufacturing and chemicals, in which British companies had initially been slow to invest, Britain's market share rose rapidly (Marquand 1988: 132).

Table 2.1   Annual average growth rates (% / year)

	1913–50	*1950–73*
Britain	1.3	3.0
France	1.0	5.1
Japan	1.8	9.7
Germany	1.3	6.0
USA	2.8	3.7
Italy	1.4	5.5
Sweden	2.8	3.8

Source: Adapted from Maddison (1982, 1991), quoted in Crafts and Woodward (1991: 8).

Table 2.2   Share of world manufactured exports (%)

	1950	*1960*	*1970*	*1979*	*1988*
UK	25.5	16.5	10.8	9.1	8.3
USA	27.3	21.6	18.5	16.0	14.9
France	9.9	9.6	8.7	10.5	9.1
Germany	7.3	19.3	19.8	20.9	20.6
Japan	3.4	6.9	11.7	13.7	18.1

Source: Brown and Sherrif (1979) and DTI (1989), quoted in Crafts and Woodward (1991: 12).

It is during the postwar period that Britain's industrial performance rapidly deteriorates. Although economic growth in the 1950s and 1960s was impressive in historical terms, it was disturbingly poor relative to other countries. As table 2.1 clearly illustrates, British growth between 1950 and 1973 was considerably lower than in the other leading industrial nations. Further, as table 2.2 demonstrates, Britain's share of world manufactured exports fell dramatically during the same period, especially in the face of German and Japanese expansion. The gradual realization that the favourable postwar economic climate concealed a deeply worrying acceleration of Britain's relative economic decline led to an explosion in explanations of decline. By far the most influential of these accounts has been the cultural thesis.

The cultural thesis

The basic premise of the cultural thesis is that economic decline is primarily attributable to the stultifying influence of a uniquely resilient, parasitic aristocracy. The reduction of Britain's economic malaise to the mismanagement of a myopic and hopelessly gentrified ruling class has led to the emergence of some unlikely bedfellows. This thesis has a strong pedigree in both the neo-Marxist and neo-liberal literature. Indeed, it is remarkable that a thesis which first emerged in the pages of the neo-Marxist journal *New Left Review*[1] was subsequently highly influential on the emergence of Thatcherism.[2]

In its initial Marxist guise the cultural thesis attributed decline to the 'exceptional' nature of British capitalism. Britain's industrial revolution arrived at a time when the old feudal ruling class, following an alliance with a nascent financier class, remained a powerful socio-economic grouping. The subsequent failure of the industrial bourgeoisie to become hegemonic and the concomitant political weakness of the working class led to a strangely stagnant historical process. The ancient institutions of the British state were left intact as the industrial bourgeoisie was content to coalesce with the aristocracy in a new historical bloc, albeit as a junior partner. Through the development of the Victorian public school system and the pervasive influence of Oxbridge and an elite civil service, the middle classes were imbued with a decidedly anti-industrial value system. This resulted in the development of a uniquely British 'gentlemanly capitalism' which is skewed towards the interests of financial capital and is essentially anti-industrial in character.

The culture thesis, as espoused by Weiner (1981) and C. Barnett (1986; 1996) emerged at a particularly opportune moment for the New Right.[3] The attraction of the Weiner / Barnett thesis to the New Right is that it suggests that Britain's economic problems are cultural rather than structural. Furthermore, it legitimizes the New Right's emphasis on the need to create a more business-friendly culture and value-system. Further, Barnett's emphasis on the debilitating economic effect of a conservative trade-union movement and the failed priorities of postwar welfarism proved particularly attractive for the New Right agenda.

An archaic and anti-industrial ruling class and obstructive and selfish trade unions were powerful rhetorical symbols of Britain's declining global status. The traditional Establishment and the trade unions were cited as the principal engineers of Britain's decline. Jettisoning the traditional Conservative emphasis on tradition and continuity, Mrs Thatcher fought the 1979 election on a commitment to clear out the staid and corrupt nooks and crannies of the British Establishment.[4] In addition, she emphasized her commitment to undermine an over-powerful and highly destructive trade-union movement.

The commitment to put the Great back into Britain was premised on the reinvention of the entrepreneurial spirit which had been the bedrock of Victorian industrial success. This necessitated the removal of a failed liberal ruling class from the higher echelons of the British Establishment and its replacement with a modern, dynamic (i.e. Thatcherite) capitalist class. Sir Keith Joseph argued, in terms eerily reminiscent of the Nairn / Anderson theses, that Britain's main economic weakness was that it 'never had a capitalist ruling class or a stable *haute bourgeoisie*'. Consequently, 'capitalist or bourgeois values have never shaped thought and institutions as they have in some countries' (quoted in Weiner 1981: 8).

Although Joseph conflates the capitalist class with the bourgeoisie, the thrust of his argument remains the same as the Nairn / Anderson and Weiner / Barnett theses; the British economy has suffered from the debilitating backwardness of its ruling class. The logic of both positions is that in order to halt Britain's decline there has to be a completion of the bourgeois revolution. In particular, there was an urgent need to get rid of a parasitic aristocracy whose pernicuous influence continues to block the development of British industry. In this respect we can see why the Barnett / Weiner thesis was so attractive to the New Right (which presumably saw itself as the vanguard of the bourgeoisie).

Unlikely bedfellows

Despite their radically differing normative assumptions, the Weiner / Barnett and Anderson / Nairn theses offer remarkably similar historiographical accounts of decline. Here, I will focus on a number of similarities between the neo-liberal and neo-Marxist positions:

- Britain's poor economic performance is primarily attributed to the absence of a technocratic elite and the failure to develop state institutions which can regulate the British economy within an increasingly complex and competitive capitalist economic system;

- the failure to develop such a state is viewed as the consequence of the continued hegemony of a backward-looking liberal political elite and the failure of the industrial middle class to realize its economic success at a political level;
- the hegemonic position of the traditional aristocracy is reproduced primarily through an elitist education system and an anti-business ethos;
- the trade unions are seen as obstructive and narrowly corporatist.

The archaic state

Within much of the leftist literature on decline there is a strong emphasis on the historical failure to modernize the British state; for example, as Marquand argues, 'Britain's inability to adjust to the economic upheavals of the 1970s and 1980s lies in her failure to become a "developmental state" ' (Marquand 1988: 5; see also Nairn 1964, 1976; Anderson 1964, 1987; Cain and Hopkins 1993b; Gamble 1994; Hutton 1995). Here, decline is attributed to a historical failure to develop the institutional capacity necessary to lead the British economy in an increasingly complex and competitive capitalist economic system. In contrast to countries such as Japan, Germany and France, where the state has an active role in economic affairs, Britain is constrained by an institutional settlement which has remained virtually unchanged since the seventeenth century.

Here, the focus is on the peculiar durability of the institutional deal which was forged in the aftermath of the Glorious Revolution, as a result of which, Hutton argues, 'The Conservative Party found itself in charge of a ruleless state, handed down almost intact from the settlement of 1688' (1995: 4). Similarly, Gamble argues: 'The British state has not suffered a major break in the pattern of its development since the civil war in the seventeenth century' (1994: 65; also Anderson 1987: 48).

The early development of commercial capitalism within Britain resulted in the creation of a politically powerful financial bourgeoisie which formed a historical alliance with the old landed gentry. Consequently, the aristocracy was able to obtain an institutional settlement which restored much of its power and maintained many of its ancient privileges. In return, the financiers were assured of the continuation of Britain's imperial role, which gave them privileged access to lucrative foreign markets. The international success of the British economy served as a bulwark for the ancient institutions of the state. Britain's imperial role facilitated privileged access to foreign markets, which British businesspeople eagerly exploited.

Nairn and Anderson argue that it was this imperial role which allowed a 'transitional state' to survive despite the backwardness of the domestic economy. The archaic nature of the state meant that there was no attempt to formulate a leading role in the development of British industry. Consequently, as the extent of Britain's economic difficulties became apparent, the state was peculiarly ill-equipped to remedy the deep-rooted structural problems which plagued British industry: 'A constantly weakening industrial base, a dominant financial sector oriented towards foreign investment rather than the re-structuring of British industries, a non-technocratic state quite unable to bring about the "revolution from above" needed to redress this balance: everything conspired to cause an inexorable spiral of decline' (Nairn 1964: 5; see also Anderson 1987: 75; Hutton 1995: 286–94). In continental Europe the state acted as a major player in promoting industrial advancement, whereas in Britain manufacturers were left to fend for themselves. This prevented the modernization of the economy during crucial periods of development, notably the postwar period. Within this narrative the principal explanation for Britain's economic decline is the absence of a modernizing 'second revolution'. Unlike all its principal competitors, the UK never experienced a major period of social and political upheaval, which would have radically remoulded the outdated institutions of the state formed after 1688 (Anderson 1987: 47).

We would expect a left-leaning literature to posit the virtues of greater state intervention; however, this position is also developed by Barnett, who advocates a more interventionist state. Despite his popularity within the New Right, Barnett's thesis does not extol the virtues of laissez-faire economics. In reality, as Addison argues, 'Barnett is a withering critic of nineteenth-century laissez-faire capitalism and its legacy for twentieth-century Britain' (1987: 19). In his criticism of the wartime National government, Barnett claims that the only viable cure for Britain's postwar economic ills was the creation of a ruthless interventionist state based upon a Bismarckian model (Barnett, C. 1986). As Morgan argues, this implied 'an injection of vigorous Prussian interventionism in the economy in place of sentimental utopianism and woolly models of voluntary partnership' (1992: 10). Only through the creation of a state dedicated to maximizing national efficiency was economic salvation plausible. Instead, crippled by the British tradition of 'collectivism', a historic opportunity to reconstruct the state was squandered and real economic difficulties ignored: 'instead of planning for an economic miracle, the government planned for a New Jerusalem' (Addison 1987: 19–20).

Barnett bitterly attacks both the Churchill and Attlee governments for failing to employ the resources of the state to restructure Britain's ailing industrial base. Rather than developing the institutional capacity

which was necessary forcibly to modernize the economy, a liberal political elite proposed an *ad hoc*, voluntary and conciliatory partnership
between government and the two sides of industry. Barnett is savagely
critical of this approach. In particular, he derides the liberal establishment's penchant for 'advice', 'persuasion' and 'consultation'. The severity of Britain's structural economic difficulties demanded 'ruthless and
wide-ranging intervention in British industry' (1996: 205).

The failure to introduce the 'vigorous intervention from above'
needed to alleviate economic decline is also attributed to the absence of
a 'state-class of "technocrats" or administrators' (ibid.). Instead, as
Nairn argues: 'the political and administrative class is irremediably
compromised, socially and intellectually, with the old patrician order'
(1976: 35). Unlike in France, for example, where an influential technocratic class is capable of leading economic restructuring from above, no
such class existed in Britain. In particular, Barnett bemoans the Attlee
government's failure to create a powerful executive agency such as the
French Commissariat du Plan with the necessary resources and institutional legitimacy to lead Britain's industrial recovery.[5]

A feudalistic ruling class

A central theme within the decline literature is the notion that the
industrial bourgeoisie failed to develop a real political voice. As
Robbins has argued, 'Britain has lacked a political / business class which
has played a directing role in its affairs either in the nineteenth century
or since' (Collins and Robbins 1990: 12; see also Cain and Hopkins
1993a: 70). Even at the height of their economic prosperity, the Victorian industrialists were unable to gain political power. Instead, both the
Weiner / Barnett and the Nairn / Anderson theses identify a fusion
between the bourgeoisie and aristocracy during the mid-nineteenth
century. The industrial middle class, meanwhile, lacking any real ideological and cultural justification for its interests, remained the junior
partner within this new class alliance.

Despite the extensive success which the industrial bourgeoisie
enjoyed, it never managed to transform its economic dominance into
political supremacy: 'Economically, English capitalism had triumphed
completely; but no commensurate political advance by industrial capital
had followed' (Anderson 1987: 23). It achieved some political success,
such as parliamentary reform in 1832 and the repeal of the Corn Laws
in 1846, but on the whole the industrial middle class remained on the
margins of the political process (Weiner 1981: 12; Cain and Hopkins
1993a: 40). As a result, it was never able to occupy a hegemonic posi-

tion within the state, and its interests remained subordinate to those of financial capitalists who had formed a cultural, political and economic alliance with the traditional landowning aristocracy. The state continued to pursue a global political and economic agenda which strongly favoured the financial and commercial sectors. *Ipso facto*, the early priorities of the state were not industrial development and domestic economic growth but the defence of empire and the search for new overseas markets – an imperial role.

Gentlemanly capitalism

Within both the neo-liberal and neo-Marxist variants of the cultural thesis it is argued that the traditional ruling class was able to remain hegemonic through the permeation of an entire set of beliefs, values, attitudes, morality, etc. In this way it was able to absorb and neutralize the interests of the industrial class. The cultural thesis, then, is Gramscian in the sense that the hegemonic class is 'one which has been able to articulate the interests of other groups to its own by means of a hegemonic struggle' (Mouffe 1979: 181). The primary basis of this hegemonic struggle was the prominence given to acquiring a 'gentlemanly' status within society. As Bertrand Russell has argued, 'The concept of the gentleman was invented by the aristocracy to keep the middle classes in order' (quoted in Weiner 1981: 13).

In order to strengthen its hegemonic position, the aristocracy sought to imbue the industrial bourgeoisie with its own values and traditions: 'In return for accepting the values and lifestyles of the landed class, the most prominent manufacturers were to be admitted as full members of the status group of "gentlemen" ' (Scott 1982: 104, quoted in Overbeek 1990: 44). The main basis of these gentlemanly values was a feudalistic penchant for rural life and a marked hostility towards technological 'progress' and urban life generally. Weiner, for example, cites numerous pieces of Victorian literature and polemical articles to illustrate the tension which existed between England's schizophrenic existence as the 'workshop of the world' and a 'green and pleasant land'. The English garden became the principal metaphorical antidote to the horrors of the dark satanic mill.

It was this hegemonic diffusion of gentlemanly values in the Victorian age that led to the development of Britain's 'exceptional' form of capitalism. An emphasis on maintaining a gentlemanly lifestyle with an income from the service and financial sectors led to the growth of a decidedly anti-industrial ethos: 'In an order dominated by gentlemanly norms, production was held in low repute. Working directly for money,

as opposed to making it from a distance, was associated with dependence and cultural inferiority' (Cain and Hopkins 1993a: 23). The cultural significance of the finance and service sectors was that they
provided the aristocracy with an alternative means of generating
income which was still deemed acceptable to the leisurely lifestyle of
the gentleman. As income from these sectors was largely invisible and
indirect, a discreet distance could be maintained from the demeaning
business of working for a living. Characterized by a lofty disdain for
vulgar materialism and a distrust of scientific progress, this anti-business
ethos was antithetical to the development of a dynamic, entrepreneurial
capitalist economy.

British industrialists, grown fat on their profits from the first industrial revolution, became dazzled by the grandeur of such a 'gentlemanly' lifestyle. Not wishing to have their hands dirtied by the grime
of the bleak industrial cities, they invested their profits in the more
discreet financial sector, seeking to attain the leisurely lifestyle of the
country gent by living off the dividends and interests of their financial
dealings.

The maintenance of an imperial role was crucial in this respect.
Britain's imperial amibitions were primarily about securing more
outlets for financial investment and high rates of return for aspiring
gentlemen: 'The purpose of Empire was as much the generation of
invisible, gentlemanly sources of income as international aggrandise-
ment' (Cain and Hopkins 1993a: 115). The industrial bourgeoisie was
content to accept the traditional ruling class's hegemonic position in
return for the state's continued commitment to an imperial role. Consequently, Anderson argues, 'The late Victorian era and the high noon
of imperialism welded aristocracy and bourgeoisie together in a single
social bloc' (1992: 29; see also Desai 1994: 34). Similarly, Weiner contends that the late Victorian era saw the resumption of 'English
history's normal pattern of ready absorption of new into old wealth'
(1981: 12).

The reproduction of aristocratic hegemony

The principal hegemonic apparatus which the ruling class employed to
disseminate this essentially feudal culture among the industrial bourgeoisie was an elite education system. Unable to acquire the necessary
acres and rural background, the growth of the 'public' school system
provided the urban bourgeoisie with the opportunity to imbue their
sons with 'gentlemanly' values. The basis of a sound and moral education was deemed to be theology and the Greek and Roman classics,

while vocational subjects, including the sciences, were eschewed as being too closely associated with industry: 'science was linked in the public mind with industry, and this damaged its respectability in upper class eyes. Industry meant an uncomfortable closeness to working with one's hands, not to mention an all-too-direct earning of money' (Weiner 1981: 18). As a result, a rigid demarcation was drawn between a morally virtuous and elitist education and an inferior vocational education: 'The public school and Oxbridge ... taught the future governing elite and intelligentsia to despise "trade" as beneath a gentleman' (Barnett, C. 1996: 15; see also Anderson 1987: 41; Overbeek 1990: 44; Cain and Hopkins 1993a: 31).

This bias against industry was continued within the university system: 'Victorian Oxbridge, too, followed the example of the public school, believing with John Ruskin that the purpose of a university was to provide a liberal education, and the purpose of a liberal education ... was to train young men to "the perfect exercise and knightly continence of their bodies and souls" ' (Barnett, C. 1986: 14). In emphasizing such values the elite education system performed a crucial role in ensuring the continuing hegemony of an archaic ruling class, enabling it to absorb only the most talented individuals from subordinate stratums (Nairn 1976: 12).

An obstructive proletariat

Both neo-liberal and neo-Marxist variants of the cultural thesis also blame narrowly corporatist and obstructive trade unions for Britain's economic decline. An essentially conservative trade-union movement, in seeking to defend its members' interests, has historically opposed the modernization and development of British industry: 'British trade unions from their birth saw their principal role as the defence of existing crafts and existing industrial technology against replacement by new machinery and new methods' (Barnett, C. 1996: 16). From the outset, the trade unions have been dominated by a relatively affluent group of skilled workers whose priority has been to improve their terms and conditions while defending existing manning levels (Anderson 1987: 49).

Within much of the neo-liberal and Marxist literature it is argued that the trade unions have been decidedly successful in realizing their narrow economistic aims;[6] for example, as Glyn and Harrison argue, 'The UK working class's strong organization at factory level thwarted many of capital's attempts to increase productivity. New techniques, involving a sharp increase in the technical composition of capital, were often effectively vetoed by unions which did not want to lose jobs'

(1980: 50; see also Kilpatrick and Lawson 1980; Hall, P. A. 1986a: 44). Similarly, Barnett derides the trade unions' power 'to hold down productivity, to insist on overmanning and to obstruct technological change' (1996: 355). Fearful of job losses, a relatively powerful skilled workforce frequently challenged the introduction of new technology,[7] thereby contributing to the UK's economic decline.

Nairn and Anderson argue that the tragedy for the British working class was that it emerged prior to the intellectual development of socialist ideology: 'The tragedy of the first proletariat was not that it was immature; it was rather that it was in a critical sense premature' (1992: 23). The early development of industrial capitalism meant that the working class emerged as a political force prior to the development of a coherent socialist ideology. The high point of English working-class radicalism, Chartism, predated the emergence of Marxism. As such, the English proletariat was denied the political and ideological leadership of Marxist intellectuals and was forced to rely on bourgeois intellectuals such as Owen.

Marxist theory became politically influential at a time when the British working class was licking its wounds, following the defeat of Chartism. Consequently, the British working class, bruised and lying low as Marxist revolutionary fervour swept across Europe, simply missed the boat. This lack of revolutionary impetus within the British Labour movement was further exacerbated by a 'supine bourgeoisie' whose ideological passivity left the working class with no immediate class antagonist. Having missed the Marxist revolutionary train, the English working class fell victim to the influence of 'stunted bourgeois ideology' in the form of utilitarianism.

Central to Nairn and Anderson's explanation of decline is their belief that the industrial bourgeoisie and the working class failed to develop more than a corporate consciousness. Gramsci identifies three moments of political consciousness which it is necessary to transcend before achieving a hegemonic position. First, there is an 'economic-corporate' phase in which the corporate group is aware of its collective interests but not of its class interests. Second, there is a 'political economic' moment in which class interests begin to be expressed but only on an economic level. The third moment is the realization of hegemony, 'in which one becomes aware that one's own corporate interests, in their present and future development, transcend the corporate limits of the purely economic class, and can and must become the interests of other subordinate groups too' (1971: 181).

As such, the revolutionary struggle is not a purely economic one, but a 'universal' struggle in which political, intellectual and moral objectives become as important as economic aims. Nairn and Anderson argue that both the industrial bourgeoisie and the proletariat fail to develop their political consciousness beyond a narrow corporate-economism. Consequently, in failing to struggle at a political and ideological level the hegemony of the traditional ruling class remained relatively unchallenged.

The determinist / voluntarist tension within the cultural thesis

A strong tension exists within the cultural thesis between a deterministic historiography and a short-term voluntarism. Throughout the literature there is an inherent tension between a structural-determinist historical narrative and an instrumentalist-voluntarist account of the perceived failings of postwar governments. On the one hand, the incomplete nature of Britain's bourgeois revolution and the subsequent failure to modernize the British state meant that economic decline was inevitable. Yet, once having established the inevitability of economic decline, the narrative shifts to the failings of individual governments. Historical inevitability has somehow become political ineptitude.

Much of the literature is dominated by a historical narrative, which is overly structural, and a short-term narrative, which is overly voluntaristic. On the one hand, there is an attempt to construct a historiographical explanation for the apparently relentless downward trajectory of the British economy. In this narrative the main culprits are a hopelessly archaic British state and a fossilized ruling class. On the other hand, as the narrative jumps to the postwar period, a succession of governments are implicated as the principal felons in this sorry tale. In this voluntarist account it is the ill-judged policy priorities of successive governments which are viewed as the main cause of Britain's continuing postwar demise.

Contradictions within the Barnett thesis

There is a considerable tension between Barnett's deterministic historiography and his agency-centred critique of the Churchill coalition and the Attlee governments. On the one hand, he argues that one hundred years of economic decline since the zenith of Victorian entrepreneurialism was the inevitable consequence of a peculiarly British anti-industrial ethos. Within this narrative, as shown in the previous section, decline is attributed to the hegemony of a backward-looking feudalistic liberal political elite. Accordingly, a self-serving ruling Establishment was able to forward its own interests through its cultural hegemony, allowing a pernicious anti-industrial culture to filter down through the state and education system. However, on shifting to his analysis of postwar decline, Barnett launches a blistering salvo against those who dominated the Churchill coalition and the Attlee governments, although there has been no discernible shift in the hegemonic domination of the traditional ruling elite. Indeed, Barnett is at pains to emphasize that the New Jerusalemers are but the latest manifestation of a long line of 'small-"l" liberal intelligentsia' who collectively form the 'enlightened' Establishment (1986: 11).

Although Barnett argues that the same traditional liberal political elite which is culpable for one hundred years of decline remains the dominant influence on the Churchill and Attlee governments, he somehow expects it to perform a volte-face and abandon its own interests to promote national reconstruction. Given the pathological trajectory of decline outlined in the historical narrative, it seems implausible that we would expect the ruling elite suddenly to jettison the very cultural ethos which was the historical basis of its hegemonic position. Barnett fails to develop an adequate explanation of why the National and Attlee governments should have acted any differently than previous governments when faced with economic realities. He clearly believes that the wartime leaders missed a historical opportunity to modernize the British economy. However, in seeking to blame the New Jerusalemers for prioritizing welfare over industrial regeneration, Barnett accords the wartime coalition and Attlee governments a political autonomy which he denies previous governments.

Contradictions within the neo-Marxist historiography

Within the Marxist historiography it is arguable that the period from 1688 to the 1960s is viewed as a unified conjunctural moment; for example, as Nield argues in a critique of Anderson's 1964 article in *New Left Review*, 'Anderson operates with a notion of conjuncture hugely expanded to embrace some three hundred years of historical process' (1980: 496). This leads to the development of a deterministic analysis in which economic decline is attributed to the historical hegemony of an archaic ruling class.

Fine and Harris argue that Nairn and Anderson's historicist methodology leads to a 'curiously monolithic view of British history', which understates the complexity and dynamism of economic, societal, cultural and political change (1985: 55–80). Similarly, Barratt Brown criticizes the Nairn / Anderson thesis for analysing historical movements from a great height: 'History is more complex than what appears in the Olympian view from great arches' (1988: 24). He argues that it is a preoccupation with identifying historical continuities which has led authors such as Nairn and Anderson to take a synoptic view of the overall picture while ignoring the underlying detail. Consequently, Nairn and Anderson develop a deterministic analysis of Britain's economic position in which recent economic difficulties, such as unemployment and industrial decline, are explained in terms of the continuing hegemony of a seventeenth-century alliance between financiers and the traditional aristocracy.

Yet, on the other hand, we jump effortlessly from 1688 to 1945 and the failings of the Attlee government to implement radical institutional change. Within this narrative, political actors are deemed to have a large degree of autonomy in pursuing policy preferences. Here, economic decline is attributed to the catastrophic policy priorities pursued by specific governments. However, given the inevitability of decline outlined in the historical narrative, there is a failure to develop an adequate explanation of why postwar governments have the political autonomy to address Britain's economic malaise. If the state has remained essentially unchanged since the seventeenth century and it is the specific character of the state which is the major problem, it seems pointless to address the policy priorities of postwar governments, which are surely irrelevant to the onward march of a historical process set in stone three hundred years earlier. As Hay argues, 'The tension between a structural-determinist account of British decline ... and an instrumental-voluntarist account of specific political projects and their institutional effects is once again starkly exposed' (1996b: 12). As such, there is an inherent contradiction between an instrumentalist view of the state and a historical determinism.

However, in rejecting the Nairn / Anderson theses as inherently deterministic, there is a real danger of throwing out the baby with the bath water. For, it is implied that the schematic approach which is utilized by Hutton, Nairn and Anderson inevitably leads to a deterministic and teleological analysis. Yet, the principal critique of the Nairn / Anderson theses is empirical rather than theoretical. E. P. Thompson berates Nairn and Anderson for over-simplifying three hundred years of English history, arguing that 'the real history will only disclose itself after much hard research' (1978: 66). While this is certainly a truism in respect of the study of history, it is rather disingenuous within the context of Nairn and Anderson's original aim. As Nield argues, Thompson's critique of Anderson relies: 'on (unequivocally solid) empirical correction and the insinuation that "Origins" is illicit as a historical account' (1980: 493). Cries of empirical paucity can easily stifle theoretical generalizations within an academic environment which favours the rigour and parsimony of a scientific approach.

Anderson argues that this thesis was not intended to provide the definitive account of the history of English capitalism. Rather, it was intended to 'start discussion at the point where it should properly begin'. In this vein, he accuses Thompson of treating 'a 10,000 word article as if it were a Cambridge History' (1966: 4). Rather, as Leys points out, 'Their intention was not to write the history of the previous three hundred years, but to quarry it, using new concepts and asking different questions, for information which would help explain the present crisis. They wanted to "think" the present crisis "historically"' (1983: 13; see also Nield 1980: 501). While we may take issue with Anderson's success in achieving this aim, this does not necessarily undermine the basis of his approach.

In seeking to cover three hundred years of history, thematic considerations are bound to dominate over empirical detail. Clearly, the methodological difficulties in providing an informed analysis of an extended historical period inevitably leads towards a more stylized account; what Anderson refers to as the methodological necessity 'of compression'. However, the aim is never to provide a definitive account of the historical period which is examined. While it does not provide a full explanation of historical events it can be used as the framework for more empirical work: 'the real justification of the theory is that it has yielded concepts that can be cashed empirically' (Anderson 1966: 39).

The real failure of the Nairn, Anderson and Hutton approach is not their methodology, but their failure to develop sufficiently robust theoretical concepts which could inform our empirical analysis. In particular, the Nairn / Anderson thesis is idealistic and, as such, places almost exclusive emphasis upon the superstructure. For example, Nairn and Anderson work with a deterministic notion of hegemony which is clearly contrary to its Gramscian origins. Within their thesis, economic decline is primarily attributed to the hegemony of an archaic ruling class. However, there is a failure to explain the processes and mechanisms through which that hegemony is reproduced. As Johnson argues:

> the Anderson / Nairn view is very undialectical. Stuck in its corporate mode, the working class seems incapable of any kind of challenge. Secure in its hegemony, the dominant class is spared the trouble of continually refurbishing its armoury, accommodating new elements, constructing hegemony from a selection of the materials offered by real relations. (1976: 23)

As such, hegemonic domination is viewed as being static and unchanging. In contrast, we need to develop a much more dynamic and Gramscian conception of hegemony which allows for a continual struggle, not only between different social classes, but also between the different fractions of the ruling bloc. Again as Johnson argues, 'one would want to insist on a pattern of challenge and response, action and re-action, problem and "solution", threat and containment, but containment always on a higher level' (ibid.).

In their haste to demonstrate the dominance of a moribund economic class within the British state, Nairn and Anderson unwittingly remove class conflict from their historical analysis. The historical failure of the industrial bourgeoisie to become hegemonic and the concomitant political weakness of the working class supposedly blunted class conflict within Britain. Nairn and Anderson's emphasis on the weakness of the 'two great hostile camps' implies that they were not 'directly facing each other' in a continual struggle. In contrast to orthodox Marxism, in which, 'the history of all hitherto society is the history of class struggle', Nairn and Anderson construct a static historical snapshot of untroubled aristocratic hegemony. History is no longer a series of class conflicts.

Clearly, the principal aim of analysing the *longue durée* is to identify structural continuities. However, in developing a totalizing view of history there is a danger in constructing a teleological analysis in which there is little room for human agency. In suggesting that politics is of little importance to the unrelenting pathologies of a political process set in motion in 1688, Nairn and Anderson negate the usefulness of empirical enquiry. As such, if political actors have had a negligible impact on history it surely seems futile to investigate their role empirically. Paradoxically, it also absolves those very governments which they hold responsible for Britain's decline.

The contested nature of the English ruling class

Within structuralist accounts of decline it is also argued that Nairn and Anderson ignore the extent to which the state has historically forwarded the interests of industrial capital. Variously, it is argued that the aristocracy survived as a capitalist class, that the industrial middle class achieved a hegemonic position within the state, or that Britain did not have a second revolution because the bourgeoisie was able to prosper without one (Mooers 1991). In reality, the state has always acted in the interests of industrial capital: 'The fact is that laissez-faire implied a powerful state framework within which capital could operate freely' (Barratt Brown 1988: 35). Further, while Nairn and Anderson claim that Britain's imperial role was uniquely favourable to financial and commercial capital, here it is argued that it also favoured the development of productive capital.

Thompson contends that Nairn and Anderson misinterpret the fundamental nature of the English ruling class (1978: 53). Although certain elements of the aristocracy retained some political influence, this was due to their metamorphosis into a capitalist class. Consequently, Thompson argues, the industrial bourgeoisie gradually became the dominant political class during the Victorian epoch. Similarly, Nicholls holds that 'Anderson seems to have forgotten the quintessential point about the English aristocracy ... namely, its remarkable wealth, enterprise and longevity as a *capitalist* class. It is precisely this point which makes a second revolution unnecessary' (quoted in Mooers 1991: 177). Whereas Nairn and Anderson emphasize the gentrification of the bourgeoisie, Thompson argues that the aristocracy survived as a subordinate stratum within a formidable new ruling bloc, formed by the Victorian middle classes. This point is emphasized by Walter Bagehot's *The English Constitution* (1867): a *'locus classicus* which Anderson and Nairn appear to have overlooked' (1978: 53). Bagehot divides the British constitution into its 'dignified parts', including the monarchy and aristocratic institutions which are essentially ceremonial, and its 'efficient parts', principally the House of Commons where government business is largely conducted. Thompson argues that Bagehot was clearly convinced that the latter was 'under the "despotic" control of the middle-classes' (ibid.).

In similar vein, Mooers argues that Britain failed to have a second modernizing revolution precisely because the bourgeoisie was able to prosper without recourse to such a struggle. Whereas Nairn and Anderson argue that an archaic state proved deleterious to the development of the British economy, Mooers claims that the state performed a central role in facilitating the development of British capitalism. The state was not backwards; instead, 'In all its major respects – Parliament and the civil service, taxation, property and criminal law, foreign policy and war – the British state in the eighteenth century was uniquely suited to the requirements of capitalism' (1991: 171). However, although the state performed a crucial role in terms of legitimizing property rights of nascent capitalists, it had no direct role in the running of the economy.

The negative impact of early industrialization

There are also a number of authors who explain the development of the British economy in terms of its initial development (Jessop 1980; Zysman 1983; Ingham 1984; Hall, P. A. 1986a, 1995; Marquand 1988; Radice 1995; Cain and Hopkins 1993a, 1993b; Hutton 1995). The basis of this argument is that the huge economic advantages which early British companies enjoyed as a consequence of being the first nation to industrialize meant that they were able to fund their own expansion and development through retained profits. Consequently, there was no need to develop the institutional links between finance and industry which are seen as the foundation of economic success in countries such as Japan, Germany and France.[8]

Further, the majority of early industrial firms were relatively small, family-owned enterprises which were largely self-financing (Hutton 1995: 118). Any coherence within industry tended to occur at a regional or local level. Significantly, there was no need for the national industrial banks such as those that developed on the Continent. As investment was largely met from retained profits, companies tended to borrow only small amounts from the banks and on a short-term basis. Consequently, 'the banks generally saw no need to take an equity share in firms or play an active role in their management' (Hall 1986a: 38).

The development of an arms-length relationship between industry and finance and a limited role for government was initially compatible with the interests of British capital generally. As the first country to industrialize, Britain enjoyed a huge advantage in the initial staple manufacturing products. The early success of British manufacturers prompted them to plough most of their resources back into the areas where they had a market advantage. As a result, there was little interest in diversifying into developing markets which were much more science-based, such as the chemical industry (Marquand 1988: 118).

The early advantage of British manufacturers was strengthened by the country's military dominance. UK companies had privileged access to a number of overseas markets as a consequence of British imperialism. In contrast to the Nairn/Anderson theses, Barratt Brown argues that this imperial role furthered the interests of productive capital as much as financial capital: 'The Empire was an economic business, involving production as much as commerce' (1988: 37). The Empire offered privileged access for many British manufacturers to invest in production (ibid.: 31–40).

Additionally, industrialists also had the option of investing their profits in the rapidly expanding financial and commercial sectors. By investing in these areas, additional profits could be realized with far fewer risks and much more quickly than through risky and long-term investments in industry. The concentration of investment in commercial and financial activity was not the consequence of a markedly anti-industrial culture but was the inevitable consequence of profit-maximizing capitalists. This has led a number of authors to argue that Britain has never been a primarily manufacturing and industrial economy (Ingham 1984; Leys 1986; Anderson 1987; Rubinstein 1990, 1994). Rubinstein's claim is indicative of this position. He argues that

Britain, 'was always, even at the height of the industrial revolution, essentially a commercial, financial and service-based economy whose comparative advantage always lay with commerce and finance' (1994: 40).

In contrast to the cultural thesis which seeks to explain the UK economy in terms of an anarchic state and cultural backwardness, Ingham views Britain's role as being integral to the international capitalist system. This is a position which is also supported by Leys, who argues that global capitalism requires a centralized financial centre which can settle international accounts through a trusted world currency. As such, the distinctive nature of the British economy can be explained in terms of its role as a global finance centre (Leys 1986: 117). Global capitalism needs an international currency and a state committed to defending the value of that currency: 'the political requirement of a world currency is above all that the issuing state can be relied not to subordinate the interests of foreign users of that currency to purely national needs' (Ingham 1984: 114). Ingham suggests that the essentially commercial character of British capitalism meant that it was uniquely placed to perform this role.

Despite pointing to a Hegelian fallacy in Nairn and Anderson's work, Ingham remains broadly supportive of their theses and has explicitly acknowledged the particular influence of Anderson on his own work (1984: 225). In turn, both Nairn and Anderson have accepted Ingham's overall argument. As such, they now provide a more materialistic explanation of ruling-class hegemony than in their earlier writings; for example, Anderson now attributes the peculiar development of British capitalism to:

> The sum of perfectly rational choices for particular capital – to persist in traditional sectors in which investment had already been sunk, to move into those overseas markets where competition was least, to avoid reorganisation of labour processes at home, or simply to shift from profit-making altogether into rent or interest – all together determined a creeping loss of competitive capacity for British capitalism as a whole, confronted with Germany or the USA. (1987: 72; see also Rubinstein 1994: 40; Hobsbawm 1969: 187–92)

Therefore, in his later work Anderson attributes Britain's decline, not to the bewitching allure of a leisurely lifestyle, but the consequence of 'perfectly rational choices for particular capitals'.

Conclusion

A dominant theme within the literature on Britain's relative economic decline is an alleged political failure to modernize the state in order to meet the demands of a highly competitive and increasingly globalized capitalist economic system. From all sides of the political spectrum, political scientists, economists and historians have rued the failure to create new institutions with the power and autonomy to reverse the spiral of decline. From neo-Marxists such as Nairn and Anderson, through centre-left critics such as Marquand and Hutton to right-wing authors such as Correlli Barnett, the lament is strangely cognate. While Britain's close competitors, such as France, Japan and Germany, benefited from highly active state / economy relations. Britain remained encumbered with an anachronistic state unable to lead industrial development. In key areas such as investment, rationalization, training and research and development Britain lagged well behind its European neighbours. However, within these accounts there is a strong residue of determinism. In particular, there is a failure to explain why the numerous political attempts at developing the institutional capacity which they call for were so unsuccessful.

Too often, in wandering through the mists of time, the discerning historiographer loses sight of politics. In particular, in providing a generalized historical overview there is a tendency to develop a schematic model which emphasizes structural continuities and leads inevitably towards a teleological analysis in which the absence of political actors is telling. The teleological nature of their historical analysis means that it is of little heuristic utility in explaining the role of agency in postwar British politics.

Clearly, I reject any suggestion that Britain's relative economic decline was inevitable. Comparatively slow levels of economic growth in the postwar period cannot be explained solely by the absence of a modernizing bourgeois revolution or by the initial character of British industrialization. While these factors may have indeed been highly influential on the particular development of British capitalism, they do not provide an adequate explanation of why successive postwar governments have failed to create a more developmental state. In particular, there is a failure to recognize the increasing support for a more interventionist state, not only within the Labour Party but also within some sections of the Conservative Party and British industry (see chapter 7). Arguably, as the extent of Britain's relative decline became more and more apparent a conjunctural moment emerged during the early 1960s in which there was the possibility of a structural shift in the balance of class forces within the state. Indeed, in Ingham's view, 'The significance of 1964 cannot be overestimated: for the first time in British history, the progressive forces of industrial capital were in accord with a political party in power' (1984: 208). This suggests that from time to time *real* possibilities do open up for radical governments to exploit.

Ultimately, what is missing from most accounts of Britain's economic decline is any analysis of the political. While an historical analysis is useful in identifying the nature of the structured environment in which political conflict occurs, we also have to account for the manner in which political actors evaluate the possibility for change and devise a strategy for achieving their party's goals and aims within contingent structural constraints. However, this is not to suggest that we privilege the political in explaining change. Rather, we need to contextualize the political response to Britain's economic malaise within the ideological, economic and political constraints which postwar governments faced.

Notes

1   In particular, see Anderson 1964 and 1996 and Nairn 1964. For an orthodox Marxist critique of the Nairn / Anderson theses, see Thompson 1965.

2   The impact of the cultural thesis on the Thatcherite agenda can be illustrated by Sir Keith Joseph's 1985 Green Paper on Education. In it, he warned that universities needed 'to be concerned with attitudes to the world outside higher education, and in particular to industry and commerce, and to be aware of anti-business snobbery. The entrepreneurial spirit is essential for the maintenance and improvement of employment' (quoted in Rubinstein 1990: 3). Mrs Thatcher's frequent reference to her status as a science graduate also comes to mind here.

3   Weiner's work in particular gained a great deal of publicity. Published in 1981 at the height of a crippling recession it was widely reviewed within the mainstream media and formed the basis for two Granada TV *World in Action* programmes (Baxendale 1986: 171). Arguably, this helped to legitimize the Thatcherite assault on the whole fabric of British society.

4   The 1979 election was the first to be fought primarily around the question of Britain's economic decline (Weiner 1981: 162).

5   There are a number of authors who argue that the Attlee government was committed to developing a much more interventionist industrial policy. The work of Helen Mercer (1991) is especially instructive in this area. In contrast to Barnett, who argues that the Attlee government's preoccupation with building the New Jerusalem meant that it ignored the needs of industry, she argues that it developed a number of institutional initiatives aimed at improving industrial performance. However, it was thwarted in its attempts at greater state intervention by peak industrial organizations such as the Federation of British Industries (FBI). This position is also supported by Johnman

who argues that 'both the Labour Party and the Board of Trade had developed highly credible industrial strategies which had become homogenous by 1944' (1991: 30; see also Tiratsoo and Tomlinson 1993). Although I accept the argument that industry has traditionally opposed greater state intervention, I also question the extent of the Labour Party leadership's commitment to large-scale intervention (see chapter 7).

6 For a critique of this position, see Fine and Harris 1985: 29–37. They argue that the British trade-union movement has been historically weak. This is illustrated by the relatively poor wages which British workers enjoy in comparison to other European workers. Richardson also argues: 'the limited hard evidence that was and is available, as opposed to anecdotes and newspaper headlines, gives surprisingly slender support to the view that trade unions or industrial relations arrangements were themselves major contributors to our economic difficulties' (1991: 416).

7 In contrast to Barnett, Tiratsoo and Tomlinson (1993) argue that the trade unions were fully committed to improving industrial productivity in the postwar period. For example, they emphasize the 1946 document produced by the General Council of the TUC, 'Production Under Full Employment', which accepted the need to increase productivity. Additionally, the TUC was fully behind the attempts of the various initiatives of the Attlee government to improve productivity levels and furiously lobbied its member unions to do likewise.

8 For example, Japan, France and Germany all have long-term development banks aimed at securing the long-term finance required for sustained investment: Japan has its Industrial Bank of Japan; Germany its Kreditanstadt für Wiederaufbau (KfW); France its Crédit National. They are all given tax privileges in order to encourage long-term investment. Additionally, each nation has a close network of industrial banks such as the *banques d'affaires* in France, which have developed a close involvement with many domestic companies and take an active interest in their performance (Zysman 1983; see also Hutton 1995: 132–68).

3

The Postwar Consensus: A Woozle That Wasn't?

Pooh was walking round and round in a circle . . .
'Hallo!' said Piglet, 'what are you doing?'
'Tracking something', said Winnie-the-Pooh . . .
'Tracking what?' said Piglet, coming closer.
'That's just what I ask myself. I ask myself, What?'

A. A. Milne, *Winnie-the-Pooh*

In A. A. Milne's classic children's story, from which the excerpt above is taken, Piglet discovers Winnie-the-Pooh following a set of animal prints in the snow. In response to Pooh's confusion over which type of animal made the tracks, Piglet volunteers the suggestion that it could have been a 'woozle' and then proceeds to join Pooh in the hunt. After a short time, however, the tracks which Pooh and Piglet had been following turn into three sets of prints and, then, five. Pooh and Piglet have been unwittingly walking in a circle. The 'woozle' which they thought they had discovered turns out to be nothing more than their own sets of prints.

My aim in this chapter is to argue that Pooh and Piglet's hunt for the woozle provides us with a useful metaphorical device for highlighting some of the problems inherent in a different kind of storyline. The storyline in question is one which the vast majority of political scientists and historians hold dear in the study of postwar British politics; specifically, that for a period of about thirty years after the war a consensus emerged amongst Britain's political elite over the need to increase levels of state intervention and co-operation between government and other key political and economic actors.

The so-called post war consensus, which is also commonly referred to as the postwar settlement or, by some state theorists, as the Keynesian welfare state settlement, has become one of the most central and recurring themes within narratives of postwar political development. Considered to have been constructed primarily around the ideas of Keynes and Beveridge, the consensus has been viewed as a distinct policy paradigm which shaped the strategic choices of Britain's leading political actors as they sought to build and then to preserve a 'New Jerusalem' from the damage created by the war.

This chapter takes issue with the consensus thesis, arguing that in many senses the postwar consensus is as much a myth or fantasy as Piglet's woozle. More specifically, I shall suggest that the origins of the consensus thesis are relatively recent and the concept was developed, in large part, to explain the origins of Thatcherism. In addition, I argue that the consensus thesis does not stand up to detailed empirical examination. First, there is doubt that early postwar governments ever really embraced social democracy and / or Keynesianism. Second, there were significant and fundamental conflicts on many of the putative pillars of the postwar consensus. Third, the dominance of the interests of the financial sector over other key groups has, perhaps, provided the greatest continuity in the postwar period and indeed earlier, yet the literature on the postwar consensus plays down this important aspect of British political development (see chapter 2).

The postwar consensus: an enduring thesis

In recent years, appraisals of the postwar consensus have assumed a certain vogue (see, for example, Marquand 1989; Dutton 1991; Butler 1993; Kavanagh and Morris 1994; Seldon 1994a). Nevertheless, the concept has not been devoid of its critics. A growing number of authors appear to be questioning the extent to which policy in both the wartime and postwar periods can be considered the product of bipartisan accord (see, for example, Pimlott 1988; Jefferys 1991; Brooke 1992; Rollings 1994). Yet, despite these efforts to revise conventional wisdom, the idea of the postwar consensus has remained an enduring theme within the majority of attempts to narrate the development of British politics since the Second World War.

The postwar consensus thesis can be traced to the work of Paul Addison (1975; 1987; 1993) and Dennis Kavanagh (1987; 1992; see also Kavanagh and Morris 1994). Addison's work popularized the idea that the experience of the Second World War created the circumstances for a consensual effort by Britain's political elite to develop policies aimed at combating the deep divisions in British society. In recent years, a plethora of authors have championed Addison's thesis, or at least a qualified version of it. They accept his view that the war led to a new agenda forged around a bipartisan consensus on the need for greater social security and welfare reforms, full employment and more interventionist fiscal and industrial policies. To date, Kavanagh and Morris provide the only systematic analysis of the consensus, which, they conclude, consisted of two key elements. First, there was an adherence to a particular policy approach or style of government. This entailed the practice of institutionalized consultative arrangements between government and the major economic interests. Second, there was a shared commitment to a broad set of policies. This involved a bipartisan accord in the following areas (see Kavanagh and Morris 1994):

- full employment, underpinned by Keynesian demand management techniques;
- the mixed economy, including the public ownership of core industries;
- active government, including a widening of the perceived responsibilities of the state and a move towards greater intervention in the economy;[1]
- industrial relations, entailing the conciliation of trade unions and their subsequent involvement in policy-making;
- the welfare state, underpinned by Beveridge's ideas for universal national insurance;
- foreign and defence policy, entailing the maintenance of Britain's role as a nuclear power and membership of the Atlantic Alliance.

Focusing exclusively on the continuity which they detect in public policy, these authors conclude that 'in no sense was post-war Britain a country without politics or without disagreement; our argument is that political disagreement took place within a broad set of shared assumptions about the goals – and the mechanisms – of government action.' (Kavanagh and Morris 1994: 110). More specifically, they define the consensus as 'a set of parameters which bound the set of policy options regarded by senior politicians and civil servants as administratively practicable, economically affordable and politically acceptable' (ibid.: 13).

Few supporters of the consensus thesis dispute its origins or, indeed, its terms. However, as we will see, it is possible to detect differences in accounts of when the period ended. Nevertheless, the increased polarization of the two main parties, coupled with the apparent breakdown of Keynesian economics and corporatist-style government, has led most to assume that the consensus gradually eroded throughout the 1970s, with Mrs Thatcher knocking the final nails into its coffin.

The consensus 'debate'

This brief summary allows us to follow the broad contours of the consensus thesis. What is particularly striking is the extent to which the thesis has become a received wisdom. The vast majority of authors who have sought to interpret the evolution of the postwar period have eagerly rushed to embrace the conclusions drawn by Addison. Of the few who have attempted to revise his views, most make only small amendments, whilst a small minority have chosen to reject it outright. Both these positions will be outlined in the following section. However, I will argue that neither has the capacity to enhance our understanding of the postwar period. For, whereas the former merely engage in semantic and pedantic squabbling, the latter miss their target altogether. As a result, the consensus 'debate' emerges as something of a misnomer, since neither of these attempts at revision has taken us beyond Addison's original work.

Semantics and pedantics: qualified acceptance of the consensus thesis

The majority of authors who have contributed to the limited debate on the postwar consensus confine themselves to persistent wrangling over both the meaning and subsequent depth of the consensus. Thus, whilst some authors refer to a convergence over policy, others argue that the consensus consisted of a deeper, more profound commitment to a set of common beliefs, moral values and social aspirations. The result, as Seldon explains, is one in which various commentators confer 'different intensities of consensual expression' (1994a: 506). For example, Turner regards the situation after the war as involving '*a compromise* between hostile groups, not a consensus' (1989: 18; emphasis added). Likewise, Ritschel (1995: 270) remarks that 'while "consensus" may be too strong a word, there did emerge during the war, if not an absolute accord, then at least *a widely shared agenda* of social and economic reform' (emphasis added).

Here, we can begin to get a measure of the limited scope of the existing debate. For it is clear that this type of discussion does more to entice us into a protracted exercise in semantics than to resolve the complexities of governmental activity in the period under review. Indeed, it is interesting to note that the parameters of this debate become so circumscribed that even Addison is able to concede that 'the term consensus is open to question' (1987: 5). Yet, in his revised judgement he is still able to assert that 'by 1945 the areas of agreement within the Coalition were of more importance for the future than the party conflicts bubbling up from below' (1993: 93). In effect, then, despite having made such a key concession to his opponents, the constricted terms of the debate allow Addison to emerge with a revision of his thesis which does absolutely nothing to alter its fundamental character.

Of course, this is not to say that the meaning and depth of the consensus remain the sole areas of dispute within this type of literature. There are a number of broader concerns which various authors have identified. Foremost amongst these remains the issue of how long the consensus lasted. Whilst there is considerable agreement that its origins lay in a cumulative process between 1940 and 1948, the question of when it ended continues to provoke a plethora of different opinions. The years 1960, 1964, 1967, 1970, 1973, 1975 and 1979 have all been forwarded as possible dates (Butler 1993: 439). Moreover, the issue of who shared in the consensus has also sparked a significant degree of controversy, with answers varying throughout the literature. As Butler explains, different analysts tend to 'pick and choose people – one minute we examine the population at large; the next we focus on parliamentary sentiment; then successive chancellors of the exchequer are in the frame, before we swing suddenly to "political elites" ' (ibid.: 438–9). However, it should be noted that much of the irregularity here has stemmed from theoretical inconsistency rather than any thorough analysis. As a result, these concerns do little to elevate the terms of dispute within the debate beyond even the most pedestrian level. In essence, they reflect a desire to amend the 'fine print' of the thesis, rather than any serious attempt to erase it altogether (Seldon 1994a: 507).

A feeble barrage: outright rejection of the thesis

There are contributors to the debate who appear increasingly inclined to adopt a more sceptical stance. Foremost amongst these is Ben Pimlott, in whose view 'the consensus is a mirage, an illusion that rapidly fades the closer one gets to it' (1988: 503). In this respect, Pimlott stresses that fundamental ideological conflicts divided the two main parties throughout the supposed consensus era. He asserts that politicians throughout the postwar period were enmeshed in deep inter-party wrangles over a wide range of policies. In particular, he cites the Conservatives' inherent hostility towards universal welfare benefits, as well as Anthony Crosland's (1956) call for the left to oppose Conservative ideas, as evidence of a fundamental lack of agreement across the political spectrum.

It is important to emphasize that Pimlott's thesis has been widely viewed as a powerful and convincing polemic against the use of the term consensus to describe postwar British politics. Moreover, as Seldon puts it, his views have attracted support from 'an army of mostly younger historians ... using documents at the Public Record Office and in party archives ... to cast doubt on the existence of consensus in key areas of policy' (1994a: 502–3). The evidence collated by Pimlott and others suggest that 'consensus might appear to have existed ... when looked at from a very broad perspective. But when viewed from close to the ground, or the documents, the reality was very different' (ibid.). This is by no means a small point. For, quite clearly, the approach taken by Pimlott and his supporters takes us beyond the threadbare rejoinders to the thesis which have so far dominated the debate. The aim of these authors is to highlight the fact that the consensus amounts to nothing more than a construct created by those who wish nostalgically to portray the postwar period as a 'golden era' in British politics. Yet this task appears to have eluded them, because, however convincing their arguments, the overall commitment to the thesis by most authors has remained resolute. As Seldon explains in relation to Pimlott's own views 'this high calibre pounding from the artillery of one of Britain's most senior contemporary historians in fact makes as little impression as the seven-day British barrage before the Battle of the Somme' (1994a: 503).

Aiming short of the target: why the consensus thesis has endured

We may then ask ourselves why the consensus thesis has remained such a central part of our understanding of the postwar political scene. In particular, we need to explain the inability to purge the thesis from our collective consciousness, despite the existence of cogent and often convincing evidence for so doing. In this section, I will argue that the main reason for this lies in the fact that the emphasis upon the consensus thesis serves a purpose which goes beyond merely explaining the period to which it has been applied. Primarily, it has been used to highlight the supposed radicalism of both the Attlee and Thatcher governments. In effect, then, it is as inextricably bound to our understanding of these administrations as it is to the era of supposed bipartisan convergence after the war.

In order to illustrate this point, I will, first, examine the origins of the consensus thesis and, second, locate the pivotal role which it plays in bolstering broader claims about the supposed radicalism of the Attlee and Thatcher governments. Overall, I will contend that the consensus has tended to be constructed around a set of pejorative assumptions which most authors have a vested interest in maintaining.

The hunt for the woozle: the origins of the consensus thesis

As we saw at the beginning of this chapter, the woozle in A. A. Milne's story turned out to be in the mind of the beholders. The tracks which Pooh and Piglet had been following were, in actual fact, ones which they themselves had created. Similarly, once we begin to locate the origins of the consensus thesis, we soon find that the same process has taken place; in this case, however, it is the persistent discovery of the supposed 'consensus', by political scientists and historians alike, which are the tracks created by those following them.

This point has been expressed by Marlow, who contends that the idea of the postwar consensus has become 'a taken-for-granted idea that remains something of an unexamined assumption' (1996: 131). In this respect, Marlow points out that the consensus thesis emerged without any detailed and systematic evidence or study to support it. In place of a distinct body of literature on the topic, what we mainly find is an assortment of 'tangential references and allusions to the existence of the once-said consensus' (ibid.: 128) which provide: 'a superficial but nevertheless mutually-supporting framework of validation for the idea' (ibid.: 131). As a result, Marlow concludes that the thesis emerged as the product of a process which postmodernists often refer to as 'inter-textuality'. This denotes a practice whereby an abstraction becomes defined through its repeated use within a variety of texts. When we trace the origins of the consensus thesis, what we discover turns out to be nothing other than 'a universe of texts that collectively sanction the ... thesis, primarily, by dint or their sheet persuasiveness' (ibid.: 132). As we noted earlier, Kavanagh and Morris (1994) have provided the only systematic study of the consensus to date, and by the time they did so the concept had already become taken for granted.

Why then have so many authors been happy to claim the existence of the postwar consensus without having a substantive body of evidence to support their views? The answer to this question soon becomes clear if we consider *when* the thesis became popular. As Pimlott (1988) reminds us, the idea came to the fore in the context of the bitter conflicts and party divisions which were characteristic of the late 1970s and early 1980s. In other words, its origins corresponded with the ascendancy of Mrs Thatcher and the emergence of New Right ideas within the

Conservative Party.[2] This is no small coincidence, especially if we consider that Kavanagh's (1987) original work on the consensus appeared within his analysis of the Thatcher governments and that the majority of the 'tangential references' to the postwar consensus are to be found throughout the literature on Thatcherism. These points help to highlight the fact, discussed in more length below, that the consensus thesis emerged, in large part, as the product of authors' attempts to draw conclusions about the Thatcher governments rather than about the so-called consensus era itself. Specifically, most authors have utilized the thesis as a crude means of underpinning their views that the Thatcher governments were radical in dismantling a set of practices which were initiated by previous postwar administrations.

Contextualizing the consensus thesis

From this, then, we can infer that the postwar consensus thesis has not essentially been directed towards describing bipartisan convergence in the period after the war. Instead, it is, in essence, an heuristic framework designed to highlight specific contrasts between Thatcherism and its historical antecedents. What is particularly illuminating, therefore, about the literature on consensus is the limited clarity which it bestows upon the period which is supposedly under scrutiny. The consensus debate does very little to elucidate governmental activity between 1951 and 1979. Rather, it offers a static representation of the period which gives greater definition to the achievements of the Attlee and Thatcher administrations than to the so-called consensus era.

At the heart of the consensus thesis, then, is the implied claim that the structures of the state were fundamentally transformed after the Second World War and then again after 1979. By supporting this claim the thesis can be said to suit the pejorative assumptions of those who have utilized it. For, as Dutton explains: 'both supporters and detractors of the [Thatcher] government[s] have had good reason to exaggerate the extent to which 1979 marks a break with the past' (1991: 95). Thus, much of the debate over consensus has been dominated by an 'attempt to engage in political myth-making' (Eatwell 1979: 158). The thesis's ability to organize a contrast between the pre-1979 and post-1979 eras and thereby provide definition to the extent of supposed transformation in both periods, has meant that the idea of consensus remains an important myth across the whole political spectrum. In particular, most have a vested interest in keeping alive the idea that consensus politicians were successful in constructing a Keynesian, social democratic state settlement which was later dismantled by the Thatcher governments. To liberals and social democrats, this thesis helps to demonize the latter, whilst proclaiming the paternalistic virtues of the former. Meanwhile, to both the left and right, it emphasizes the fact that, as Marquand explains, 'Keynesian social democracy collapsed because it was bound to collapse. It was a philosophy of the middle way and there cannot be a middle way' (1989: 2).

Broadening our focus

So far, I have argued that the idea of the postwar consensus, and with it the implied claim that the structures of the state were fundamentally transformed in the immediate postwar period, is, to an extent, a myth created by those who wish to exaggerate the extent to which Keynesian social democracy became inscribed into the parameters of the state after the Second World War. In this section, I will contend that this myth has been successfully maintained through the highly selective information which most authors highlight in order to support their views. This selectivity manifests itself in two different ways. First, the majority of accounts on offer provide us with a very circumscribed view of the 'political', thereby focusing almost exclusively on party politics to the neglect, or exclusion, of other key actors. Second, they also pay too much attention to the power of particular ideas in shaping government policy to the neglect, or exclusion, of others.

Circumscribing the political: the overemphasis on party politics

Throughout the literature on consensus, most authors' focus is directed, almost entirely, towards an analysis of the behaviour of Britain's two leading political parties. Indeed, in many cases, the primary focus becomes the leading personalities within both parties. As a result, these analyses offer a narrow framework within which we might seek to view legitimate political activity. In effect, they are implicitly driven by the idea that the power to influence government policy rests primarily with government actors.

The problem, however, is that such accounts fail to appreciate both the subtleties and the complexities of the power relations which influenced the postwar political scene. In particular, they fail to acknowledge the complex interactions between class fractions, leading institutions, government and, indeed, the leading pressure groups, which all combined to influence policy over this time-frame. As I shall argue in the following sections, once we broaden our focus beyond the arena of party politics and personalities, we begin to get a better measure of the true dynamics within the postwar British state, and of the constant interaction and articulation of interests between politicians, unions, producer groups, financiers and leading institutions, such as the Treasury, the City and the Bank of England. When we consider the sum of these interactions, the picture which emerges is one of continual and often fundamental conflicts between the key actors involved in the formulation of policy, rather than one of consensus.

Circumscribing the ideational: the overemphasis upon the power of particular ideas

Related to the problem outlined above has been the persistent tendency within the literature to overstate the impact of particular types of ideas throughout the postwar period. Most authors have been highly selective in emphasizing the impact of ideas geared towards the implementation of statist measures to promote economic growth, welfare reform and full employment. Generally, if not invariably, the principal emphasis has been placed upon the role of both Keynes and Beveridge, and more broadly of social democratic ideas in general, in helping politicians from both parties to formulate, or come to embrace, a coherent policy paradigm which could achieve these aims. The problem, however, is that these accounts tend to exaggerate, first, the unity and coherence of the ideational paradigm around which the consensus supposedly resolved; second, the actual impact which statist ideas made upon the implementation of policy; and, third, the extent to which the dominant ideas of the period differed from both prewar and post-Keynesian beliefs.

Overall, it has been easy for authors to overstate each of these points. At the heart of the problem has been the way in which the definition of Keynesianism has been widened within the literature to the point at which it has become synonymous with broader statist ideas such as those we equate with corporatism and social democracy. Thus, the sum commitment to Keynesian, social democratic, planned interventionist strategies is presented as a unitary set of beliefs. As such, no attention is paid to the tensions, contradictions and, of course, conflicts, both within Keynesianism, and between Keynesianism and other dominant ideas of the period. As Keith Smith explains: '[although] the "Keynesian" policy-makers have been condemned as full-scale interventionists ... their belief in markets was scarcely less extreme than that of the monetarists' (1989: 182). This means that the attempts to stretch the notion of Keynesianism to include the ideas of corporatism and social democracy fail to consider the crucial conflicts which existed between the commitments of Keynesian policy-makers, on the one hand, to the promotion of statist, interventionist strategies and, on the other hand, to more traditional monetary beliefs and non-interventionist policies. More broadly, however, they fail to acknowledge the conflict which these ideas created between the desire to implement radical policy initiatives and the more conservative instinct to maintain the *status quo*.

As I will demonstrate below, the extent to which Keynesianism, in any form, let alone in the interventionist and radical guise which most authors assume, was ever fully incorporated into economic management is questionable. Nevertheless, this issue is most often sidestepped within the literature. By linking Keynesianism to such a broad church of political practices, the awkward fact that Keynesian ideas were often both inconsistent and indeed inconsistently pursued becomes almost irrelevant, and the false assumption that we can detect continuity based around a strictly statist ideational paradigm is successfully maintained.

Revising the consensus debate

This, then, leaves us with the question of how we can advance the debate over consensus in order to gain a fuller understanding of the evolution of the state in the postwar era. Here, however, I will argue that the only way to advance the present debate is to move beyond it entirely and to redirect our focus away from the question of consensus to the key issue at the heart of the thesis; that is, the question of the extent of state transformation in the early postwar period. Once we start to examine this issue, it soon becomes clear that the concept of consensus, and with it the claim that the consensus brought about state transformation based around a coherent set of governing expectations and assumptions, has little resonance. For, as a review of the supposed planks of the domestic consensus clearly indicates, the aims of postwar politicians were invariably thwarted by the residual contradictions and tensions within those aims and by the overall conflicts which existed between the leading political and economic groups and key institutions of the period.

Keynesian demand management and full employment

To most commentators, the Keynesian revolution in economic policy derived from the success of Keynesian ideas in penetrating the orthodox Treasury view. Traditionally, Treasury control over government finances stood as a powerful impediment to collectivist expansion. Driven by 'two powerful logics' – namely, the logics of tax-cutting and of fiscal responsibility – Treasury officials were 'mainly restricted to the habit of saying no' (Cronin 1991: 12). Consequently, if Keynesian ideas had succeeded in piercing this monolithic arbiter of monetary vigilance, then we could conclude that they had become properly institutionalized.

However, it is essential to remain cautious as to how far the Keynesian ethos successfully penetrated, or indeed challenged, the existing orthodoxy within the state. Throughout the postwar period, pre-Keynesian beliefs continued to dominate the Treasury, thereby serving as a major obstacle to the introduction of an effective demand management strategy for achieving full employment. Consequently, many of the 'supportive' policies advocated by Keynesians during and after the war were ultimately sacrificed, leading to the development of a much more 'modified', or 'simple', variant of Keynesianism which displayed an enormous degree of continuity with previous practice (Thompson, G. 1984; Booth 1986). As a result, an 'oral tradition' in favour of sound monetary policies persisted within the Treasury and was reflected in the economic policies of all postwar governments (Bulpitt 1986).

Overall, the expansion of limited statist measures in the early postwar period, designed to promote both full employment and welfare reforms, should be more readily seen as the result of a temporary loss of Treasury control, rather than as a fundamental conversion by the Treasury to Keynesian ideals (Cronin 1991). By 1947, this control had been re-established and the two 'political logics' of tax-cutting and financial rectitude took their traditional precedence in the minds of Treasury officials and, subsequently, politicians. Thus, by 1951 and the re-election of the Conservatives, the Keynesian revolution in macroeconomics had begun to assume 'a pattern that bore a strong resemblance to the budgetary history of the inter-war years' (ibid.: 208).

However, traditional Treasury orthodoxy and monetary concerns remained only one obstacle to the efficient use of Keynesian budgetary policy. The various attempts by all postwar governments to manage sterling and the exchange rate were a more crucial impediment. The attempts in the years 1957, 1960, 1964, 1966 and 1973 to protect the balance of payments meant that postwar governments were continually forced to throw their apparent commitment to Keynesianism, and with it major planks of their domestic policy, into reverse in the defence of sterling. These attempts at deflation rather than devaluation highlight the crucial fact that the consensus on domestic policy was, in many ways, overshadowed by the persistent hegemony of the sterling lobby. According to Blank, 'this lobby shared the belief that Britain's international position and responsibilities constituted the *primary policy objectives* and that the international role of sterling was vital to this position' (cited in Grant 1987: 81; emphasis added). Thus, the financial sector, with its ability to sanction governments by withholding investment, has played a crucial role in deflecting most postwar governments from the Keynesian policy of maintaining full employment.

Therefore, rather than extending the idea of Keynesianism to describe the institutionalized parameters of the state, it is more important to recognize that preinscribed institutional bias, within the state, coupled with conflicting policy objectives, served to hamper the full implementation of even the most basic Keynesian techniques. In particular, it is clear that the oft-cited consensus on Keynesian, interventionist strategies coincided with a rarely emphasized, often diametrically opposed and, indeed primary, commitment to more traditional monetary concerns and an arms-length approach to economic management. This rival monetarist ethos meant that macroeconomic policy throughout the postwar era displayed an enormous degree of continuity with both prewar and post-Keynesian practice.

The mixed economy

The nationalization programme, although viewed as a litmus test of the Attlee government's commitment to socialist transformation, reflected a more pragmatic commitment to dealing with short-term economic imperatives. Most of the industries taken into public ownership directly after the war were in vulnerable positions within the economy, facing either underinvestment or declining demand and, in the later period, fierce competition from abroad. In this sense, the government had merely taken limited interventionist measures to secure Britain's core industries. Moreover, the provision of cheaper fuel, transport and communications services served, both directly and indirectly, to reduce the costs of private sector business and commercial interests (Thompson, G. 1984: 89). Consequently, as Thompson argues, the nationalization programme 'fitted into a strategy of moderately radical reform under conditions of support for the existing social structure and economic and political relations ... it did not mark a fundamental break with the previous set of state economic practices' (ibid.: 86).

Although public corporations were formally responsible to ministers, the ministry became merely a sponsoring department and key decisions were left to boards and chairmen, who enjoyed complete autonomy from parliamentary accountability. The relations between nationalized industries and sponsoring departments were characterized by tensions and mutual misunderstanding; as such, they were not fully integrated into the control of the state. Therefore, although nationalization did represent a potential redefinition of the relationship between state and society which was consistent with a broadly statist policy paradigm, the reality was that there was little or no commitment to bringing these industries under state control. More importantly, from around 1967 most of these industries were subject to the investment rules and financial criteria of private firms. This effectively meant that they were 'progressively integrated back into the market economy long before the question of their "privatisation" came onto the political agenda' (Thompson 1984: 91).

Of course, to an extent these points are accepted by the majority of political scientists and historians. Nevertheless, the desire to demonstrate the radicalism of both the Attlee and Thatcher governments, and in particular their respective commitments to diametrically opposed policy paradigms, has meant that the bulk of the literature on the postwar period has emphasized the contrast between nationalization and privatization, rather than stressing the crucial continuity in the structure of the state which has predominated.

Planned intervention and active government

As we have seen from our review of both Keynesianism and the nationalization programme, the commitment of postwar politicians, other leading groups and, indeed, key institutions within the state to implement statist measures in order to promote economic growth remained weak. Thus, the third plank of the so-called consensus, a broad commitment to active government, emerges as yet another myth within the literature. Certainly, it is possible to identify a broad coalition across the political spectrum in favour of greater intervention. However, this element of the dominant ideational paradigm co-existed alongside an even stronger commitment to arms-length government and an overall reluctance to institute radical reform.

On the few occasions when governments did reveal their commitment to intervene, they found that the tools which they could use to take supportive measures to aid industry were severely limited. Thus, they found themselves at odds with both the existing structures of the British state and the conflicting interests of other leading groups and institutions. In particular, the separation of the Bank of England and financial capital from the state has effectively prevented all governments from having effective control over the flow of funds in the economy. Similarly, the Treasury has remained isolated from the co-ordination of industrial policy. This has meant that the views of industrial capital have generally been subordinated to the interests of the financial sector and this remained so throughout the postwar period. Indeed, this is one area of continuity in policy which existed between the wars and in the entire postwar period. Overall, these factors all combined to prevent serious attempts at planning until the creation of the National Economic Development Council (NEDC) in 1962.

Between 1962 and 1976, it became increasingly clear to governments that the range of facilitative policies aimed at budgetary management required supplementary interventionist strategies. During this period, therefore, governments began to pursue more active policies aimed at supporting industry. However, this change did not prove to be either fundamental or, indeed, long-standing. The extent to which the government exercised control over capital, even during this more interventionist period, has been grossly overestimated. As a result, these initial attempts failed when, in 1966, in the face of a balance of payments crisis, the Treasury forced the abandonment of economic planning and, indeed, full employment, in the defence of the value of sterling. Similarly, although the 1974–9 Labour government came to power with a commitment to pass an industry act which would provide for the establishment of planning agreements between the government and the country's top firms, coupled with the creation of the National Enterprise Board, by the time the act was passed, it had become substantially deradicalized in the face of major opposition from the Confederation of British Industry (CBI) and the City.

These points highlight the crucial need to distinguish between the statist, interventionist rhetoric which underpinned both parties' policy choices and the actual implementation of policy. It is certainly clear that, whilst a broad commitment to active government remained an important element of the paradigm governing postwar policy, this coincided and indeed conflicted with a more long-standing conservative ethos which sought merely to preserve the *status quo*. After 1962, when governments did start to initiate limited interventionist strategies to promote industry, these strategies found themselves at odds with pre-existing institutional practices and the rival interests of the business and financial sectors.

Industrial relations

There are two distinct, though related, myths often cited regarding the position of trade unions within the so-called consensus. On the one hand, it is argued that throughout most of the period the relationship between government and unions was a harmonious one. On the other, it is suggested that within that relationship unions enjoyed considerable power. Certainly, it is possible to concede that a period of relative consensus did exist between unions and government between 1945 and 1966; however, thereafter this consensus was replaced by persistent conflict in which the balance of power was firmly weighted in favour of capital and the state. Prior to the mid-to-late 1960s there were two main reasons for the relative accord between unions and government. First, the unions were generally content to rely upon wage bargaining within a voluntarist framework consistent with the practice of simple or modified Keynesianism described earlier (Marsh 1992). Ironically, rather than incorporating unions into the decision-making process, this model allowed them to preserve their autonomy and resist integration into any concrete consultative relationship with government. Second, relatively full employment ensured that the unions' bargaining power was stronger.

The unions' devotion to voluntarism has meant that for most of the postwar period they have, contrary to popular belief, resisted direct involvement in the political sphere. Moreover, the increased union involvement after 1966 was the result of government, rather than union, initiatives (Marsh 1992: 56). In this respect, the politicization of trade unions occurred primarily as a consequence of the political elite's search for a quasi-corporatist solution to the country's increasing economic malaise and, subsequently, as a direct result of the imposition of successive incomes policies. As Coates explains, 'with the arrival of incomes policy, industrial relations were, so to speak, politicised at a stroke' (1989: 50).

Nevertheless, it is crucial that we do not lose sight of the extent to which union power throughout the postwar period remained 'overwhelmingly negative' (Dorfman 1979: 6). Any assessment of the relationship between government and unions throughout the postwar period needs to take account of the limited power over and, indeed, involvement with, government which the unions had prior to 1979 (Marsh 1992). Even more crucially, most analyses of the political power of trade unions have neglected the enormous positive veto which capital has had over government in comparison to trade unions. As Hay explains, 'far less visible, yet ultimately of greater significance were ...

the private and informal channels linking the City of London, the Bank of England and the Treasury' (1996c: 56).

Overall, then, much of the literature on the postwar period over-emphasizes the transformation which the consensus brought about in the relationship between government and unions. Whilst exaggerating both the extent of union power and, indeed, their involvement with govern-ment, most authors have also neglected to acknowledge the considerable influence which the 'City–Bank–Treasury nexus' (Hay 1996c: 56), com-pared to trade unions, had over successive postwar governments.

The welfare state

In contrast to the previous policy areas which we examined, the sub-stantial package of welfare reform introduced by the Attlee administra-tion indicates one area of the so-called consensus within which it is possible to identify significant structural transformation. The founda-tions of the welfare state settlement, which was to emerge in the after-math of the Second World War, were laid down by William Beveridge. Beveridge's plans for a radical restructuring of welfare based upon a national insurance scheme were accepted by both main political parties throughout the postwar era and, as Kavanagh and Morris point out, remain 'the most solidly implanted of all the planks of the domestic post-war consensus' (1994: 89). The essential ingredients of the welfare state were fourfold: the extension of existing social security provision; the creation of the National Health Service; the extension of a compre-hensive education system; and the creation of a public housing service.

The creation of a universal welfare state system remains the least dis-puted of the achievements of the Attlee administrations. Indeed, for authors such as C. Barnett (1986), it remained the sole priority of postwar governments and, thereby, had a concomitant effect upon Britain's failure to adjust to the changing conditions of a restructured world economy. Of course, this is a contentious point within the liter-ature. However, when we compare the achievements and the commit-ment of postwar politicians in erecting and then preserving the welfare state system with their lack of success in fulfilling most, if not all, of their other rhetorical commitments, then Barnett's point has some potency. Overall, the enormous successes in welfare reforms contrast starkly with the magnificent failures to implement radical reform in most other areas of the so-called domestic consensus. Ultimately, the welfare state emerges as a spectacular achievement by comparison to the efforts by postwar politicians to enact their other statist commit-ments.

The conflictual character of British politics in the postwar period

Having looked at each of the individual planks of the domestic policy consensus, we are now in a better position to assess which and, indeed, whose particular sets of governing assumptions and expectations succeeded in penetrating the institutional architecture of the postwar British state. Undoubtedly, there is no simple or easy answer to this question. Clearly, the answers vary from policy area to policy area. Thus, for example, the extension of the welfare state emerges as one policy area in which politicians successfully translated their rhetorical pronouncements towards social democracy and active government into actual policy achievements. In this area, we can see that significant structural transformation was brought about by a genuine consensus amongst Britain's political elite. However, beyond the issue of welfare, once we start to examine the achievements in areas such as demand management, nationalization, industrial relations and support for industry, the picture which emerges is a somewhat more complex one. For example, it is clear that the limited efforts by politicians to implement measures to support industry were ultimately thwarted by conflicting pressures from key institutions such as the Treasury and the Bank of England as well as by the rival interests of the business and financial sectors.

Moreover, the issue of locating any real continuity both within and between these distinct policy areas is further complicated by the fact that, in some areas, the direction of policy changed over time. Thus, for example, in industrial relations, it was the assumptions and expectations of trade unions which were primarily satisfied by government acceptance of voluntarism in the early postwar period. However, by the latter half of the so-called consensus era, the sudden interference in industrial relations by the state served to threaten the interests of the unions, whilst satisfying the broader aims of postwar politicians. Similar changes of direction in policy occurred with regard to nationalization, when, after 1967, nationalized industries were gradually integrated back into the market economy; and Keynesian demand management, when the initiative gained by politicians prior to 1947 was lost in the face of a resurgence of Treasury control.

The situation becomes no less complicated once we start to look at which particular ideas came to dominate the scene. Clearly, in the area of welfare, the liberal paternalism of Beveridge, coupled with a commitment to social democracy were in the ascendancy. However, in contrast, with regard to nationalization, we see a semblance of socialism, giving way to pragmatism, before being ultimately replaced by an emphasis on market solutions. Similarly, in macroeconomic policy, the Keynesian concern for full employment is consistently abandoned in favour of traditional monetary concerns. Likewise, when it comes to planning, we are confronted by a commitment to active government, coupled by a concomitant commitment to laissez-faire.

Of course, it would be possible to go on highlighting more and more of the complexity of the postwar political scene without ever reaching any clear or firm conclusions. Yet, this may not be a futile exercise, because it presents us with at least one clear conclusion; that it is more or less impossible to capture the complexity of postwar British politics by utilizing a simple, formulaic thesis. However, this is the aim and indeed the claim of advocates of the consensus thesis, at the heart of which lies the assumption that postwar British politics can be characterized by a clear trajectory of continuity, both in policy and in the governing ideas and assumptions which shaped policy. Once we begin to get a measure of the true complexity of the period, the thesis emerges as an heuristic device of limited value. Unfortunately, it diverts attention away from the inherent conflicts, tensions and contradictions which characterized British politics in this period. It selects the ideas, such as Keynesianism and social democracy, which its adherents wish to emphasize, whilst at the same time neglecting and excluding others, such as the commitment to arms-length government and to traditional monetary orthodoxy. It also selects which groups we should focus upon, emphasizing parties and leading pressure groups, whilst diverting our attention away from others, such as the financial sector. It chooses which institutions are important to look at, such as the nationalized industries or the NEDC, whilst neglecting others, such as the City of London or the Bank of England.

Overall, then, we can only conclude that the postwar consensus is a harmful construct, in the sense that it severely blurs our understanding of the true dynamics behind governmental activity in the postwar period. Once we begin to examine these, it becomes clear that the real dynamic behind policy was the inherent conflicts which characterized the postwar political scene, between groups such as politicians, producers, trade unions and financiers; institutions such as the Treasury, the NEDC and the City of London; and ideas, such as Keynesianism, monetarism, laissez-faire economics and corporatism. The sum total of the interactions between these conflicting elements is a continual struggle between different groups, institutions and ideas to resolve the residual tensions and contradictions within the constantly evolving state settlement which each combined to create.

Conclusion

The postwar consensus thesis has been utilized by the majority of those interested in analysing the development of postwar British politics. However, as this chapter indicates, the concept of consensus has limited heuristic value in helping us to understand the complexities of governmental activity following the Second World War. Rather, its value to most authors lies in the fact that it helps to emphasize the impact of ideas such as Keynesianism and social democracy in bringing about the structural transformation of the state in the early postwar period, as well as highlighting the impact of Thatcherism in reversing these developments. However, once we begin to interrogate these assumptions, we soon find that the extent of state transformation brought about by the so-called consensus was limited. Most importantly, the major reason for this is that too many conflicts and contradictions existed both within the aims of postwar politicians, and between the aims of politicians and other key actors. In other words, we can say that very little change occurred in the structure of the state in the early postwar period primarily owing to the overall lack of both coherence and consensus governing the implementation of policy.

Clearly, in order to gain a better understanding of the complexities of postwar British politics, we need to abandon the consensus thesis altogether. In its place, we need to begin to reappraise the dynamic and constantly evolving relationships and conflicts which structured the development of postwar public policy. This would enable us not only to develop a more sophisticated understanding of the earlier postwar period, but also to generate a better conception of the Thatcher years and beyond.

Notes

1. Kavanagh and Morris do not directly cite this as a separate pillar of the consensus. However, the move towards active government is recognized by most authors, including Kavanagh (1987) himself as a central feature of the policies pursued by all postwar governments up until the election of the first Thatcher government in 1979.

2. This point requires some qualification. For, it is possible to find an assortment of (often implicit) references to the consensus dating from the 1950s onwards (see, for example, McKenzie 1955: 581; Beer 1965: 357; Calder 1969). Moreover, it is widely accepted that the concept has a strong genealogical linkage to the phrase 'Butskellism', coined by *The Economist* in 1954. However, as Rollings (1994) reminds us, it is clearly wrong to assume that the term

'consensus' is directly synonymous with Butskellism. Although we may re-cognize a manifest connection between both concepts, it is important to remain clear as to the obvious differences between them. Whereas the former refers to a broad spectrum of policy agreement, the latter relates only to a narrow convergence between the parties over their specific economic outlook. Therefore, although we can point to the earlier term 'Butskellism' as providing a tenuous clue to one area of policy convergence, it by no means leads us to the overall origins of the consensus thesis itself. As a distinct thesis, used to describe the nature of the political system as a whole, the idea of consensus did not start to cement until after Addison's publication in 1975. Therefore, although we can point to previous points of reference, Addison's work is normally regarded as being the closest we come to a seminal piece in the literature (see Kavanagh and Morris 1994: 1; Seldon 1994a: 501). Overall, we only need to examine any detailed bibliography on consensus politics to realize that the growth in the literature is a relatively recent phenomenon.

4

Crisis and Political Development in Postwar Britain

A state without the means of change is without the means of its conservation.

Burke 1790: 106

The crisis of the British state, economy and society in the 1970s – its existence in the first place, its causes and its consequences – continues to divide political scientists, political historians, sociologists and economists, as indeed it did the principal political protagonists, commentators and public of the time. Indeed, even the most fleeting glance at the vast literature on this topic cannot but reveal the enormous range of contending and mutually incompatible accounts: of crisis and of the absence of crisis; of endogenous (internally precipitated) crisis and of exogenous (externally precipitated) crisis; of a minor crisis for the incumbent government and of a profound crisis of either liberal democracy or western capitalism itself; of a crisis calling forth a decisive intervention, now happily made, and of a permanent and ever-more intractable crisis locking Britain into a seemingly inexorable spiral of precipitous decline.

Much is at stake in this debate and in the complex issues that lurk beneath the surface of these disputes. For, arguably, our understanding of the temporal rhythm and indeed of the whole texture of political development in the postwar period hinges on the significance we ascribe to moments of crisis (Hay 1997a). Whether we see British political and economic development in terms of a succession of relatively static institutional settlements punctuated periodically by crises, or in terms of a more gradualist conception of institutional adaptation, learning and evolution, will clearly make a very significant difference to our understanding of the process of social and political change. Moreover, even if we accept the existence of a crisis in the 1970s, the level at which we choose to locate the crisis (whether we identify a crisis of the government, the state or western capitalism, say), the extent to which we regard the crisis as threatening the system in question (whether we identify a crisis *in* or *of* the system, say) and the related degree to which we see the crisis as irresolvable within the parameters of the existing system, will also influence significantly the likelihood that we interpret the crisis as marking a moment of determination and a break with the past.

In the sections that follow we consider some of the crucial conceptual, analytical and theoretical issues involved in identifying a condition of crisis, before considering the range of positions advanced to account for the widely identified crisis of the British state of the late 1970s. We concentrate on the process of change itself, emphasizing the role of ideas in mediating systemic change and arguing that the ability to offer a compelling narrative of crisis may hold the key to state and governmental power in a condition of widely perceived crisis, such as that of Britain in the late 1970s.

Conceptualizing crisis

As is so often the case, the disarming simplicity of the concept of crisis and the frequency with which the term is deployed masks a range of complex theoretical and conceptual issues. Indeed, the very use of the concept is fraught with potential difficulty. For the effects often attributed to moments of crisis tend to rely upon the identification of a situation by the principal political protagonists of the time as one of crisis – and hence upon the use of the term in the first place. Is crisis, then, a neutral analytical category describing a particular state or property of a system, or is it in fact a term whose (often strategic) deployment by political actors may well be profoundly implicated in and, indeed, integral to the transformation of that system? This raises some important and complex issues regarding the status of the concept within political analysis, to which we will return. Before immersing ourselves in such thorny dilemmas and paradoxes, however, it is perhaps useful to engage in a few preliminaries.

First, it is important to emphasize the sheer diversity of uses to which the concept has been put. Thus, within the existing literature:

> Crises may be singular, exceptional, recurrent or periodic; momentary, ephemeral, enduring or eternal; linear or cyclical; destructive or creative;

underdetermined or overdetermined; inevitable or contingent; pathological or regenerative; organic or inorganic; paralysing or liberating; immanent, latent or manifest. They may be appealed to as mechanisms, processes, properties or conditions; failures, contradictions, ruptures or catastrophes; endings, beginnings or transitions. And they may refer to subjects, objects, systems or structures: to personality, identity or subjectivity; to modernity, history or Enlightenment; to state, economy or polity; to the environment, the world or the planet; to life, the universe ... and everything. (Hay 1996a: 422)

When one recalls that few political commentators and social scientists seem to exhibit any great desire to consign their understanding of the concept to the page – at best relying on a clear if implicit conception, at worst vacillating erratically between a host of implicit, ambiguous and mutually irreconcilable formulations – then the need for at least a measure of conceptual precision becomes transparent.

By and large, the concept implies a pejorative assessment of the existing state of affairs or condition of the system in question (the state, say); the identification of a significant, singular and potentially cathartic moment of political time; and the closely related sense that the system is currently unstable and that a catastrophic and potentially terminal event threatens or is in some cases inevitable unless an adequate response (in the form of a decisive and path-breaking intervention) is made. Moreover, the concept is often deployed in such a way as to conflate the normative (or value-laden) and the analytical (or value-neutral), implying that the *modus operandi* of the existing system is both inefficient and hence practically sub-optimal and, at the same time, normatively suspect (being premised, say, upon a conception of the political 'good' that is distorted or perverse).

As should by now be apparent, the concept of crisis is highly contested both theoretically (in the sense that it has been taken to refer to a wide diversity of rather different things) and politically (in the sense that the identification, diagnosis and response to crisis is, essentially and irreducibly, a political activity of great potential significance). The term has been used with great, if varying, frequency by journalists, analysts, commentators and political actors throughout the postwar period. There has been considerable dispute about whether specific events or circumstances qualify as examples of political or economic crisis, and even where there is apparent unanimity in identifying a situation as one of crisis, commentators have tended to disagree over its form, causes and consequences. Thus, although the concept is simultaneously both theoretical and analytical, it is also, and crucially for our concerns, an integral part of contemporary political discourse.

The objectivity and / or subjectivity of crisis

This brings us to the difficult problem of the objectivity and / or subject-ivity of crisis. Is the identification of a situation as one of crisis an objective, analytical or even empirical claim, or does it necessarily imply a subjective and hence a normative judgement? Should we define crisis in terms of objective factors such as the 'volume' of contradictions within a given system, or in more subjective terms such as the percep-tion of the need for rapid and decisive intervention in the context of widely experienced political and economic contradiction?

'Crisis', from the Greek, *krino* ('to decide') means, literally, a moment of decisive intervention. Yet in most contemporary accounts it has come to refer to an accumulation of contradictions. It is tempting, then, simply to relate the two, defining crisis as an accumulation of con-tradictions leading to a moment of decisive intervention. This is all very well, but it does raise a potential problem. For it is effectively to imply a theory of crisis: that decisive interventions are made once a certain crit-ical mass of contradictions is reached (an assumption frequently made within the existing literature and rarely exposed to critical scrutiny).[1] As a theoretical proposition it is at best dubious. Different political systems exhibit markedly different sensitivities to contradictions. This sensitivity is in turn dependent upon a range of factors such as their more or less democratic nature, the scope and development of their public sphere, the pervasiveness and character of media intervention and so forth. Moreover, a moment's further reflection reveals that the decision as to which contradictions require a response (and indeed what constitutes a contradiction in the first place) implies an act of subjective judgement. Such judgement is in turn likely to be reflective of pervasive norms, codes and conventions specific to a political system at a particular moment or stage in its institutional development. More fundamentally still, to make a decisive intervention requires a perception of the need to make a decisive intervention. It requires an awareness and an under-standing of current political and economic circumstances as indicative of contradictions and as indicative of contradictions that not only must be dealt with but that can be dealt with.

If we are to define crisis as a moment of decisive intervention then we must also recognize that crisis is in one sense an essentially percep-tual and hence subjective matter. If we wish to understand the making of decisive interventions and hence the transformation of social and political systems that such decisive interventions may initiate, then we must consider the mechanisms and processes by which perceptions of crisis, and indeed of the responses that such crises necessitate, are mobilized and shaped – often in hegemonic struggle (Hall et al. 1978; Hay 1996b). Crisis, within such a formulation, is a condition of a system brought about by the pervasive perception of political and economic contradiction or failure and the perceived need for a decisive intervention.

It is this 'narrativity of crisis' that political scientists seem so reluctant to acknowledge. Accordingly, they tend to revert to an objectivist formulation of crisis as a simple accumulation of contradictions. In so doing they generally either conflate contradiction and crisis (at the cost of emptying the latter term of its specificity) or fall back on the assumption (problematic, as we have seen) that the gradual accumulation and articulation of contradictions eventually and inevitably precipitates a qualitative shift from a condition of contradiction to one of crisis, initiating a period of institutional innovation. The former strategy strips political analysts of the conceptual armoury required to interrogate the process of transformation. For, as we have suggested, contradictions only result in transformation if they are responded to and they can only be responded to if they are identified as contradictions (whether such contradictions are, in turn, held to be constitutive of a condition of crisis or not). A theory of contradiction, then, and a theory of crisis constructed in its image, can tell us very little about the mechanisms of institutional development. The second strategy arguably does not help us understand and interrogate the process of change so much as assume that it takes a specific form – an assumption that is overgeneralized, rarely if ever exposed to critical scrutiny and ultimately deeply problematic, as we have seen. It is, in short, to rely upon a theory of change for which there is little or no evidence.

It would seem that if we wish to analyse the mechanisms of institutional development, we have little choice but to acknowledge the perceptual or discursive quality of the moment of crisis and hence to consider the processes through which competing narratives of crisis struggle for ascendancy in a battle to shape the course of subsequent institutional development. This suggests the importance of maintaining a clear and unambiguous distinction between contradiction and failure (an accumulation of contradictions) on the one hand and crisis on the other. For if it is narratives of crisis that are responded to and not the contradictions themselves, we cannot in any sense (theoretical or otherwise) derive the response to crisis from a static analysis of the contradictions of the existing system. Note, however, that this is not to suggest that there is no relation between the contradictions of a political / economic system and the narratives of crisis to which these (may or may not) give rise. The crucial point is that a given constellation of contradictions can sustain a multitude of differing and incommensurate conceptions of crisis, apportioning responsibility and culpability very differently and calling forth widely divergent interventions. Moreover, crisis narratives do not compete in terms of the sophistication or indeed accuracy of their understanding of the crisis context. Indeed, their success as narratives generally resides in their ability to provide a simplified account sufficiently flexible to narrate a great variety of morbid symptoms whilst unambiguously apportioning blame. To become sufficiently ascendant to alter the trajectory of institutional change in the post-crisis world, crisis narratives must make sense to individuals of their experiences of the crisis (whether direct or mediated); they must also be sufficiently general and simple to identify clear paths of responsibility and an unambiguous sense of the response that must be made if catastrophe is to be averted.

This in turn suggests that there can be no critical mass of contradictions that, once exceeded, guarantees a crisis scenario, not even for a particular political system at a particular stage in its institutional development. Crises, within such a schema, are as much made and constructed as they are determined by the weight of contradictions. Although the late 1970s stands out as the moment in the postwar period in which narratives of crisis became most ascendant, there were perhaps other moments (such as that of the late 1980s and, perhaps, the mid-1990s) when the volume of political and economic contradictions alone might also have sustained popular narratives of crisis calling forth decisive interventions at the level of the state and the economy (see, for instance, Hay 1996c: 174–7; 1996b: 242–52).

The struggle to impose a new trajectory upon the institutions of the state and the economy in a situation of widely perceived contradiction is essentially a struggle to find purchase or 'resonance' with individuals' experiences of such contradictions, enlisting them in support of a crisis narrative. This has important implications for the (rather paradoxical) status of the concept of crisis within political analysis. For it should be noted that many of the narratives of crisis that have proved successful in mobilizing perceptions of pervasive contradiction and of the need for a decisive intervention and a shift in the dominant political-economic paradigm originated (or at least had clear antecedents) within the social sciences. Arguably, this is precisely what happened in Britain in the late 1970s, where a conception of crisis advanced by the so-called New Right became popularized and ultimately ascendant (on the New Right, see Levitas 1986; King, D. S. 1987; Gamble 1988; Hay 1996c: 130–6). This was to pave the way for a paradigm shift from the Keynesian social democracy of the postwar years to the Thatcherite neo-liberalism of the 1980s (Hall, P. A. 1993).[2]

Here, we might usefully recall Giddens's notion of the 'double hermeneutic' discussed in chapter 1. The understandings we reach of the social and political world are part of that world and may serve to shape it, in many cases profoundly and irreversibly. The notion of crisis illustrates this in a particularly acute form. Thus, when deploying the concept of crisis, particularly with respect to contemporary political experience, we may well be crossing the always rather fragile and inde-terminate boundary between political analysis and political inter-vention. Social and political analysis does not always leave its subject-matter unscathed. This is particularly so, as we shall see, when that subject-matter is political crisis, raising interesting questions about how we should assess and evaluate the various interpretations of the crisis of the 1970s offered by political analysts and social scientists at the time. Should they be judged in terms of their ability to reflect accurately the events precipitating such a crisis, or in terms of their impact on the subsequent course of institutional change in postwar Britain? As we shall see, the two are not easily reconciled.

The crisis of the 1970s: a crisis of regulation, legitimation or overload?

In turning our attention to the existing literature on the crisis of the British state and economy in the 1970s, a number of contending per-spectives can be identified. We will here restrict ourselves to just two: the thesis of political overload and ungovernability popularized by the New Right and the regulation theorists' diagnosis of the crisis of the dominant postwar mode of economic growth. We consider each in turn.

Political overload and ungovernability: the fable of the hungry sheep

> The hungry sheep look up and reckon that they have at least a reasonable chance of being fed. (King 1975: 286)

The overload thesis was advanced at the time to account for what its proponents saw as an ongoing and pathological process rendering the advanced liberal democracies 'ungovernable' (see, in particular, Brittan 1975, 1979; Crozier et al. 1975; King 1975; Douglas 1976; Jay 1977). In such a situation, the concern of the overload theorists was to demon-strate the need for a withdrawal of a monolithic and overbearing state from its regulation of the economy, civil society and the public sphere. Their account, whether because, or in spite of, its crude and simplistic form, was to prove extremely influential, offering as it did a convenient diagnosis of the social democratic malaise and of the affliction assailing the British economy in the 1970s.

The overload theorists identified a self-reinforcing politicization of the economy and civil society. This they associated with the more interventionist state of the postwar period. Enticed perhaps by the promise of the scientific management of the economy and society offered in particular by Keynesianism, the state of the postwar period came to claim for itself greater expertise. In so doing, it sanctioned ever-spiralling social expectations (Brittan 1975; King 1975; Douglas 1976). The result was to reward those organized political interests most active and strategic in lobbying a state which now claimed to bend an ear to all concerns. This was to provide a powerful incentive for heightened pressure group activity. The unintended consequence, in turn, was to establish a political market place in which the parties would vie for votes, yet one lacking the discipline provided by formal market mechanisms.

In such a context, political competitiveness (measured in electoral terms) is achieved at the cost of economic competitiveness as interest and voter constituencies are bought off one by one, by offering ever greater concessions to ever wider sections of society. The economic cost is either deferred to future generations in the form of a heightened public sector borrowing requirement and diminished prospects for future economic competitiveness, or is manifest more immediately in terms of economic stagnation combined with increasing unemployment and inflation – the widely identified 'stagflation' of the 1970s (for a rather different account of which, see Glyn et al. 1990). The consequence, as Anthony King argued at the time, was that the state 'has come to be regarded, in Britain at least, as a sort of unlimited-liability insurance company, in the business of insuring all persons [and, one might add, interests] at all times against every conceivable risk' (1975: 286). The casualty in all of this was the ability of political parties in power to deliver what they promised: '[J]ust as the range of responsibilities of governments has increased, so ... their capacity to exercise their responsibility has declined. The reach of government exceeds its grasp; and its grasp ... is being enfeebled just at the moment when its reach is being extended' (ibid.: 288).

Within such an undisciplined political market, fiscal irresponsibility is rewarded electorally. In what amounts to a form of political corruption entirely compatible with the liberal democratic system, 'rational' political parties are encouraged to buy off a sufficient share of the electorate by promising to accede to the demands of ever more pressure groups, thereby raising the price of a vote and the stakes of fiscal irresponsibility. This can only serve to precipitate overload, ungovernability and, ultimately, fiscal crisis. The result is a profound 'crisis of democracy' as, in Michel Crozier's terms, 'the operation of the democratic process ... appears to have generated a breakdown of traditional [presumably undemocratic] means of social control, a delegitimation of political and other forms of authority and an overload of demands on government, exceeding its capacity to respond' (1975: 8; see also Crozier et al. 1975).

The image is a simple one: of a vicious political whirlpool out of whose clutches political parties can only escape at considerable cost to their electoral prospects, but which cannot fail to produce economic irresponsibility and the looming 'political bankruptcy' (Rose and Peters 1978) of an 'overloaded crown' (Douglas 1976). The solution, however politically unpalatable to an electorate that has come to conceive of government as a simple relay for its preferences, is simple: a severe bout of fiscal austerity, tight monetary control and a programmatic withdrawal of an overloaded, overburdened, yet beleaguered state. The spirit of the diagnosis is again well summarized by King: 'our image of government is that of the sorcerer's apprentice. The waters rise. The apprentice rushes about with his bucket. The waters rise even faster. And none of us know when, or whether, the magician will come home' (1975: 286). The sorcerer, as it happens, was a sorceress, first arriving on the scene shortly after these words were written and entering Downing Street in May 1979.

Though in many respects a simple, indeed simplistic, account – a simplicity, it might be suggested, making it all the more politically attractive – the overload thesis contains a number of profound internal contradictions and tensions. For, on the one hand, its proponents conjure up the impression of a cynical and self-serving electorate responsive only to political bribery and looking to the state to satisfy its every whim and desire. This is the fable of the 'hungry sheep' with which we began: 'Once upon a time, man [*sic*] looked to God to order the world. Then he looked to the market. Now he looks to government' (King 1975: 288). Yet this ultimately somewhat patronizing and condescending depiction of the electorate as greedy, unprincipled, opportunistic and, above all, simply too stupid to consider the costs (both economic and political) of their unrealistic expectations, stands in marked contrast to much of the rest of the analysis. Thus, in his opening reflections on the notion of overload, King explains: 'It was once thought that governments would be extremely difficult to remove from office, given their ability to manage the economy. Now we are inclined to assume the opposite: that the tenure of governments is precarious and that for the foreseeable future it will be a lucky government that survives for more than a term' (1975: 282).

This implies, and indeed the evidence would certainly support such a claim, that the principal factor determining success at the polls throughout the postwar period (particularly since the mid-1960s) has been the perceived state of the economy and not the ability of parties to outvie one another through exaggerated claims, counter-claims and concessions. As noted elsewhere, 'this rather puts paid to the image of growing fiscal irresponsibility and the "buying off" of the electorate by Machiavellian social democrats' (Hay 1996c: 101). Once it is considered that re-election is likely to prove conditional upon perceived fiscal probity, the incentive to court interests with promises that cannot be realized seems to evaporate and with it much of the credibility of the overload thesis. Moreover, in its call for a decisive break with the practices that have led, supposedly, to overload and ungovernability and, in particular, in its advocacy of welfare and state retrenchment and the politics of diminished expectations, the overload theorists appeal to precisely the good sense of the electorate (presumably now no longer mere 'hungry sheep') that they had previously dismissed. The argument would then appear at best somewhat opportunistic, cynical and disingenuous, at worst profoundly self-contradictory.

More worrying still perhaps is a certain disdain for democracy that so often seems to creep into such accounts (see especially Brittan 1975; Crozier et al. 1975; Jay 1977). It is, for instance, somewhat unclear whether the 'crisis of democracy' which Michael Crozier, Samuel Huntington and Joji Watanuki identify in their report to the Trilateral Commission (1975) is really a crisis of democracy at all or a fiscal crisis to which their preferred solution is a significant attenuation and curtailment of liberal democracy and its 'economic contradictions' (Brittan 1975). For, as they suggest, 'it is the democratic idea that government should be responsive to the people that creates the expectation that government should meet the needs and correct the evils afflicting particular groups in society' (Crozier et al. 1975: 164). Given that for them, and indeed for many of the theorists of overload and ungovernability, this is the heart of the problem, it is difficult not to suggest that given the choice between democracy and governability most would happily trade off the former for the latter. Arguably, this is precisely what has happened since 1979 (see, for instance, Ewing and Gearty 1990).

In one sense, however, such contradictions and tensions are insignificant. For to assess the contribution of the overload and ungovernability thesis purely in terms of its intellectual cogency is to ignore altogether its most important contribution – that to the political debate of the time. The thesis, as diluted and refracted by the think-tanks of the New Right and in the pages of the tabloid and broadsheet papers alike, offered a compelling, rhetorically rich and ultimately persuasive narration of the events of the crisis as it was to develop in the late 1970s. It would steer and mould perceptions not only of the nature of the contemporary British affliction, its culprits and villains, but of the necessary response to a crisis of an overextended state. In this, its simplicity, its flexibility, its nostalgia for a deferential past that arguably never existed and perhaps even its internal contradictions were a significant advantage.

A crisis of regulation: bringing the economic back in

The second account of the crisis of the British state and economy of the 1970s, that offered by the regulation theorists, can be dealt with rather more swiftly. Whereas the theorists of political overload and ungovernability considered above were concerned principally, if not quite exclusively, with political factors in accounting for the crisis of the 1970s, the regulation school seeks to bring the economic back into central focus. Unlike these politicist accounts, regulation theory was developed, or at least applied to the British experience, *after* the events it purports to explain. For although Michel Aglietta's pioneering account of capitalist regulation, *Régulation et crises du capitalisme* was first published in the mid-1970s, it was not translated into English until 1979.

Regulation theory is concerned with the reproduction of capitalist economic and social relations over time. As a distinctive theoretical approach to the problem of capitalist reproduction, it was first advanced in France in the 1970s in and through a critique of existing approaches within Marxist political economy. The central contribution of regulation theory can be stated simply. It relies on two key claims, the first theoretical, the second empirical: first, capitalism as a mode of production is inherently unstable, characterized as it is by class conflict and social antagonism; second, the history of capitalism is one of a succession of patterns of economic development and expansion, punctuated only infrequently by structural crises. This presents a central paradox: how is it that despite the fundamental contradictions of capitalism it exhibits apparently stable periods of sustained economic growth? The answer to this question is found in the concept of regulation itself. Indeed, Alain Lipietz goes so far as to define 'regulation' as the way in which a social system reproduces itself despite, and indeed through, its own contradictions (1985).

The approach is characterized by a concern with and focus upon the evolution and transformation of capitalist social relations and institutions over time. Regulation theory produces a nuanced and sophisticated periodization of capitalist development into a succession of stages, each distinguished by a particular *regime of accumulation* and its attendant *mode of regulation*. The view of capitalist development that it presents is one of 'punctuated equilibrium': capitalism requires regulation for its expanded reproduction; specific modes of regulation emerge in the context of crisis and become institutionalized; such regulatory forms (institutions, norms, conventions and so forth) serve to displace, manage or attenuate the contradictions of the accumulation process for a particular period of time in a particular context; external shocks, technological developments or other contingent factors, however, may have the effect of destabilizing the mode of regulation, such that latent contradictions and tensions now return to the surface; under such conditions a structural crisis of the mode of regulation and regime of accumulation can be said to exist, initiating a period of (class) conflict; the outcome of the moment of crisis cannot be predicted in advance, contingent as it is upon the nature of the ensuing struggle, the strategies of the protagonists and the alternatives offered; eventually, a new mode of regulation may emerge and become institutionalized, restoring the conditions of capitalism's expanded reproduction (for an exemplary summary, see Boyer 1990).

The sheer diversity of regulationist approaches has ensured that there is no single periodization of capitalist development to have emerged from regulation theory. Yet by far the most influential account has been that offered by Aglietta and the Parisian school. In his seminal study, Aglietta distinguishes between two basic forms of capitalist development (1979). In the former *extensive* phase of capital accumulation, capitalism expands by spreading into new areas of activity. By contrast, in the later *intensive* phase, expansion is conditional upon the reorganization of existing areas of capitalist activity to increase efficiency and hence the rate of relative surplus-value. Although the mode of regulation within the intensive phase was first competitive, this proved incapable of generating sufficient demand to complement the expansion of production enabled by Taylorism and the principles of 'scientific management'. The result was a severe structural crisis of over-investment and under-consumption precipitating the great depression of the 1930s. In the context of this crisis a new 'monopolistic' mode of regulation was to emerge in the postwar period. This was to encompass collective wage bargaining backed by the unemployment and insurance provisions of a significantly expanded welfare state. The so-called Fordist 'golden age' of the 1950s and 1960s was characterized (within this somewhat stylized account) by the diffusion of mass-production techniques (as the principles of scientific management became automated) and by the stimulation of mass demand through the interventions of the state (associated in particular with the principles of Keynesian demand management and, latterly, corporatism).

Yet the Fordist mode of development would in turn give rise to its own distinctive structural crisis in the changed circumstances of the mid-1970s as the perfection of Fordist production techniques left no space for further growth in productivity. On this much the Parisian regulationists agree. Yet here there is a significant divergence of opinion. Some argue that a new and distinctive post-Fordist mode of development has already emerged and that it is characterized by 'flexible specialization', the search for economies of scope rather than scale and a workfare rather than a welfare state (Jessop 1993; Piore and Sabel 1984); others suggest that we are in the midst of an extended period of transition towards a post-Fordism that has yet to become firmly rooted and institutionailized and whose precise form thus remains unclear (Boyer 1990); still others regard the politics of neo-liberalism and welfare retrenchment that seems to pervade the advanced capitalist economies as a symptom of the continuing crisis of Fordism, suggesting that no resolution is as yet in sight (Peck and Tickell 1994).

As an account of the crisis of the 1970s, and indeed of the more general development of contemporary capitalism, regulation theory has much to commend it. It concedes the possibility, indeed the likelihood, that capitalist accumulation can persist during and after periods of crisis, resisting the temptation (to which so much previous Marxist theory succumbs) to associate each and every contradiction of the capitalist system with a potentially terminal crisis of capitalism. In so doing it suggests that capitalism evolves through a series of crises, but that, by and large, these are crises *within* capitalism as opposed to crises *of* capitalism. It usefully suggests that widely identified crises of the state in the 1970s at the national level may be linked to a more general crisis of the international regime of accumulation, precipitated at least in part by the consequences of the exhaustion of the Fordist mode of growth that had developed and become consolidated in the postwar period. Above all, it demonstrates the significance of economic mechanisms and processes often operating at spatial scales above the national to the development of the political institutions of the contemporary capitalist state, emphasizing the importance of locating the evolution and transformation of the state in terms of the changing context provided by a dynamic international political economy (see also chapters 5 and 6).

Nonetheless, an adequate account of the crisis of the British state and economy of the late 1970s it is not. Regulation theory tends to reduce the state to a functional agent of capitalist regulation, whose form emerges miraculously from the ashes of the moment of crisis in conformity with, and in subordination to, the functional requirements of the capitalist economy. It thus tends to summon the form of the state, as it does the mode of regulation, as a 'functional fix' for capitalism's crisis tendencies. It tends to treat periods of sustained economic growth as the product of essentially static institutional complexes functional for capitalist accumulation. As a consequence it can offer no account of the origins of the tensions, contradictions and ultimately the crises which it suggests periodically punctuate such stable phases of economic growth. Accordingly, it does not consider how economic crises are reflected and mediated politically, far less how they are identified or constructed as crises and hence responded to. Nor, for that matter, does it consider or demonstrate how such processes might result in the emergence of the common institutional responses to crisis across the advanced capitalist economies that it observes. Regulation theory is then perhaps not so much a theory of crisis as an assumption (based on an observed empirical regularity) that in and through crisis capitalism will renew itself institutionally, thereby paving the way for a new phase of sustained economic growth. The precise mechanisms by which this is achieved remain unspecified (Hay 1995b).

Towards an alternative perspective: on crisis as paradigm-shift

Despite their flaws and internal contradictions, both of the above perspectives offer important insights into the moment of crisis and the process of institutional change. The thesis of overload and ungovernability reminds us that to prove 'successful' in narrating a crisis, an account must be simple, flexible and compelling and not necessarily complicated, sophisticated or even accurate. The regulation approach demonstrates the importance of reconciling exogenous and endogenous economic factors in any adequate account of the crisis of a national regime of the state. For it suggests that capitalism itself evolves through a series of stages of more or less sustained economic growth punctuated by moments of economic crisis in which the dominant mode of growth is exhausted. Such crises may in turn serve to render obsolete the existing mode of regulation, precipitating a crisis of the state, the principal agent of capitalist social and economic regulation.

This suggests that an adequate account of the crisis of the British state in the 1970s must prove itself capable of integrating the political, the economic and the ideological. In this final section, we begin to outline the form that such an account might take.

If, as we suggested in chapter 1, political subjects can be conceived of as strategic actors located within a strategic context which favours certain strategies over others and, moreover, their access to that context is mediated by their understandings and perceptions of what is possible, feasible and desirable, then we might make a strong case for the importance of political-economic paradigms in shaping the course of institutional change. Following Peter Hall's pioneering work, we might suggest that policy is made within the context of a policy paradigm (1993). This interpretative schema is internalized by politicians, state managers, policy experts and the like. As such, it comes to define a range of legitimate policy techniques, mechanisms and instruments, thereby delimiting the very targets and goals of policy itself. In short, it comes to circumscribe the realm of the politically feasible, practical and desirable.

This allows us to differentiate between periods in which a particular policy paradigm (such as that of Keynesianism) is ascendant and periods in which the very parameters that had previously come to delimit the realm of the politically possible are called into question, rejected and ultimately replaced. We might recognize this distinction as one between periods of evolutionary or incremental (yet often cumulatively radical) change on the one hand, and periods of crisis or paradigm-shift on the other (Hay 1997a). Such an understanding of crisis has a number of important implications for an analysis of the British state in the late 1970s (for a more detailed account of which, see Hay 1996b).

First, it suggests that with respect to the development of the ideas animating and informing policy, crises may mark fairly abrupt moments of significant change, as the old paradigm (say, that of Keynesian economics) is cast aside to be replaced by the new (that of monetarist or neo-liberal economics, for instance).[3]

Second, it suggests that the process of institutional change following a period of crisis is likely to be much slower. Thus, even if a new paradigm becomes ascendant relatively swiftly within the corridors of Westminster and Whitehall, it may take an extremely long period of time before its consequences are reflected to any significant extent in the institutional architecture of the state itself. As argued at greater length in chapter 8, the institutions of the state did not look remarkably different six months, or even five years, after Mrs Thatcher entered Downing Street, despite her obvious commitment to a radically different conception of the political 'good' from that of her predecessor. This suggests, in turn, that the development of the state in and through moments of crisis is not, as is often suggested, a process of 'punctuated equilibrium' (Krasner 1984) – of long periods of relative stability punctuated by rapid and intense periods of institutional innovation. Rather, it takes the form of 'punctuated evolution' – of iterative yet cumulative change animated and informed by particular political-economic paradigms.

During moments of crisis these may be challenged and replaced to alter the trajectory, if not necessarily the pace, of institutional change.

Finally, it emphasizes once again the crucial role of ideas in any understanding of the process of political and institutional change. Political-economic paradigms are never simply exhausted. For them to be replaced and superseded they must be perceived to be obsolescent, and an alternative must be perceived to exist. The moment of crisis is, then, essentially a discursive or hegemonic struggle often taking place in the context of widely experienced contradictions, to demonstrate the obsolescence of the old 'ruling ideas' and the possibilities offered by a new paradigm.

In the context of the late 1970s, the contradictions were indeed widespread and widely experienced. In the final section we consider briefly their precipitation as contradictions and their narration as crisis in the context of the exhaustion of postwar economic growth in Western Europe in the 1970s.

From growth to contradiction to crisis

Even the most cursory of reflections on the catalogue of events leading to the exhaustion of the long 'golden age' of economic growth that had characterized the postwar period and, seemingly inexorably, to the crisis of the British state of the late 1970s reveals the significance and interconnectedness of political, economic and ideational factors.

The first, and perhaps most widely identified, of these, is the Yom Kippur War of October 1973. This would result in the Organization of Petroleum-Exporting Countries (OPEC) limiting the production and export of crude oil and quadrupling its prices virtually overnight (Cairncross 1992: 182–7; Cleaver 1997: 177–8). The 'oil shock' became the catalyst, if not the direct cause, of the longest and deepest world economic recession since the Great Depression. Its economic consequences were devastating for the (Fordist) phase of growth that had characterized the postwar years in Western Europe and, ultimately, for the ascendancy of the Keynesian economics widely held to be responsible for that sustained growth phase (Glyn et al. 1990: 98–113). The rise in the cost of crude oil led to price explosions across the economies of the advanced capitalist world, further escalating already rising inflation and generating higher wage demand from trade unions anxious to protect real incomes in the face of such inflationary pressures. The result was to set in place what Fritz Scharpf terms an 'accelerating cost-price-wage-spiral' (1987: 42). Moreover, the increase in oil prices significantly eroded the buying power of the advanced industrialized nations, whilst massive surpluses accrued to the OPEC countries. As Scharpf again notes, '[t]hese OPEC surpluses corresponded with equivalent reductions in aggregate demand in the industrial nations ... in the absence of effective remedial action, the consequence ... had to be decreased production and rising unemployment' (ibid.). The Yom Kippur War, then, in the context of the transition to a system of flexible exchange rates since 1971 (which rendered unilateral reflationary responses much more difficult), served to bring about the desperate combination of high and rising inflation on the one hand with high and rising unemployment on the other. To this inauspicious constellation of circumstances Keynesianism had neither an explanation nor a solution (Hall, P. A. 1986a, 1993).

The Yom Kippur War could scarcely have come at a worse moment for the incumbent Conservative government of Edward Heath, for it was, at the time, engaged in delicate wage negotiations with the National Union of Mineworkers (NUM), negotiations whose strategic context was altered significantly by the quadrupling of oil prices, to say nothing of the (further) inflationary pressures this injected into the domestic economy (Kavanagh 1996; Taylor, R. 1996). Predictable intransigence on both sides, combined with the rapidly deteriorating fuel situation, led to the government declaring a State of Emergency on 13 November and, later, to the infamous three-day-week (during which electricity was only supplied to industry for three specified days per week) starting on New Year's Day 1974. Heath resisted the mounting pressure (from within his own party and from the media alike) for a general election early in the New Year, but could only delay the inevitable, as the NUM balloted for an all-out strike for early in February. The election was called for 28 February 1974 and was fought, perhaps inevitably, primarily over the issue of 'who ran the country – the trade unions or the government?'. The electorate decided, though by no means unequivocally, that whoever ran the country it was not to be the Conservatives, restoring Labour to power (with Wilson, once again, as Prime Minister) as the largest single party, but without an overall majority.

That Labour won the general election (and indeed won again six months later, this time with a meagre overall majority of three), was testimony to the impression (one that it had done much to cultivate) that Labour was better placed to keep the unions on board. This was undoubtedly the case, and was reflected in its social contract with the unions (negotiated in opposition but taken with it into government). Yet it was to help little in managing the contradictory economic settlement that Labour inherited from the Conservatives (Coates 1980). In the early years, the incoming Labour administration followed the broadly Keynesian strategy of the Heath government, engaging in reflationary policies by increasing social expenditure and public sector wages. Consumer spending rose, restoring economic growth, but only at the cost of heightened inflation (peaking at 25 per cent in the spring of 1975) and an escalating balance of payments crisis (Hall, P. A. 1986a: 93–6). In late 1975 and 1976 matters came to a head. Open, if unguarded, speculation about the need for a competitive devaluation (though never really actively contemplated) led to a disinvestment of the OPEC countries' funds from sterling, bolstering a wave of self-reinforcing speculation against the pound. The consequence was to increase the cost of imports massively, generating further inflationary pressures, hence undermining the government's social contract with the unions. The Bank of England's attempts to defend the pound on the international exchanges failed to convince investors of the govern-ment's commitment not to devalue the currency, whilst exhausting regular lines of credit from the International Monetary Fund (IMF) (Barnett 1982: 97–117; Scharpf 1987: 80; Burk and Cairncross 1992: 20–58). It was in this context that the government was forced to con-template a longer-term 'special loan' from the IMF. Yet this came with strings attached and only after a detailed investigation of Britain's predicament by the IMF's monetarist converts. As Scharpf notes, the government's 'reluctant conversion to monetarism', though already evi-denced in the Treasury's moderately restrictive stance since the winter of 1975, was reaffirmed and reinforced here (1987: 82; Epstein and Schor 1990: 147).

Yet, if monetarism was already being deployed as a technique or instrument of economic management by the Labour government even prior to the IMF loan (with its rather punitively anti-Keynesian con-ditions), then it is important to note that the conversion to monetarism as an economic doctrine was, at this stage, by no means secured (Hall, P. A. 1986a, 1986b: 96; 1993; Scharpf 1987: 239; Epstein and Schor 1990). Monetarism, like corporatism (and the incomes policies and compul-sory wage restraint on the part of the unions that they facilitated) was deployed by Labour as a crisis-management technique. The Labour government of 1974–9 never abandoned its overarching policy commit-ment to full employment, a mixed economy and a comprehensive welfare state, even if the instruments and techniques which it deployed were hardly compatible with such goals. From 1973 to 1979, a clear gulf opened up between the instruments of economic management deployed by the British state, which were increasingly monetarist in inspiration, and the governing economic paradigm (and attendant political goals), which continued to be broadly Keynesian and welfarist (Panitch and Leys 1997: 121–3).

It was only with the election of Margaret Thatcher in 1979 that the paradigm shift was completed, as economic and political goals were brought up to date with the monetarist techniques that had increasingly come to characterize the management of the economy since the 1970s in Britain as elsewhere (Hall, P. A. 1986a; Scharpf 1987; Panitch and Leys 1997). Arguably, this was, in turn, dependent upon the events, the humiliation and the ignominy of the 'Winter of Discontent' in which a wave of industrial stoppages shattered the social contract, with the trade unions bringing Britain to a standstill during the worst winter in living memory (Hay 1996b). All hopes for a corporatist (far less monetarist) solution to the problems of Britain's peculiar (and perhaps peculiarly pathological) Keynesianism were abruptly terminated. If there is one single point in postwar British political development that can be referred to as a cathartic moment of crisis, it is surely this.

It is in this context that the appeal of the New Right's account of a crisis of an overextended, overloaded and ungovernable state 'held to ransom' by the trade unions must be sought. It was this narrative and the resonance that it found and constructed that brought Thatcher to Downing Street in May 1979, promising, in the words of St Francis of Assisi, 'harmony' where there had been 'discord'. It is to the consequences (immediate and continuing) of the crisis of the 1970s for the transformation of the state, to Thatcherism and to its ability to translate rhetoric and diagnosis into reality that we return in the final chapters of this book. For the time being we concentrate, however, on the European and global aspects of British political development, so crucial, as we have seen, to the processes of social and political change in postwar Britain.

Notes

[1] Precisely such an understanding of crisis is found in the work of the regulation theorists. Robert Boyer, for instance, in his admirable summary of the regulationists' conception of crisis, suggests that within this schema, 'crises are held to correspond to the phase in which tensions and disequilibria accumulated during periods of expansion are wiped out' (1990: 50). Unfortunately, the mechanisms by which such contradictions are first identified and subsequently understood and responded to (a condition, presumably, of their being 'wiped out') are not discussed within the regulationist literature, leaving the (unfortunate) impression that once a certain critical mass of contradictions is exceeded some functional safety device will spontaneously kick into action.

[2] Of course, as we have been at considerable pains to point out throughout this book, the extent to which the postwar period was genuinely Keynesian, or for that matter social democratic, and indeed the extent to which the Thatcher

and Major governments were unequivocally neo-liberal, has tended to be exaggerated within much of the existing literature (see in particular chapters 1, 3 and 8). Nonetheless, it is the argument of this chapter that a clear qualitative break can be identified in the late 1970s which can conveniently be described in such terms.

[3]   Nonetheless, even this can be a relatively protracted process. The first term of the Thatcher administration was, for instance, characterized less by political radicalism than by the attempt by Thatcher and her supporters to win the 'battle for hearts and minds' within the Cabinet.

5

Britain's Relations with the European Union in Historical Perspective

All we can do is to press every button we've got. We don't know which, if any, of them will have the desired results.

Tony Crosland, quoted in Castle 1984: 223

Since the end of the last century it has been an article of faith with the British that they were wealthy and prosperous – or to pitch it at a lower level, they survived – because Britain was at the centre of a world-wide Empire ... So in-built was this belief that, when the Empire dissolved ... the people of Britain suffered from a kind of vertigo: they could not believe they were standing upright, and reached out for something to clutch.

Enoch Powell 1971: 59

The quotations above betray the main argument to be pursued in this chapter. As Crosland suggests, the performance of the British economy could often prove a perplexing problem for British politicians after 1945. Chapters 2 and 3 have explored the question of British decline and the response of the British state since 1945. The purpose of this chapter is to explore the link between these themes and the external statecraft of successive British governments. With the increased Europeanization of British foreign policy since the 1960s, particular attention is paid to the domestic–European connection.

Many accounts of Britain's relations with the European Union (EU) view this association in static terms. Britain is described as an 'awkward' or 'semi-detached' partner, continually prevented from pursuing a more *communautaire* approach by powerful domestic institutional constraints (George 1992; 1994; Armstrong and Bulmer 1996; see also Buller 1995a; George 1995; Wilks 1996). In particular, four features of the British polity are stressed. The first is the legacy of institutional continuity in Britain (see Radice, G. 1992: 11–62). Having avoided invasion and internal revolution since the mid-seventeenth century, British policy-makers remained heavily influenced by the 'myth' of national sovereignty (Wallace, W. 1986). Second, Britain's adversarial political culture militates against the more consensual style of decision-making undertaken at the European level (Ashford 1992: 199–200). Third, British statesmen are constrained by political parties which remain divided over the issue of European integration (Ashford 1992; Wallace, H. 1995). Finally, these politicians continue to operate against a backdrop of public opinion which remains sceptical of the benefits of EU membership (Nugent 1992). Listed in this way, it seems foolish to deny that powerful institutional obstacles frustrate the adoption of a more co-operative diplomatic style by London.

However, whilst 'awkwardness' may have been a continuous feature of Britain's negotiating style at the European level, this chapter argues that there has been significant change in the substance of policy during the postwar period. British policy (both foreign and domestic) has increasingly become Europeanized. That is to say, all Whitehall departments have become increasingly influenced by legislation emanating from Brussels. Obviously, part of this process is the result of Britain signing the Treaty of Rome and its amendments (the Single European Act, the Treaty of European Union and the Amsterdam Treaty). However, this Europeanization of public policy has also been encouraged by the day-to-day process of greater informal co-operation between Britain and its partners in the EU. The question remains: how can we account for this change?

It will be argued below that we need a historical perspective which employs a more dialectical approach to the relationship between agents (state actors) and structures (both domestic and external) as it unfolds over time. Existing accounts of Britain's relations with the EU are right to highlight the domestic institutional constraints on state action. However, as other chapters in this book suggest, these constraints stem as much from the structure of British economic markets as from domestic political institutions. Moreover, the effects of these economic constraints on state action have been markedly different from what the awkward partner thesis would suggest. To compensate for this 'weak' position, successive British governments have sought solace in external solutions to domestic economic problems. As Powell's quote indicates, before 1961 the Empire / Commonwealth provided this external support function. After 1961, membership of the EU represents the latest version of this strategy. In an era of increased globalization, an increasing number of British politicians now conclude that the scope for national solutions to economic problems has further diminished (see chapter 6). In the light of this dilemma, an increasingly attractive solution has been to hive off the whole problem of economic management to the European level.

Domestic economic management and foreign policy, 1925–61

An awareness of the relationship between domestic and external policy before 1961 is important if we are to understand the connection between British economic policy, state strategy and membership of the EU. As far back as 1918, two particular features of the British economy have frustrated experiments with more interventionist industrial policy instruments. The first is the dependence of the British economy on the international trading system. After the repeal of the Corn Laws in 1846, Britain had become increasingly reliant on agricultural imports to feed its population. At the same time, the Treasury increasingly depended on so-called 'invisible' exports – income from financial services provided by the City of London to the rest of the world – to avoid a deficit on the balance of payments (Hobsbawm 1969: ch. 7; Cain and Hopkins 1980; Gamble 1990a). As a result, economic policy gave preference to the interests of finance capital over the concerns of domestic industry. The second is the tradition of voluntarism and self-government, which became increasingly important in the conduct of industrial relations, with the result that British business and unions took great exception to the British state poking around in their internal affairs (Morgan 1984: 95–6; Weir 1989: 75; Marsh 1992: 1–21).

Given these structural constraints, the British state demonstrated little sustained enthusiasm to confront the task of industrial restructuring head-on. Comparatively speaking, Britain was peculiar in not developing a 'developmental state' during this period (see chapter 2). Of course, the 1930s witnessed various *ad hoc* initiatives designed to restructure specific industries, such as steel and chemicals (Middlemas 1994: 464–9; Tomlinson 1994: 113–35). In addition, one cannot ignore the Attlee government's sustained programme of nationalization and planning during the second half of the 1940s. However, as other authors in this book have noted, the Labour government's supply-side strategy had a more limited impact on the British economy than traditional surveys of this period would suggest (see chapter 7). For example, the Lord President's Committee, the main planning arm of the Attlee government, suffered from uncertainty and ambiguity concerning its role, failed to plan a coherent response to the coal shortage of 1947 and was 'gutted' after the 'bonfire of controls' in the following year (Budd 1978: 58–9; Morgan 1984: 127–35; Weir 1989: 68–9). Moreover, Labour's programme of nationalization, particularly its reliance on the Morrison model of public boards, actually served to strengthen the ability of British business to regulate its own affairs (Tomlinson 1994: 188–200).

Instead, the most notable characteristic of Whitehall's approach to economic management at this time was the narrow and limited way in which it defined its responsibilities. Before the 1940s, primacy was given to the task of maintaining low and stable inflation. This meant resurrecting the neo-classical framework of the balanced budget and putting sterling back on the Gold Standard (Middleton 1985: 47–51; Weir 1989: 60–2; Tomlinson 1994: 84–111). However, a brief review of the 1950s, after the so-called Keynesian revolution in British economic policy, suggests more similarities than differences with the interwar period. Having locked the pound into a new Bretton Woods fixed exchange rate system in 1944, British policy increasingly became concerned with the problem of cost-push inflation to maintain foreign confidence in sterling (see chapter 3). Although full employment was achieved throughout this period, this seems largely to have been the result of world economic conditions. It was certainly not the result of the conscious pursuit of Keynesian demand management. As Matthews has noted, successive governments ran a budget surplus at this time (Matthews 1968).

In short, the pursuit by Whitehall of more interventionist national solutions to Britain's economic problems was constrained by powerful structural forces. Faced with such a problem, the role of external policy was to support the weak position of the British state throughout this period.[1] On the one hand, foreign economic policy was designed to provide some image of policy activity in the absence of significant domestic initiatives. Since the late seventeenth century the Empire always played this role, providing important markets for British financiers and manufacturers, thus helping to secure state revenue, domestic employment and public order. However, with the collapse of the Gold Standard in 1931, the newly formed National government showed an ability to appropriate external structures to support its domestic position. It created the Sterling Area in 1932 (formally the Overseas Sterling Area in 1940), which gave British industrialists preferential access to imperial markets. Some authors have questioned the material benefits of imperial preference. Capie, for example, has argued that this policy added only 1 per cent to industrial production during the interwar period, hardly a significant figure (quoted in Holland 1991: 115). However, Holland has noted the psychological boost which this external policy conferred; it allowed British manufacturers imperial shelter from an increasingly competitive economic climate (Holland 1991: 130–3). This psychological benefit continued to be important throughout the 1940s and the 1950s.

As some authors have noted, politicians were also capable of seeing the benefits of this weak position. By putting off the development of policy instruments which could be used to intervene in the supply-side of the economy, successive governments avoided direct and continual contact with a multitude of interest groups, all claiming special treatment from the state. The immediate fear was that these policies would lead to unsustainable levels of public spending and the threat of hyper-inflation. More generally, there was the concern that this strategy would involve large amounts of time and energy, especially when there were powerful structural obstacles to its implementation. In this context, it was hoped that returning the pound to its fixed rate against gold in 1925 would serve as a neutral discipline to be slavishly worshipped by all domestic forces. As a result, governing would become easier. Economic policy could be run almost on 'automatic pilot'. All that would be needed was the occasional adjustment of the odd fiscal and monetary lever (Winch 1969: 83; Middleton 1985: 83–90; Holland 1991: 104, 110–12; Tomlinson 1994: 9).

In other areas too, British foreign policy was managed in such a way as to disguise the impact of the country's decline on the British public. After 1945, the special relationship with the USA was of particular benefit. In general, this relationship conferred a status and prestige on British leaders which set them apart from their European counterparts. More particularly, it allowed Britain to acquire a defence capability unrivalled in Western Europe, a fact crowned by the Polaris deal signed with Washington in 1962. Of course, these benefits meant additional responsibilities for London. A defence presence east of Suez had to be maintained, leading to higher levels of military expenditure than other European economies had to shoulder (Buller 1995b: 226–8). By the 1960s, these high levels of defence spending became a consistent theme of the criticism of Britain's comparatively poor industrial performance.

Britain and the European Community, 1961–79

If this was the relationship between domestic and external policy before Britain contemplated EEC membership, it was clear that by 1961 Whitehall could no longer avoid giving more serious attention to supply-side economic matters. The problem of Britain's relative economic decline had now entered the public arena and demanded some kind of response. Critics drew attention to issues such as the relationship between finance and industry, the relatively low levels of domestic investment, poor management practices and the deteriorating state of industrial relations in Britain. At the same time, commentators observed that Commonwealth preference had also become part of the problem, insulating British manufacturing industry from the invigorating winds of international competition (Sanders 1990: 203–4). These problems provoked feelings of increasing bewilderment and fear within Whitehall, as Harold Macmillan's memoirs show (Macmillan 1972: 217–35; Horne 1989: 62–70, 245–9).

During this period, Whitehall's response was twofold. Domestically, it attempted to forge a more modern British economy by subjecting it to the 'white heat' of a new interventionist industrial strategy. However, despite notable achievements,[2] by the end of the 1970s this domestic experiment was not considered to have been a great success (see, for example, Gilmour 1977: 252–3; Barnett 1982: 74–5; Lawson 1992: 437; Thatcher 1993: 93; 1995: 223–30). Wilson's failure to devalue the pound on coming into office in 1964 meant that the implementation of the National Plan was frustrated by international economic structures and concerns (for an interesting account of this episode, see Ponting 1989: 48–58). Instead, successive attempts to introduce a sustainable prices and incomes policy to contain wage rises only politicized relations with business and the trade unions, which resented any erosion of the principle of voluntarism in industrial affairs. Finally, more ambitious attempts at industrial relations reform met the same fate. For example, the Industrial Relations Act (1971) created a new National Industrial Relations Court, as well as empowering the Secretary of State for Employment to call for a cooling-off period and a ballot before industrial action went ahead. However, this legislation only had the effect of strengthening the position of the trade unions. Separate disputes involving the dockers and the railwaymen in 1972 were testimony to this fact (Campbell 1993: 457–65).

Second, Whitehall continued to search for external solutions to these intractable problems. For many politicians at this time, the idea of Common Market membership provided an attractive solution to this conundrum. It seemed obvious that unrestricted access to this new dynamic market of 170 million customers would allow British firms to take advantage of greater economies of scale, leading to greater investment and profits. However, as Hall has noted, the importance of economic ideas in their own right is based on a number of assumptions. Two are particularly important to the argument being pursued here.

First, if ideas are to be influential in their own right, those responsible for promoting their merits should be reasonably united. Put a different way, policy-makers are likely to be less receptive if the so-called experts find it impossible to agree on the likely outcome when these ideas are translated into policy practice. Second, policy-makers should receive these ideas with a relatively neutral and open mind. All too often politicians are only attracted to doctrines (or parts of doctrines) because they fit in with existing governing principles. Ideas are not important in themselves, but serve as a cover for cruder political needs (Hall, P. A. 1989: 8–10).

Unfortunately, once these assumptions are made explicit, it is possible to question explanations which seek to explain British policy towards the EC as being the product of ideological factors. Economists and policy advisers have never been united over their assessment of the effect of Community membership on the British economy (for more sceptical views, see Cohen 1983; Jacquemin and Sapir 1989; Davis et al. 1989: 8–9; Cutler 1992). Moreover, a number of accounts of policy at this time show that political leaders were not entirely neutral and open-minded about the ideas they used to make their decision to apply for EC membership. Of particular interest here is the account of Douglas Jay. He accuses Wilson of deliberately trying to marginalize the more sceptical case for membership during the mid-1960s. As he concludes, 'the tragedy was that Brown, Wilson, Jenkins and others mainly in the Foreign Office, reached conclusions before they had made any serious effort to estimate the economic consequences at all. That was indeed the basic truth in the whole tangled story of Britain's plunge into EEC membership' (Jay 1980: 386–8).

Whilst the economic case for joining helped support pro-European ministers in the public battle of ideas (often in direct conflict with other ministerial colleagues), other explanations lie behind the decision to join the EEC in the 1960s. Faced with the structural limitations on its position, EEC membership provided an 'escape' from the failure of Whitehall's supply-side initiatives (see Crossman 1975: 557–8; Castle 1984: 245). Put another way, this external association provided a sort of neutral European 'invisible hand', which would shock or discipline British industry into modernizing its practices, whilst at the same time providing a new base from which Britain could regain its influence on the world stage (H. Macmillan, in *Hansard* (Commons) 2 August 1961 cols. 1488–9; R. Maudling, in *Hansard* (Commons) 2 August 1961, col. 1605; Roll 1985: 102; for the opposition viewpoint, see Crossman 1963: 743). At the same time, responsibility for the difficult business of supply-side reform could be partially contracted out to the European level.

The exception to this argument was, of course, Edward Heath, who took up the policy of Community membership with genuine enthusiasm. Even then, the EEC was to play a supporting role to his domestic concerns. Once the 'Quiet Revolution' had modernized the supply-side of the British economy, the Common Market would provide a much-needed external outlet to channel the increased exports which were expected to result. Of course, this revolution did not survive the U-turns of 1972, but the EEC still provided an important, if slightly altered, support function. Now, the intense competition in the Common Market would provide a useful way of disciplining the union's incessant demands for wage increases. Moreover, in the event of future balance of payments problems, the EEC would provide a valuable additional source of funds to ward off speculators (Holmes 1982: 5; Lord 1993: 23).

However, as noted in the Introduction, attempts by agents to use structures in the pursuit of their objectives may produce unintended consequences which can stem from the fact that actors misunderstand the structural properties they are 'appropriating'. At this time, successive British governments misunderstood (or choose to ignore) the structural qualities of the EEC in two senses which were to have important repercussions for future British policy in this area. First, Whitehall misunderstood the principles on which the EEC was founded. At the heart of the Community's structure was the principle of supra-nationalism. This principle had its origins in the so-called 'German Question' which haunted Western European governments after 1945. In more graphic terms, the issue was how to 'tie-up', 'tie-in' and 'tie-down' the resurgent power of Germany as it went through a period of reconstruction after the war. If a revival of German economic and political power could not be stopped, it would have to be contained within a new supra-national organization which committed itself to the development of common policies. At the heart of this arrangement was a French promise to allow German industry access to its markets in return for the development of a Common Agricultural Policy (CAP) which protected French farming interests. These policies would be included in a legally binding treaty, closely monitored by a new Commission (French-dominated) and policed by a new European Court. In short, the Community would serve simultaneously as an institution which would allow Paris to control future German economic development and as an internationally recognized base from which Bonn could set about rebuilding German power (on British self-delusion, see Charlton 1983; Denman 1996; Beloff 1996).

Second, if ministers persistently misunderstood the importance of supra-nationalism to the original Community members, British statesmen overestimated London's ability to build alliances 'at the heart' of the Community to promote their own interests. This is perhaps best demonstrated by regular British attempts throughout the period to achieve an acceptable settlement on the question of British budgetary contributions. Pompidou, although more sympathetic to British membership than de Gaulle, failed to consider the renewal of Britain's application for membership until the final details of the CAP had been worked out in 1969, suspecting that the British would want to alter a policy which penalized their budgetary position within the Community (George 1994: 38). Once Heath had accepted the principles of the CAP, it took the threat of negotiation and referendum under Wilson and the histrionics and 'hand-bagging' of Mrs Thatcher before a deal was finally agreed at Fontainebleau in 1984. Even then, the Thatcher government did not secure the automatic and permanent system of rebates it had been seeking, let alone broader structural reform of the CAP (George 1994: 155–9). In short, then, despite the reassurance of ministers at the time, the EEC could not be promoted as 'just another international organisation', like NATO or the OECD. Because of the importance of supranationalism and the balance of power that dominated the Community structures, there was always the danger that the EEC would be an external structure which was capable of continually and explicitly penetrating domestic politics with adverse consequences (Bulpitt 1992: 266).

The Europeanization of British economic policy, 1979–97

Whilst the arrival of the Thatcher government promised a new departure in British politics, the gradual Europeanization of British economic policy was not part of the strategy. Certainly, party publications consistently employed the theme that the Conservatives were the 'party of Europe' (Conservative Research Department 1979; see also comments from Roy Jenkins on *The Poisoned Chalice*, BBC2, 23 May 1996). Moreover, the party accepted the need for increased European co-operation in certain policy areas as long as this co-operation did not contribute to the undermining of the nation-state as the principal actor in international relations. However, this positive approach did not extend either to a more general enthusiasm for the 'Community ideal' (Conservative Research Department 1979: 3–4) or to the 'greatest' single policy achievement of the Community to date – the CAP. There was certainly no acceptance of the argument that Community membership was vital as an external discipline to push through the modernization of British industry.

Of course, the modernization of the British economy and the reversal of Britain's decline were key themes of the new monetarist strategy. Hence, it was clear that this intractable problem was to be faced squarely by employing national economic policy solutions. Interestingly, monetarism resurrected the distinction between the two levels of the economy which Whitehall had favoured during the interwar period (Lawson 1992: 1054; Ridley 1992: 167). At the macro-level, ministers defined the provision of a sound nominal framework for the pursuit of low and stable inflation as their primary responsibility. To achieve this objective, the Medium Term Financial Strategy (MTFS) was set up to provide a published framework of rules and targets for the growth of the money supply (measured by M3), public expenditure and interest rates over a four-year period. Significantly, although the exchange rate was to be monitored, sterling would continue to float and not play a central role in Whitehall's calculations (see Keegan 1984; Smith, D. 1987).

If macroeconomic management was to be dominated once again by the goal of controlling inflation, monetarism also off-loaded direct responsibility for 'real' economic variables such as demand, growth and employment on to groups in the supply-side of the economy. Of course, the government accepted that it would have to undertake specific supply-side measures to help these groups adjust to the realism of increased international competition. Most notable here were policies concerned with taxation, industrial relations reform and privatization. However, the burden of responsibility remained clear. Governments could not create growth and jobs. These tasks were the responsibility of British entrepreneurs, competing freely and efficiently in newly 'liberated' markets.

It would be foolish to deny that the Conservative government implemented monetarism because certain Thatcherite ministers in key policy portfolios believed in the verities of these New Right ideas. However, while ideology remained important to Thatcher and her supporters, these policies were attractive because they conferred additional advantages on ministers at this time. Lawson has said as much himself: 'to describe the New Conservatism purely in terms of an approach to economic policy would be manifestly inadequate – it goes a great deal wider than that' (Lawson 1992: 1041). The beauty of monetarism was that by rejecting the cost-push theory of inflation and reviving faith in the domestic discipline of the MTFS and the magical qualities of the market, Conservatives could reject the need for interventionist planning instruments and incomes policies and, with this, the need for direct and continuous contact with societal groups. Instead, by arguing that inflation was the government's primary responsibility, which could be controlled by manipulating the level of the money supply at the Treasury, these economic ideas seemed to make governing relatively easy again. Policy could be run by pushing buttons and watching dials in the relative isolation of Downing Street (Lawson 1992: 66–7, 1021, 1040).

However, although the Conservatives had won the 1983 election with an increased majority, it was clear by 1984 that monetarism was experiencing a number of implementation problems. At the macro-level, both Howe and Lawson experienced real difficulties in establishing a reliable relationship between the measurement of the money supply in the economy and the rate of inflation. As Lawson himself admitted, although inflation had been reduced to 3 per cent by 1984, the government had only managed to hit its M3 target twice (Lawson 1992: 447–55). As a result, ministers gradually fell back on the policy of controlling inflation through the manipulation of the exchange rate. However, by the mid-1980s, as the level of the pound oscillated wildly on the waves of an increasingly global financial market, more and more Cabinet members came to the conclusion that this strategy was also vulnerable to the vagaries of international economic forces. Indeed, Lawson himself began to argue that exchange rate volatility could, in the short term, contribute to inflationary pressures. It followed logically that, for any government serious about controlling inflation in the medium term, 'benign neglect' of the exchange rate was not an option (Lawson 1992: 483–96).

At the same time, monetarism was generally perceived to be largely responsible for generating three million unemployed by 1983. With the opposition in disarray, the Conservatives were able to argue, with some success, that this monetarist experiment was a necessary response to Britain's economic malaise, especially given the continual neglect of this issue by previous administrations. Furthermore, the fact that the shake-out of British industry coincided with a worldwide recession was helpful to the leadership, which was able to off-load some blame for unemployment onto international forces. However, by 1984, with the British economy on the up-turn and unemployment stuck stubbornly at three million, both Howe and Lawson accepted that the government needed to do more to address this economic issue (Howe, G. 1982; Lawson 1992: 423). It was also argued that, although the party had won in 1983, evidence suggested that the electorate did not view the monetarist experiment with any enthusiasm (Crewe 1988; Young 1989: 299). In other words, Conservative leaders began to search for additional ways to institutionalize this monetarist experiment (on the question of policy entrenchment, see Lawson 1992: 250–3).

Having spent five years locked in a pitched battle with its Community partners over the issue of Britain's budgetary contributions, the government gradually accepted (with different degrees of enthusiasm) that it could promote reform at the European level as a way of institutionalizing its monetarist strategy. In other words, ministers acquiesced in, or positively encouraged, the process of transferring more and more responsibility for policy to the Community level. The first evidence of this change of strategy occurred in 1984, as it became increasingly common for ministers to publicize the link between Britain's unemployment problem and the need to complete the single market (G. Howe, in *Hansard*, vol. 63, 10 July 1984, col. 898; see Thatcher in *The Times*, 1 November 1984; G. Howe, in *Hansard*, vol. 81, 25 June 1985, col. 803; see also Thatcher, in *Hansard*, vol. 82, 2 July 1985, col. 188). These arguments were codified in the White Paper, 'Europe – the Future', which was presented without much effect to the European Heads of Government at the Fontainebleau European Council in June. Lord Cockfield was eased into the relevant Commission portfolio, where he proceeded to produce a detailed programme and timetable calling for the reduction of all non-tariff barriers by December 1992. Ironically, it was Thatcher herself who had real reservations about the policy once other member states called for the single market project to be accompanied by institutional reform and a new treaty. However, she was persuaded that, overall, the policy package was in British interests.

Although it was not a dominant theme of the debates at the time, politicians from both sides of the Commons also understood that, by appropriating Community structures, ministers were attempting to institutionalize their monetarist strategy at home. At this time, Howe continually stressed the extent to which the Conservative emphasis on free markets was now being accepted in Europe and was rapidly lying near the international centre of gravity (Howe, G. 1994: 445; see also Howe, G. 1982, 1988: 5). Conversely, Labour politicians also demonstrated an awareness of the danger that the Single European Act would have for their own economic strategy. Both Eric Deakins and Michael Foot observed in the Second Reading of the European Communities (Amendment) Bill (drawn up to insert the Single European Act in British law) that, under these treaty amendments, future British governments would be unable to institute import controls, place restrictions on capital movements and use state aids to support declining, but politically sensitive, industries (*Hansard*, vol. 100, 26 June 1986, col. 593; 27 June 1986, col. 604).

If the Thatcher government realized that it could institutionalize its free market supply-side strategy by Europeanizing it, similar considerations underpinned the attractiveness of Exchange Rate Mechanism (ERM) membership for an increasing number of senior figures. If the exchange rate was going to replace domestic monetary targets as the desired policy instrument through which low and stable inflation was to be achieved, it was clear that ministers would have to find a way of minimizing the exchange rate volatility experienced in the first half of the 1980s. For Lawson, this meant pegging sterling to another currency with a sound record on inflation, (the 'inflation by association' argument) and securing organized international support for this pegged exchange rate. By 1985, Lawson, Howe and other Euro-enthusiasts saw the ERM, dominated by the Deutschmark, as a suitable institutional mechanism for this policy.

Just as important for the Euro-enthusiasts were the political arguments for ERM membership. These arguments began by stressing the limits to self-government in an increasingly interdependent world. As a man who had struggled with 'domestic' monetarism in the 'formative years', it is perhaps not surprising that Howe could now be seen arguing that the ability of national governments to solve their own problems in an age of increasing globalization had long declined. The logical response for these governments, including the British government, was to 'pool sovereignty'. By doing this, Britain would be better placed to solve its domestic problems and to maximize its influence in the world (Howe, G. 1990; Radice, G. 1992: ch. 7).

At the same time, Lawson understood that, by tying the conduct of British monetary policy to the external discipline of the ERM, ministers could further entrench their freedom of manoeuvre from domestic groups. Interestingly, as far back as 1981 one can find Lawson deploying this argument, although then he talked largely of the need to discipline the profligacy of his own party, particularly the so-called 'Wets': 'those of our colleagues who are most likely to be pressing for the relaxation of monetary discipline, are those that are keenest on the UK joining the EMS (European Monetary System). In other words, we turn their swords against them' (Lawson 1992: 111–12). Of course, such arguments could be applied to all domestic groups. In short, faced with unsettling forces and economic shocks emanating from an increasingly global market, a growing number of Conservative ministers (and British businessmen) sought solace in the straitjacket of the ERM. The parallels with Whitehall's enthusiasm to return to the Gold Standard after 1918 are interesting here, although it is important to remember that the EMS was only a semi-fixed system of exchange rates.

Finally, as unwelcome pressure for a move towards Economic and Monetary Union (EMU) built up in the late 1980s, the Euro-enthusiasts argued that by joining the ERM the government would be in a strong position within the EC/EU to frustrate further progress towards a single currency. The flipside of this approach was an increasing frustration with the counter-productive nature of Thatcher's strident and hectoring diplomacy. For the Euro-enthusiasts, this belligerent style, most graphically demonstrated in the Bruges speech, ruined any chance that British negotiators had of building alliances at the European level (Lawson 1992: 928–9, 1032; see also Lawson interview on *The Poisoned Chalice*, BBC2, 30 May 1996; Howe, G. 1994: 577–80). The result was the Howe–Lawson 'ambush' just before the Madrid European Council in 1989. Using the threat of joint resignation, they forced Thatcher to accept that sterling would join the ERM and Britain would participate in stage one of EMU. This conciliatory gesture, they argued, would allow Britain to work within the EC/EU to 'detach' stages two and three and thus frustrate further momentum towards a single currency.

If the Thatcher government was largely united in its enthusiasm for signing the Single European Act, the issue of ERM membership and the Europeanization of monetary policy provided the original source of the splits which were to appear in the late 1980s. A dissenting group led by Thatcher and supported by Ridley and Walters rejected many of the arguments put forward by the Euro-enthusiasts. The political arguments were rejected because of the undue defeatism which infused them. Despite the Single European Act, Euro-sceptics still saw monetarism as a national solution to the problem of reversing Britain's decline. To argue that national solutions were now 'a thing of the past' would sound like a contradiction coming from a government which had spent the first half of the 1980s championing the verities of the 'Thatcherite experiment'. Those who sought refuge in European solutions hankered in vain for some kind of 'automatic pilot' which would relieve them from the (significantly reduced) burden of discretionary economic management (Ridley 1992: 88–9, 193; Thatcher 1993: 700, 707).

At the same time, Euro-sceptics denounced arguments that the best way to achieve British interests was to work at the 'heart of Europe'. In more academic language, they accused Euro-enthusiasts of misunderstanding the developing structural properties of the Community. More particularly, Euro-enthusiasts misunderstood that attempts to frustrate progress towards EMU were futile. This policy reform was supported by a powerful alliance, including France, Germany and the Commission. Sceptics could support these arguments by pointing to the failure of British attempts to build support around their own, more limited proposals for monetary co-operation. For example, suggestions for a competing currencies or hard ECU plan aroused little interest at the end of the 1980s because they fell short of explicitly endorsing the goal of EMU. In short, Euro-sceptics perceived the 'heart of Europe' strategy to be naive and dangerous. Far from securing increased influence at the Community level, this approach would result in continued and heightened pain as the party was increasingly stretched out on the 'Euro-ratchet' (Bulpitt 1992; Thatcher 1995: 473; Cash 1996: 3).

The Major government and the 'Euro-ratchet'

In the aftermath of the leadership cull in 1989–90, with the emergence of Major as the new 'unity leader', flanked by Hurd as his Foreign Secretary, it was clear that the Euro-enthusiasts had finally gained the upper hand within the party. In this context, the government's policy during this period was driven primarily by three objectives: first, to reunite the Conservative Party after the bitter legacy of the Thatcher era; second, to resist any further movement towards centralization at the Community / Union level; and third, to achieve this by adopting a new co-operative style which would see the government working at the heart of Europe to achieve British interests. If the style was to be different from the Thatcher era, policy content remained largely the same. Major re-emphasized the importance of a decentralized, competitive Europe, in which future co-operation would respect the sanctity of the nation-state. There was a new emphasis on flexibility through the new concept of 'variable geometry'. This policy asserted that it was acceptable for some member states to integrate more quickly and closely than others as long as there was no question of exclusion and as long as these policies remained open to all. Finally, there was a renewed emphasis on the importance of enlargement as well as the need to consolidate democracy and prosperity throughout the whole of Europe (Major 1993).

If these were the objectives of the Major administration, they remained agonizingly difficult to realize in practice. Despite the Prime Minister's claim that he had halted the tide of centralism at Maastricht (a claim boosted by the collapse of the ERM in August 1993), it was clear that by 1997 the goal of EMU had once again acquired an unstoppable momentum. Most worrying to the Major government was the fact that Europe's political leaders seemed immune to warnings about the need for real economic convergence and the dangers of 'creative accounting' if the policy was to be sustainable. Second, by the end of 1996, the policy of working at the heart of Europe had crumbled into a policy of non-co-operation as the Major government prevented the passage of EU legislation in the hope of gaining concessions over the BSE affair – a tactic that Thatcher had never employed (Grant 1997: 345). Finally, instead of healing the divisions which had developed at the end of the Thatcher era, Major watched the Conservative Party drift into a state of civil war over Europe. As Baker, Gamble and Ludlum have documented, the ratification of the Maastricht Treaty was a perilous and exhausting process, which saw the leadership experience defeat on one vote and postpone a number of others it thought it would lose (Baker et al. 1993). In fact, things were so bad by the 1997 election that the leadership gave up imposing any kind of unity on the question of EMU, giving candidates freedom to issue their own statements to the electorate.

How can we explain the failure of the Major government to achieve its objectives? Why does the European issue continue to be such a divisive one for the Conservative Party? Since 1990, the external institutions of the EC/EU have been developing in a way which has led to a number of unforeseen consequences for the Conservatives. In particular, two external developments are worth noting. The first was the re-emergence of the so-called 'German Question' in the late 1980s which had its origins in complaints from Paris concerning the operation of the ERM in 1987. When the mechanism had to be realigned in response to a rapid fall in the dollar, French ministers complained loudly about the dominance of the German Deutschmark within the system. However, these worries were soon eclipsed once it became clear that German reunification was to become a reality.

Second, the response of Britain's partners was to deal with this problem by reigniting the process of European integration. Indeed, as already noted, supra-nationalism was perceived as the best method of containing German power in the aftermath of the Second World War. Faced with a resurgence of the 'German Problem', Community members fell back on this method once again. In policy terms, they used a little-noticed commitment in the preamble of the Single European Act to restart momentum towards EMU, a move which caught British negotiators by surprise. In doing so, the French, in particular, believed that they could exert decisive control over these nascent structures and thus be in a much better position to contain the increasing economic and political might of Germany. By 1988, policy papers advocating the reforms needed for a single currency had been published. By the end of 1991, the 'irreversible' goal of EMU had been enshrined in European law at the Maastricht Summit, with Britain securing an opt-out from stage three of the process.

Even from a cursory discussion of the objectives of the Major government, it is easy to see why these external structural developments posed problems during this period. British promises to work at the heart of Europe, whilst at the same time resisting most attempts at further integration, were regarded as unsatisfactory by the European partners. Not surprisingly, there have been increasing calls from within the EU to ensure that 'the slowest ship [does] not determine the speed of the convoy' (Kohl, quoted in Cash 1996: 5). For example, British calls for 'variable geometry' were met by proposals for a 'hard core' of member states pursuing their own path to faster integration. Moreover, New Labour's unsuccessful attempt to gain access to the Euro X Committee (by which representatives of all countries participating in EMU will monitor the management of the single currency) seems to confirm fears that any future hard core might pursue discriminatory policies against non-members. Similarly, Britain's enthusiasm for enlargement produced, to Major's horror, a successful move in 1994 to dilute the future blocking majority in the Council of Ministers.

The sight of the Conservative leadership struggling to contain this momentum for centralization at the European level has had the effect of aggravating the complaints of the Euro-sceptics and, thus, widening the splits within the party. For the Euro-sceptics, the problem with the heart of Europe strategy, particularly after the ratification of the Maastricht Treaty, is one of principle. Of particular importance is the acceptance by Major of the broad aims set out in Articles A and B. These state that the Treaty 'marks a new stage in the process of creating an ever closer union among the peoples of Europe', by working for the creation of EMU, a common foreign and security policy and the introduction of European citizenship. By accepting these parameters, the Major government threw away its last opportunity to promote an alternative philosophy of a decentralized Community of freely co-operating nation-states. In this sense, Britain's opt-out from stage three of EMU sent the wrong signals to her partners. It implies that Britain accepts the principle of a single currency, although it has reservations about the technical aspects of the process. In short, the Conservative Party continues in the late 1990s to remain firmly stuck on the 'Euro-ratchet'. Sooner or later, the British government will come under pressure in one form or another to opt into this legal obligation (Thatcher 1995: 470–507).

This leads to a second main criticism from the Euro-sceptics, which lies at the heart of the bitter divisions within the Conservative Party over the issue. By accepting the principles of the Maastricht Treaty, they fear that the Euro-enthusiasts aim to take Britain into a federal European superstate by stealth. Reading the speeches of the Euro-enthusiasts, Euro-sceptics highlight their defeatism and the pessimism concerning the future possibilities for independent political action in a world of increasing economic and political integration. They suspect the enthusiasts of wanting to preside over the gradual euthanasia of the British political class. Of course, in many ways this represents the logical conclusion of a strategy which has consistently emphasized the link between domestic economic problems and external solutions. Why not 'follow through' and hive-off responsibility for the whole of British government to an external body like the EC/EU? For the Euro-sceptics, this development would be disastrous for those poor politicians left to preside over the administration of the British polity. As glamorized 'local councillors' on the periphery of a federal European superstate, they would lack legitimacy in the eyes of the British public, which, having woken up to this loss of self-government, might initiate an ugly nationalist backlash.

Conclusion

Since 1945, British foreign policy has undergone significant change. With the gradual decline of the Empire / Commonwealth and of the 'special' relationship with the United States, Britain at the end of the 1990s is a more complete European power than it has ever been. However, this change should not be allowed to mask essential continuities in British foreign policy during the twentieth century. Faced with powerful institutional constraints on domestic economic initiatives, successive British governments have continually attempted to support this 'weak' position by promoting external market solutions to policy problems. Historically, the Empire / Commonwealth provided a shelter for industrialists and politicians alike, in the absence of more interventionist supply-side strategies. Initially, EEC membership represented a straight swap: one external support system for another. However, faced with the logic of globalization in the 1980s and 1990s, British politicians have increasingly concluded that the only response to these international constraints is to place additional constraints on their freedom of action by seeking further solace in the supra-national institutions of the EU. So although the Europeanization of British policy represents an example of significant change, continuities with the interwar period should not be ignored.

Notes

[1] I am indebted to Jim Bulpitt for the concept of an 'external support system' (Bulpitt 1983).
[2] In particular, the success of the Industrial Reorganization Corporation in promoting rationalization of the British computing industry.

6

Globalization and the Development of the British Political Economy

Positions in the globalization debate

As the political imagination develops over a period of time, it tends to do so with reference to a few key concepts. These ideas come to embody 'the spirit of the time'. For contemporary politics, the spirit of our time has been firmly inscribed with the rhetoric of globalization. However, the forces driving change in contemporary Britain are similar to those which have shaped much of this country's postwar political and economic development. Globalization is therefore most usefully considered not as an historical moment with relevance only to the present. Instead, the politics of globalization are presented in this chapter as a perpetuation of the politics of relative economic decline. Structural constraints associated with finance capital's position as the dominant class fraction clearly continue to impede Britain's industrial modernization; indeed, such a tendency is perhaps now more pronounced than ever before. Financial capital can now be moved around the world at the flick of a cursor. Industrial capital, meanwhile, lacks these mobility options and, consequently, finds itself increasingly subordinate to the moods of the financial markets.

This is not the impression given in the dominant discourse of globalization, however. In this depiction of 'new times', productive interests are also free to locate anywhere they wish, taking jobs with them as they go. Thus, reality and the discursive construction of reality are not always one and the same. Repeatedly in this chapter, I will point to evidence that it is the discursive construction of globalization which is driving political change in Britain, rather than globalization *per se*. Ideational constructs do have the ability to produce material effects, then. However, it should be stressed that this is not the orthodox inter- pretation of contemporary events. According to most accounts, the process of globalization is purely a material phenomenon. Frequently, moreover, this process is also assumed to be already complete: our world has changed irrevocably and should now be conceptualized as a world of 'one place' (Ohmae 1990, 1995; Reich 1992). In other accounts, though, the material changes associated with globalization are thought to be merely peripheral and, as such, should have only a marginal influ- ence on restructuring our understanding of the economy (Berger and Dore 1996; Boyer and Drache 1996; Hirst and Thompson 1996). By emphasizing the marginality of globalization, these accounts focus upon a fundamental stability of state structures (see, for example, Hutton 1996) and, as a result, a presumed stability of the relationship between state and capital (see Piven 1995; Boyer 1996; Cox 1996; Gill 1996).

To deny the existence of change *per se*, however, would surely be a mistake. For one thing, there has been a significant increase in recent years in the perception that the notion of globalization is relevant to understanding the world we live in today. It may well be true that there is no consensus about what it is in relation to globalization that is so important. For, normatively, globalization is presented to us – in acade- mic debates at least, if less so in formal politics – as good or bad in roughly equal measures. Empirically, too, the split between globaliza- tion as real and globalization as imagined is just as pronounced. Yet nonetheless, there does seem to be an emerging consensus that what- ever it is about globalization that is important, then it undoubtedly *is* important. Arguably, to get to the heart of understanding the globaliza- tion phenomenon revolves not so much around asking questions about what globalization is, but about what it is perceived to be. Put simply, it perhaps matters most that globalizing tendencies are thought to limit contemporary state actions.

In recent years, globalization has come to be used to describe the causes of an ever greater number of public policy dilemmas. However, it would appear to be necessary to believe that the notion of globaliza- tion embodies a set of empirical realities before it can be understood as an actual constraint on state action. This is a reading of the globaliza- tion debate, though, which many authors seek to challenge. Hirst and Thompson (1996) in particular have presented a whole range of empiri- cal data which undermine what they see as exaggerated claims that national economies have been effectively globalized. Their contribution to the literature has created a general air of scepticism amongst acade- mics regarding claims that globalization is an economic reality. This suggests, then, that there may well be something distinctive about the *political* context in contemporary Britain which has prompted policy-makers to 'learn' that globalization acts as a constraint on their auto-nomy.

Globalization has been used as a rhetorical device to discipline expectations of what is feasible in terms of social expenditures and welfare entitlements. This is perhaps most clearly seen in the feverish nature of government attempts to roll back the frontiers of the state. Thus, the discourse of globalization has been most frequently appropri-ated by governments which have required it in order to drive home the argument that contemporary macroeconomic policy must necessarily be inflected with a neo-liberal bias. The emergence of globalizing tenden-cies have, therefore, been identified as a means to discredit the national state in general, and anything which comes remotely close to resem-bling social democratic uses of the state in particular.

In this reading, globalization should be understood in political terms. There is a certain irony that concerted political interventions have been necessary at the discursive level to create the impression that globaliza-tion does, indeed, embody reality. For this reality has been sub-sequently appealed to in order to justify the *de*politicization of the macroeconomic sphere. However, it is only within the ideational con-fines of the late twentieth-century ascendant neo-liberal paradigm that contemporary capital flows appear so completely antithetical to distinc-tive national economic policies. Globalization may well be responsible for breeding a political fatalism about what is now possible in relation to economic and social regulation. Yet, it remains a political choice to express such fatalism, in distinctively neo-liberal terms, as the need to hand over an ever increasing number of policy spheres to private inter-ests. Certainly, there is no sense in which the late 1990s period of neo-liberal convergence in Britain (Heffernan 1996; Russell 1996; Shaw 1997; Hay 1997g, 1998) has been structurally determined through the emergence of a new, global economy. Viewed through this perspective, globalization's 'inevitable' downsizing of the state does not appear to be so inevitable after all. In fact, globalization's 'logic of no alternative' is exposed as a mere construct of neo-liberalism. However, as Piven argues, irrespective of our ability to demonstrate empirically that the dominant explanation of globalization is plain wrong, 'the explanation itself has become a political force helping to create the institutional realities it purportedly merely describes' (1995: 108).

In our 'global' world, capital is frequently assumed to be completely released from any ties of geography. As such, it is thought to be free to locate wherever perceived competitive advantage dictates. New produc-tion possibilities have consequently become feasible, enabling capital to exploit the lowest available labour costs anywhere in the world. This is a story, therefore, of an accelerating power asymmetry between relatively static labour and hyper-mobile capital. Workers in advanced industrialized societies are assumed to be increasingly powerless to resist downward pressure on labour costs in the face of ever more aggressive wage competition from workers in newly industrializing societies. All resistance is considered fruitless, for any period of prolonged political struggle over the general wage level will merely persuade capital to take advantage of its enhanced exit options from the national economy and move off-shore (see Wickham-Jones 1995).

This, then, is a sketch of the most commonly cited version of the globalization hypothesis. The remainder of this chapter is devoted to investigating, first, the ideational foundations of the globalization discourse and, subsequently, the economic realities of the wider environment of which it is a part. It is divided into four sections. Globalization has become a potent rhetorical device within contemporary British politics, being used most frequently to justify a newly emergent national state form. Whilst the size of the state, measured in terms of the proportion of GDP, has remained relatively unchanged despite the 'logic of globalization' suggesting its immanent retrenchment, the expectations of the scope of the state have been significantly reduced. The first section seeks to determine the ideological basis of this use of the globalization discourse. I then move on to ask whether the empirical data concerning the British economy's putative globalization is satisfactorily unambiguous to justify the attack on the national state which globalization is assumed to necessitate. My conclusion that there is insufficient evidence to suggest that we live in a truly global economic world raises an important question: one that sets the parameters for the discussion in the third section. Are there any distinguishing characteristics relating to the structure of the national economy which makes British politics so susceptible to the demands of the globalization discourse? The final section revisits the idea that a new national state form is in the process of being created and concentrates specifically on the political aspects of this process.

Globalization as ideology?

It has been argued that the 'logic of globalization' and, subsequently, the policy programmes which this logic is assumed to necessitate are constructed discursively. This leaves us with important questions to answer: this is globalization for what purposes and for whom? In short, whose is this narrative? Given that those political actors who refer to globalization tend to do so specifically to justify making existing economic relations ever more flexible, where flexibility equates with ever cheaper labour costs, it should be clear that the politics of globalization furthers the interests of capitalist class actors. This is not to claim that there is now an organized global business community acting as a 'class for itself'; the means through which the globalization discourse has been popularized cannot be reduced to any single collective actor in this way. There is no single subject responsible for the spread of the discourse of globalization. In this respect, there is no straightforward answer to the question of whose narrative this is. However, in so far as the politics of globalization routinely work against the interests of labour, we can still state with a high degree of certainty that we know whose narrative this is not (Watson 1999a).

The rhetoric of globalization has been used to dissolve national social compromises between capital and labour which had been forged in order to correct market failures felt most severely by labour. The collapse of national postwar social compromises can be seen most clearly in the ongoing process of systematic welfare retrenchment. It would be wrong, however, to assume that globalization has acted as the lone assassin of the postwar welfare settlement. The literature includes several arguments which suggest that the welfare state has been undermined more by domestic factors than by external constraints (on which point, see Martin 1997: 23–32). In these accounts, it is domestic political dynamics which have impacted upon the economic sphere to cast doubt upon the future viability of the welfare state. The perceived success of the British postwar welfare state was grounded in the successful reproduction of the national postwar accumulation regime. Yet, its continued expansion created a state bureaucracy which has frequently been accused of crowding out private concerns. As private accumulation rates fell in Britain with the end of the long postwar boom, the ensuing fiscal crisis created a political space for the construction of a popular image of a country attempting to 'live beyond its means' (for this articulation of the crisis narrative of the 1970s, see chapter 4; Brittan 1975; King 1975; Bacon and Eltis 1976). Subsequent calls for welfare state retrenchment were justified with the argument that any further expansion would only serve to undermine the private accumulation process upon which its very future was dependent. In this respect, globalization merely reinforces other crisis discourses which have long been articulated in relation to the British welfare state (Pierson 1991). The political settlement instituted in response to such crisis discourses has been struck on capital's terms. It is embodied in the redefinition of the context within which the reproduction of the capital relation takes place, and made concrete in the subordination of legitimation imperatives to those of accumulation. As Jessop argues, 'the crisis of the welfare state provided capital with an opportunity forcibly to reimpose the unity of economic and social policy in the interests of renewed accumulation' (1994a: 257). Johnson and Lundvall make essentially the same point when they write that 'the diagnosis of institutional sclerosis had built into itself the cure of the disease; a movement towards flexibility was assumed to demand the restoration of an institutional framework closer to the ideal of the pure, and perfectly competitive, market economy' (1991: 34).

At most in this instance then, globalization acts as some sort of *post hoc* rationalization for a political project of change which was already under way. Therefore, there is something of a chronological contradiction in the conventional wisdom of globalization, which sees the phenomenon itself as the motive force driving this change. It is important, in this case as in all others, to get cause and effect in the correct temporal order, ensuring that observed effects do not precede perceived causes. The erosion of the welfare state clearly began before the emergence of globalizing tendencies; its decline originated with the endorsement of a neo-liberal policy agenda which attempted to roll back the state in general. The adoption of this neo-liberal agenda has not been structurally determined by exogenous economic processes; it is the intentional product of political choice. As Peters observes, any pronouncement of the death of the welfare state is better understood as 'suicide' through neo-liberalism rather than 'murder' by globalization (1997: 18).

Except for the assumption that a competitive market structure is necessary to achieve the most efficient allocation of existing resources, the neo-liberal programme for institutional design is distinctive for the way in which it largely seeks to undermine the institutional context. Therefore, neo-liberal rhetoric is synonymous with the desire to create a space for deregulatory market reforms by cutting back on bureaucratic expenditures and government intervention. However, a gap clearly exists between the frequent articulation of such policy rhetoric by British government officials and observed policy outcomes (see Marsh and Rhodes 1992). As Hirsch argues, these outcomes 'do not so much involve "less state" as a new form of state' (1991: 73). Indeed, the state has been used extensively to insert market relations into an ever greater number of areas of public life. The neo-liberal experience in Britain has turned out to be less a matter of reducing the level of state activities than of reprioritizing what those activities should entail. The redistribution of political power that this has necessitated has been facilitated by a fundamental redefinition of class relations. Extra rhetorical flourishes have been added to the momentum for driving down wages through subsequently appealing to the dominant globalization discourse; yet this should not lead us to overlook that this momentum was already in full swing.

Globalization is presented in this reading as an ideational façade which is constructed in order further to facilitate the imposition of a neo-liberal economic agenda. Put another way, the globalization discourse is in most cases 'unnecessary to carry out the conceptual work which is attributed to it' (Wincott 1997: 1). Yet perhaps it is necessary to carry out the practical work of the political ventures which seem to follow everywhere that the idea of globalization goes. For there is nothing 'natural' about globalization, however much the discourse is constructed through the language of inevitability by those with the strongest ideological commitment to it. Furthermore, in circumstances in which globalization is presented to us as an adequate description of actually existing conditions, such empirical claims tend to be based on what Krugman calls 'careless, flawed arithmetic' (1994: 30). In the next section, I turn to the arguments which suggest that globalization is an economic reality, before showing that these arguments are sustained by claims which are, indeed, empirically suspect.

Globalization as economic reality?

There are three economic processes which are frequently introduced as evidence of globalization – the internationalization of trade, production and financial flows. Importantly, in the context of a study of British politics, all are assumed to entail a necessary policy response from national governments. There is little reason to doubt that financial flows have become truly internationalized. Moreover, these flows do appear to limit the choices that national governments now have in terms of monetary policy. However, there is a need to challenge the assumption that trade and production have been internationalized, for the available empirical evidence undermines such claims. The 'necessary' policy responses to these trends are, in fact, anything but necessary. That is, the British government has not been structurally bound by the logic of globalization into reformulating its fiscal and labour market policies in line with international business interests; that it has nevertheless done so is the result of political choice.

It is argued in the conventional understanding of globalization that the relaxation of spatial constraints on the location of capital has been responsible for locking national economies into an increasingly interdependent system of world trade. Success in such a system is assumed to be conditional upon national economies displaying a competitive advantage in terms of production costs. As Krugman argues, however:

> The idea that a country's economic fortunes are largely determined by its success on world markets is a hypothesis, not a necessary truth; and as an empirical matter, that hypothesis is flatly wrong ... The growing obsession in most advanced nations with international competitiveness should be seen, not as a well-founded concern, but as a view held in the face of overwhelming contrary evidence. (1994: 30)

Throughout the 1990s, the three most prominent groupings in the world economy – North America, Western Europe and East Asia, themselves assumed to be the principal agents driving the globalization of trade – exported only the equivalent of 10 per cent of their GDP (Hirst 1997: 196). In such circumstances, it is a mistake to think of national economies as being competitively aligned against one another. The world's major economies do not trade openly on any global market; instead, they supply 90 per cent of the goods and services that their citizens demand. Thus, the vast majority of Britain's national product continues to be consumed 'internally'. Contemporary changes to the structure of the world economy do not appear, then, to be undermining the significance of the national market, and nor, therefore, of national economic policies. Given the fundamentally internalized nature of economic activity, the priority which is placed upon the question of international competitiveness in popular political debates is difficult to justify.

However, the culture of competitiveness is pervasive in contemporary economic thought. In response to an assumed internationalization of production, for example, it is now not only firms and workers that are exposed to the pressure of having to be competitive, it is places too (Harvey 1989; Kearns and Philo 1993; Kotler et al. 1993). The ability of capital to be increasingly selective in its location decisions is assumed to highlight the significance of the particular production and consumption conditions prevailing in any given place. Places are thus thought to compete in terms of 'locational attractiveness', with inward investment flows acting as a suitable proxy for estimating a measure of national competitiveness. What, then, are we to make of Britain's recent 'successes' on the market for capital relocation? The government, for example, has enthusiastically embraced the fact that the British economy has become the adopted home for an increasing number of inward investment projects (see tables 6.1 and 6.2) as conclusive proof of national competitiveness (HM Treasury 1997). Are we to understand this trend in a similar way?

Table 6.1 Foreign direct investment inward flows (in millions of US dollars), 1981–91

Host economy	1981–6 (average)	1987	1988	1989	1990	1991
Canada	−173	4,198	3,795	2,883	7,018	4,534
France	2,338	5,140	8,487	10,313	13,223	15,235
Germany	1,395	1,480	870	10,630	8,390	6,590
Italy	860	4,188	6,789	2,191	6,441	2,403
Japan	317	1,170	−520	−1,060	1,760	1,370
USA	21,422	58,220	57,270	67,870	45,140	11,500
UK	5,041	15,696	21,414	30,553	32,669	21,537

Source: United Nations Conference on Trade and Development 1993, *World Investment Report: Transnational Corporations and Integrated International Production* (New York: UN)

Table 6.2 Foreign direct investment inward flows per head of population (in US dollars), 1981–91

Host economy	1981–6 (average)	1987	1988	1989	1990	1991
Canada	−6.7	163.6	147.9	112.4	273.5	176.7
France	42.0	92.2	152.3	185.1	237.3	273.4
Germany	22.9	24.3	14.3	174.4	137.6	108.1
Italy	15.0	73.0	118.3	38.2	112.2	41.9
Japan	2.6	9.6	−4.2	−8.7	14.4	11.2
USA	87.2	237.0	233.1	276.3	183.8	46.8
UK	88.4	275.3	375.6	535.8	572.9	377.7

Calculated from: United Nations Conference on Trade and Development 1993, *World Investment Report: Transnational Corporations and Integrated International Production* (New York: UN)

My answer is to warn against such interpretations. For the figures shown in tables 6.1 and 6.2 tell us neither that production flows have been globalized, nor that Britain's attraction of a large amount of these flows is evidence of national competitiveness. The data undoubtedly do show an increase in foreign direct investment stocks, but this should be understood largely as a peculiarity of the time-frame over which the data has been collected. The worldwide recession of the early 1980s depressed investment flows in the first half of that decade; this, in turn, served to exaggerate the relative strength of inward investment performances from 1987 onwards. If we widen the time-frame of the study, we find that the growth of inward investment flows in the pre-globalization era of 1967–80 was more robust than that for 1981–91 (Busch 1999: 21). And, if we widen it further still, we also discover that these flows as a proportion of GDP are the same in the globalization era of the late twentieth century as they were in 1913 (Bairoch 1996: 188). Moreover, these flows of inward investment are in no way global flows. The rhetoric of the more extreme narratives of the globalization thesis, in which capital investment, output and jobs are transferred inexorably from high-wage industrialized economies to low-wage industrializing economies, is clearly divorced from the reality of actual capital flows. In the period 1981–91, almost 85 per cent of investment flows were conducted between western countries (Hirst 1997). Furthermore, as this period drew to a close and the 1992 completion date for the European single market neared, a disproportionate amount of inward investment activity was directed towards European Union economies (see table 6.1).

The most immediate reason for Britain's success on the market for inward investment is its location within the European Union. Britain's attraction of inward investment is, to a certain extent, the result of riding the coat-tails of wider European dynamics. The creation of the European single market prompted a surge in inward investment activity. Non-European firms, especially those from North America and East Asia, scrambled to exploit the imminent expansion in the European consumption market by establishing a production foothold before the 1992 deadline date. Britain had a significant in-built advantage among the sites which vied to house these new production outlets: English remains the language of international business. This, in itself, is enough to ensure that it is the first foreign language to be taught in schools in Japan. Both American and Japanese investors found that the cultural impediments which increase the risk of relocating overseas were lessened by choosing to move to Britain rather than other European sites. Furthermore, Britain's open financial system has always been conducive to supporting non-indigenous investors (to the detriment of indigenous investors: see chapter 2). By contrast, the relatively closed systems which have operated in most continental economies have traditionally been focused towards facilitating domestic economic goals and, therefore, towards supporting only national economic interests.

London's money markets have gained a reputation for being unusually detached from domestic productive concerns. Moreover, this dissociation of money interests from productive interests has intensified as financial flows have become truly internationalized. As Hübner explains:

> [T]he world money market is not merely a place where portfolios are optimised: since the late seventies [that is, pre-dating the perceived era of globalization], the money market itself has become a genuine realm for

the valorisation of capital. This indicates a drastic increase in liquidity preference of industrial capital as well as of money capital holders, releasing a massive switch from productive to financial assets. (1991: 58–9)

Financial transactions are no longer undertaken merely to facilitate productive investments. Financial assets now act as commodities in their own right and, as such, are traded for speculative purposes. Nowhere is this change in the structure of the international economy more readily apparent than in the exponential increase in activity on currency markets. In the aftermath of the demise of the Bretton Woods fixed exchange rate regime, exchange controls were unilaterally abolished and exchange rates were allowed to float. Thus, national governments succeeded in unleashing a speculative frenzy through deregulating financial markets.

Moreover, it is generally thought that the internationalization of financial flows will now be a permanent feature of economic life, given technological developments which cannot be reversed. Quantum leaps in computer technologies have redefined the constitution of money. Money now consists primarily of electronic impulses. These impulses can be held in computer memories as a prelude to being moved to wherever in the world offers the highest returns on their investment. The ease with which financial transactions can be undertaken helps to explain the surge of activity on the money markets since the early 1980s. In 1979, the value of transactions in the international financial markets was six times greater than the value of world trade. By 1986, it represented twenty-five times the value of world trade, and by 1998 that ratio was well in excess of forty to one (Busch 1999: 23).

The sheer volume of these financial flows has served to undermine the policy autonomy of national governments. It is no coincidence that the numbers associated with these flows – which in the late 1990s exceeded an average daily turnover of US$1.2 trillion – last caused major news headlines in Britain during the collapse of the ERM in September 1992. On that occasion, an intensive bout of one-way speculation, designed specifically to 'pick-off' individual European currencies, spectacularly succeeded in overwhelming the British government's stated policy objectives. It is a sobering thought for national policy-makers that the total official central bank reserves of all IMF member countries in aggregate is less than the equivalent of the daily turnover on the world's foreign exchange markets. Given the weight of capital which can be deployed against a particular currency, then, no amount of concerted central bank resolve can ever stave off co-ordinated market attacks.

Therefore, currency speculators operating within the world's financial markets clearly possess the ability to discipline national economic policy. The mere threat of prompting such speculative activity limits the ability of state actors to shape domestic policy purely in line with the demands of the national economy. Moreover, the conditioning effects which speculative flows have had on domestic monetary policy have impacted in a systematically asymmetrical manner. Governments have found that their macroeconomic goals are most readily undermined by external pressure in circumstances in which they prioritize unemployment targets. By contrast, governments which prioritize inflation targets are much less likely to be treated as 'fair game'. Consequently, national policy-makers are presented with a clear incentive to run a tight monetary policy. In effect, it can be argued that the internationalization of financial flows has imposed a consistent deflationary bias upon western economies. However, it would be a very different claim to suggest that it is globalization which imparts this deflationary discipline onto economic policy. The two should not be conflated. The financial system is the most integrated element of the international economy; but financial integration does not, of itself, necessarily constitute a qualitatively new phase of economic regulation – that associated with the 'logic of globalization'. For there is nothing new about the international outlook of Britain's financial sectors. And there is nothing new either about the deflationary consequences which this international outlook has had for British monetary policy.

Financial capital has been the dominant class fraction throughout the postwar period. Furthermore, given that the politics of globalization have served only to reinforce this tendency, it is possible to argue that globalization merely represents more of the same. Despite the much-vaunted novelty of the globalization phenomenon, the forces which are driving social, political and economic change in Britain in the 1990s are those which have shaped most of Britain's twentieth-century economic history. The conventional wisdom interprets globalization as a historical anecdote appropriate only to the present, yet these tendencies are more usefully considered within the context of long-term economic processes. Thus, whilst phenomena such as inward investment are most commonly pointed to as evidence of the increasing globalization of the British economy, I view them as the contemporary manifestation of much longer-term economic and political dynamics. These dynamics are associated with British decline. The following thoughts are presented with direct reference to relative economic decline, which is viewed both in this account and in chapter 2 through the perspective of an unfolding history of state macroeconomic policy which has persistently prioritized financial interests at the expense of the potential of the productive economy.

Globalization as more of the same?

When attempts are made to determine exactly what it is that is distinctive about Britain's postwar economy which has led to its relative underperformance, they are often drawn to the lack of 'dedication' of capital investments. Conditioned by the experience of operating within an economic context in which their interests are subordinate to those of finance, British producers have learned to rationalize their investment strategies so that, in general, they are directed towards short-term goals. In Romer's terms, the investment stance in Britain is characterized by 'routine investment' rather than 'assimilating technology' (1993). By concentrating primarily on replacement investment, British producers have tended to focus more on short-term returns than on long-term market share. The first strategy can still facilitate the private goal of profit-chasing; but the second strategy can, in addition, also facilitate public goals by helping to drive long-term dynamics of economic growth.

The second strategy, though, demands a 'dedicated' supply of capital, thus compromising the future mobility options of capital by locking-in otherwise fluid assets. However, Pollin argues that the institutional structure of Britain's financial system impedes the attraction of such 'dedicated' capitals (1995). The high liquidity preference of Britain's capital market-based system has ensured that there is a general reluctance to free up capital to fund long-term projects. In effect, Britain's financial sectors have acted (and continue to act) as a structural constraint impeding industrial modernization. Britain's highly developed and increasingly internationalized capital markets have encouraged a diffuse ownership of equity and debt instruments. In contrast, Zysman points to the experience of Japanese, German and French firms which operate in a domestic financial context which is dominated by commercial banks rather than by capital markets. These banks have concentrated a large degree of the equity and debt of domestic firms into single portfolios. This allows them to reduce the risk which is associated with making funds available to any one firm. As a result, these banks have shown themselves willing to engage actively with the preparation of 'dedicated' capital funds for long-term investment in new productive projects. In addition, they have also frequently teamed up with their respective national states to boost national growth potentials by providing low-cost credit for domestic firms (Zysman 1983).

Under the watchful eyes of state supervision, bank / industry partnerships have flourished in a number of national economies.

Interestingly, all of these countries have consistently out-performed Britain in terms of growth rates in the postwar period. However, in contrast to these faster growing economies, the British economy has historically shown a distinct lack of integration between its financial and productive spheres. British producers have consequently approached London's capital markets in search of funds for new investments knowing that there are no state-sponsored compromises to shelter them from the markets' competitive instincts. Thus, the resources which they hope to secure are priced in line with the interests of the financial sectors, and not their own. This has ensured that the repayment terms on loans have tended to be very different for British firms operating within London's capital markets than they have been for overseas firms operating in bank-based financial systems. The overriding desire for financial liquidity has guaranteed that British firms have faced capital costs which have been higher than those faced by almost all their industrial competitors.

The means through which high liquidity preferences undermine the preparation of 'dedicated' long-term capital can be analysed by using the concept of 'exit' (on which, see Hirschman 1970; 1986). The moment financial assets are made concrete through the acquisition of corporate equity or debt, they become locked into a binding relationship with that corporation. However, the more liquid the form in which these assets are held – and the shorter the time-horizon over which repayment terms are set, the more liquid we can say these assets are – the easier it is for the owners of these assets to quit existing economic relationships. The arguments developed in the work of both Pollin and Zysman focus on the exceptionally short time-period over which British firms are expected to repay capital loans sourced in London's money markets (see also Lee 1996). They move on to suggest that the key to explaining the peculiar lack of integration between finance and industry in postwar Britain is the high liquidity demands of British finance. Thus, the structure of British finance can be seen to have facilitated exit long before the emergence of the globalizing tendencies to which enhanced exit options are so often attributed.

In general, economic relationships in which one party has a well-defined exit option, while the other does not, are clearly unequal relationships (Hirschman 1970; 1986). The owners of highly liquid financial assets possess a variety of exit options. Given the existence of these options, industrial interests are effectively powerless to prevent financial interests unilaterally setting the nature of their relationship. In this instance, finance capital's potential mobility substitutes for a politically mediated resolution of the competing interests of finance and industry (Watson 1999b). Moreover, finance capital's ability to threaten to play the mobility card gives it the upper hand, not only in its relationship with industrial capital, but also in its relationship with national governments. The international context within which financiers now operate has clearly limited the scope which national governments may once have had to influence financial market outcomes through regulation. The increased speed with which financial assets are now traded, coupled with the increased number of feasible locations for holding these assets, has ensured that there are ample opportunities to exit domestic financial systems. As Helleiner argues, 'states are being forced to become increasingly "internationalised" [in the sense of having to] respond to the judgements of those who move internationally mobile funds rather than to the opinions of their domestic citizenry' (1996: 195). The new liberal international financial environment is thus one which is dominated by 'exit' as a means of exercising influence.

As 'exit' has become ever more established as a strategic option, the pace of deindustrializing tendencies has quickened. In the context of postwar British politics, the prolonged recession of 1980–2 offers the most vivid example of accelerated deindustrialization, with one-third of the total manufacturing capacity of the British economy being wiped out in a single three-year period. However, once again the effects of financial liberalization were being felt in a period which predates the globalization phenomenon as experienced in Britain. This provides more evidence that the two are by no means synonymous. It is financial liberalization, and not globalization *per se*, which has increased the rate at which productive capital has been decommodified and converted back into money capital.

When we take a closer look at the figures for foreign direct investment, we find evidence that British finance has increasingly dissociated itself from British industry. Whilst the government has insisted on focusing exclusively on the 'good news' element of inward investment, little attention has been paid to outward investment. Britain has, in fact, been a consistent net exporter of capital. Indeed, since the worldwide relaxation of capital controls in the early 1980s, 1990 has been the only year in which inward investment flows outnumbered outward investment flows (see figure 6.1). There is nothing new, though, about Britain's status as an external investor. However, what does appear to be new is the way in which contemporary political discourses are portraying these flows of money as the economic reality of globalization. Moreover, these same discourses insist that globalization is accompanied by its own distinctive political and institutional logics. As such, the phenomenon is assumed to necessitate a qualitatively new state form, one which is capable of responding to the demands of new, global interests. The concluding section of this chapter sets out to explore this argument.

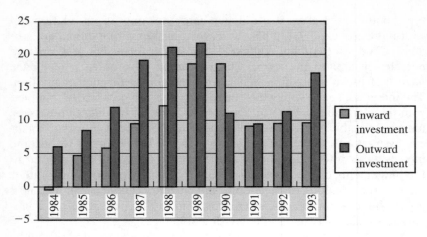

Figure 6.1 Foreign direct investment flows into and out of Britain, 1984–93 (measured in £billion)
Source: *Economic Trends*, 49, September 1994; chart B, p. 20.

Globalization and the political restructuring of the state

Both the rhetoric and the actions of the New Labour government suggest that it understands globalization almost solely in terms of an increase in the range of feasible exit options from the national economy. Consequently, its policy response to the perceived pressures of globalization has been focused consistently on the need to avoid triggering capital flight. This has been sufficient to ensure that an effective veto over domestic policy-making has been handed to those fractions of capital which are assumed to be globally mobile. However, capital exit clearly predates globalization. As such, it may well be that globalization is not the main reality in terms of explaining the trend towards the creation of a new, neo-liberal state form. The internationalization of the financial system has indeed created new possibilities for capital to quit the domestic arena, but it has impacted upon everyday life more clearly in the way that these possibilities have been used to facilitate what Piven calls 'a much more aggressive capitalist class politics': 'Capital is pyramiding the leverage gained by expanded exit opportunities, or perhaps the leverage gained merely by the spectre of expanded exit opportunities, in a series of vigorous political campaigns' (1995: 110). Thus, the policy responses to globalizing tendencies are not economically determined, but are, in fact, contingent upon political dynamics. In recent years, we have witnessed the progressive hegemonizing of neo-liberal economics at the level of both theory and practice. The ensuing shift in the focus of economic policy is to be explained by the political processes which are driving the construction of this new hegemony. As such, the changing economic environment – that is, the new global economy to which these policy initiatives are so often said to be a response – is in many ways superfluous to the explanation.

The political process is mediated, now as it has always been, through the institutions, apparatuses and practices of the state. Yet this is often overlooked in the desire to theorize globalization as the end of the national state. We must be aware, however, that what passes in so many accounts for globalization is actually the product of state action. The realities of globalization have been the cue not so much for the national state to be sidelined as for its internal structure to be reorganized. Indeed, the state is being used as an agent of its own transformation. If national states are in any sense to be swept away by a resurgent neo-liberalism, then somewhat paradoxically it is state actors who are preparing the way for this process. As Panitch observes, 'Far from witnessing a bypassing of the state by a global capitalism, we see very active states and highly politicised sets of capitalist classes working to secure what Gill ... aptly terms a "new constitutionalism for disciplinary neo-liberalism" ' (1996: 85; see also Gill 1992). The role of the national state has been redefined so that it now acts as the domestic enforcer of global norms. The discipline of the global market has been imposed at the national level via a process which has seen the number of outlets for local resistance to globalization reduced through a recentralization of state power. Globalization is thus encoded by national states. Globalizing tendencies are not merely the end result of exogenous social and economic change. They are purposely produced through the organized political activities of state actors.

Thus, the most common misunderstanding in the debate is that globalization signals the effective end of the national state. This claim is based on a false dichotomy between the international and the national. This, in turn, is grounded in the flawed assumption that capital, with its international focus, is conceptually distinct from the nationally bound state. However, it is more useful to perceive a structural relationship between state and capital. Despite their formal separation and their individual institutions, functions and logics of action, each is inextricably locked into the other. Neither the structure of the capitalist state nor its policy concerns can be understood as autonomous from the wider social forces which underpin capitalist development. The continued reproduction of the state is therefore dependent upon the continued reproduction of the capitalist economy (see chapter 4). The contingent form taken by this unfolding process of reproduction at any moment of time is, in turn, dependent upon the relative ability of competing social forces to exercise political power.

Irrespective of the presence of new, external, economic forces which are so often thought to necessitate a new role for the national state, the essence of the functioning of the capitalist state remains basically as it always has been. The activities of the national state are still directed, in large part, towards the functional imperative of guaranteeing the expanded reproduction of capital. However, whilst the functions of the capitalist state have resisted fundamental change, the same cannot be said of its form. This, though, merely reflects a change in the form of the dominant fraction of capital. Contemporary technological advances have impacted most spectacularly upon the operation of the financial sectors. The information technology revolution has decreased the time that it takes to trade financial assets to such an extent that a theoretically limitless number of new exit opportunities from the domestic economy have been created. The mere presence of alternative overseas locations for domestic finance has been translated into new resources of political power. The spectre of mass capital flight is a threat to the continued reproduction of the state. As a consequence, the state has been internally restructured so that it may now support a liberalized domestic financial environment.

Moreover, the trend towards liberalization has been framed against the backdrop of an ascendant political discourse which stresses that this, albeit necessary, trend is also one to be willingly embraced. Exit opportunities have themselves been enhanced by the way in which these dominant political ideas have been made concrete in policy outcomes. As Piven notes, 'a hegemonic ideology supporting the necessity and inevitability of the free movement of capital and goods help to create the institutional conditions which then contribute to making the free movement of capital and goods a reality' (Piven 1995: 112).

The institutional structure which is shaped in the image of neo-liberal ideas is therefore implicit in making globalization: ' "true", in the sense that people ... now experience the world in a way that confirms the ideology' (Piven 1995: 112). Consequently, my argument here is that globalization must be understood in broad political terms. For the concept encapsulates a range of ideas and normative assumptions which, when taken together, are used to legitimate certain forms of class domination. Therefore, we are able to conclude that globalization exists as a political reality. Furthermore, the grip which globalization has on the political imagination in contemporary Britain suggests that this is a political reality which we will continue to 'live' for the foreseeable future. However, it is altogether different to claim that globalization is also an economic reality. When its economic foundations are examined through a systematic, comparative and long-term perspective, it is clear that 'the notion of a quantitative leap is a wrong one' (Busch 1999: 24). As such, the most important fact of our historical moment is not economic globalization *per se*. The distinguishing feature of the present epoch of capitalist development is that it is underpinned by the institutionalization of a particular balance of social forces. Economic globalization only re-enters the story in so far as the newly dominant social forces have appropriated the globalization discourse in order to justify their command of the political agenda.

Part II

Key Narratives of Postwar British Political Development

7

Questions of Change and Continuity in Attlee's Britain

[The] absence of a theoretical basis for practical programmes of action is the main reason why the post-war Labour government marked the end of a century of social reform and not, as its socialist supporters had hoped, the beginning of a new epoch.

Richard Crossman, *New Fabian Essays*: 1–2

This volume emphasizes that much of the existing literature on postwar British politics is dominated by a positivist epistemological position. As Marsh argues in the Introduction, mainstream political science is primarily concerned with observable decision-making. In this chapter I suggest that this has led to a plethora of primarily agency-centred accounts of the Attlee government. Drawing on government archives and political memoirs, the mainstream historiography provides a micro-level account of conflict among political elites. While this is useful in encapsulating the mechanisms and processes of government, it ignores the wider social, economic and political environment in which policies are formulated.

In emphasizing some of the theoretical and methodological difficulties within the existing literature, I aim to develop a more sophisticated understanding of the Attlee years. First, I argue that we need to account for the structural constraints which the Attlee government faced. However, we must also develop a relational and dialectical notion of structures. In particular, we need to examine actors' perceptions of the structures they face; for example, a moderate Labour leadership has historically viewed the state as enabling rather than as a constraint.

In this chapter I shall locate Labour's policy priorities within the context of both its own historical development and the conservative British political tradition. In doing so, I suggest that the overarching priority of the Attlee government was to attain legitimacy as the natural party of government within the constraints of this dominant political paradigm. Additionally, I argue that this aim reflected the historical priority of an essentially conservative Labour leadership. Consequently, the reforms which Labour introduced were not legitimized on a social democratic theoretical foundation.

Much of the literature on the Attlee government focused upon the extent to which the postwar settlement was forged during the war. This debate has tended to revolve around two central questions. First, to what extent were the major policies introduced by Labour a direct consequence of wartime blueprints? And if they were, would they have been implemented, regardless of who won the 1945 election? Second, to what extent was the Attlee government committed to a radical socialist agenda?

In table 7.1, I identify four competing theories about the relative importance of the war and the Attlee government in laying the foundations of Britain's postwar political trajectory. On the one hand, what I have termed the consensus thesis and the betrayal thesis emphasize a radical shift in public opinion during the war as the principal reason for social change. In contrast, both the social democratic thesis and the neo-liberal thesis emphasize the role of the Attlee government in transforming the political landscape in the aftermath of the war.

The impact of war

The consensus thesis

Early analyses of the Attlee government emphasize the experience of war as the principal independent variable in explaining social, political and economic change (Titmuss 1950; Marwick 1968; Addison 1975). Indeed, Addison argues that a 'national consensus' emerged during the war which 'fell like a bunch of ripe plums, into the lap of Mr Attlee' (1975: 14). Labour is viewed as the fortunate beneficiary of a sea-change in the fabric of British society. In particular, it is argued that the war politicized large sections of the working class. Increasingly conscious of their own political strength, they sought assurances that the war was 'something worth fighting for'.

It is argued that the war exploded traditional hierarchies, thus facilitating the development of a much more egalitarian society. The

Table 7.1 Accounting for the postwar political landscape

	Emphasis upon war		Emphasis upon the Attlee government	
	Consensus thesis	*Betrayal thesis*	*Social democratic thesis*	*Neo-liberal thesis*
Impact of war	The wartime experience is seen as the major catalyst of social and political change. The political elite responds to an increased sense of egalitarianism by embracing a social democratic consensus.	The wartime experience engendered a radical leftwards shift in public opinion. This opened up a real political space for a socialist government to exploit.	The extent to which war fostered a national consensus is overstated. Social democratic policies were fiercely opposed by key interest groups.	The wartime experience led to increased demands from the working class which a backward-looking paternalistic elite were only too happy to oblige.
Impact of Attlee government	It is viewed as the fortunate inheritor of this consensus. Suggests that a Conservative government would have implemented similar policies.	A conservative Labour leadership is seen as betraying the interests of its own working class constituency. Reneges on socialist manifesto commitments.	It is credited with implementing a social democratic policy agenda which went well beyond that envisaged by Beveridge and Keynes.	It epitomized the historical failure of Britain's archaic ruling elite to address structural economic difficulties. Rather, its priority was the creation of the New Jerusalem.

evacuations at the beginning of the war exposed the severity of the squalor within the inner cities and stimulated public support for societal remedies. Further, the total mobilization of the war effort, which became essential after France's defeat in 1940, was dependent on the establishment of a much more communitarian ethos within British society. Addison and Marwick argue that, in fostering this ethos, the political establishment was forced to embrace the grievances of the working class. A sense of national unity coincided with an overwhelming optimism that the quality of life in the postwar period would be far superior to that of the interwar years (Marwick 1968: 322). In turn, this solidaristic impulse led to the radicalization of public opinion[1] and the emergence of a national consensus which recognized the political legitimacy of working-class interests. This consensus was built upon Beveridge's proposals for the creation of a universal benefit system and the pursuit of full employment.

As such, within this narrative it is argued that wartime blueprints such as the Beveridge Report and the 1944 White Paper on Employment were not a product of autonomous liberal idealists, but a response to working-class radicalism (Addison 1975: 270–8; Marwick 1968: 328). The driving force of social reform in this account was the politics of class. In return for their wartime efforts, the working class was rewarded with a new social contract which guaranteed the labour movement an enhanced political role within state / civil society relations. The liberal intelligentsia (Beveridge / Keynes) did not drive social change. Rather, their policy ideas were a response to a structural shift in the balance of class forces. Moreover, Addison argues that the wartime consensus had developed to such an extent that there is little doubt that 'a post-war Conservative government would have carried out its pledge to implement the social insurance plan and establish, in some form, a national health service' (1987: 14). Even on nationalization there was some acceptance by leading industrialists that basic industry would be subject to wider state regulation without state ownership in the postwar period (ibid.: 18).

The betrayal thesis

This is a position which is also prevalent within Marxist accounts of the Attlee government. However, whereas the consensus thesis contends that working-class demands were largely met by the political elite during the war, the betrayal thesis argues that the Attlee government failed to implement the radical socialist agenda on which it was elected (Miliband 1972; Nairn 1976; Anderson 1987; Blackwell and Seabrook

1988; Saville 1988). Rather, policy continuity is emphasized as the distinguishing characteristic of the Attlee years. Labour's failure to implement institutional change, its defence and foreign policies and the priority given to restoring the capitalist economic system are all cited as being indicative of its innate conservatism. Despite the radical mood of the electorate, the Attlee government marked a return to the political settlement of the interwar years.

Miliband argues that 'it was the experience of war which caused the emergence in Britain of a new popular radicalism, more widespread than at any time in the previous hundred years' (1972: 272). He identifies a number of reasons for the emergence of this popular radicalism. First, the war was defined as an ideological struggle against fascism and the defence of democratic values such as freedom and equality which were not consistent with most people's experience of the interwar years under Tory rule. Second, the need for massive state intervention, including the centralized planning of the economy in the universal rather than the particular interest, legitimized the authority of the state throughout civil society. Third, the wartime experience led to increased political awareness as illustrated by an increase in Labour Party and Communist Party membership. Additionally, Saville cites the by-election victories of the newly formed, radical socialist, Common Wealth Party[2] and the popularity of left-leaning literature such as *Guilty Men*[3] as illustrating this leftwards shift in public opinion (1988: 84–5).

Within this narrative it is argued that this shift in public opinion opened up a political space for a radical reforming government to exploit. Unfortunately, a conservative Labour leadership failed to grasp this historic opportunity, preferring instead a cautious and pragmatic approach to government. As Anderson argues:

> The post-war Labour government ... thought only of bettering the condition of the working-class within a social order taken as given and an imperial heritage it strove to preserve, by reliance on American protection. Major change in the economic foundations of the country never occurred to it. Socialism had never been on the agenda of the Attlee Administration. Its goals were social concessions from a capitalism whose strengths it accepted as besides contestation. (1987: 58; see also Blackwell and Seabrook 1988: 25)

Labour's priority was not the introduction of socialism, but the restoration of the capitalist economic system. For example, the main purpose of its nationalization programme was to improve the efficiency of the capitalist economy, rather than seeking its transformation (Miliband 1972: 288). In total, government intervention in the economy posed no real threat to the balance of class forces within society and ensured that the power to manage capital remained firmly within the private sector.

The Labour leadership's primary aim was to ensure the smooth transformation from wartime to peace. As such, there was as much an emphasis on continuity as there was on change. Nowhere was this strategy more evident than on foreign policy; for example, as James Byrne, American Secretary of State, wrote: 'Britain's stand on the issues before the [Potsdam] Conference was not altered in the slightest, so far as we could discern, by the replacement of Mr Churchill and Mr Eden by Mr Attlee and Mr Bevin' (1947: 79, quoted in Miliband, 1972: 283). Further, despite a tradition of anti-imperialism within the party, the Attlee government remained largely committed to a global military role. For example, it was actively involved in suppressing opposition to French rule in Indo-China during 1945–6, while it also supported the right-wing monarchy in Greece in its struggle against Communist insurgency (Saville 1988: 90–3).

The impact of Labour

The social democratic thesis

Whereas both of the above narratives emphasize the favourable political conditions which the 1945 Labour government inherited, a number of authors have increasingly questioned the extent to which an 'Attlee consensus' actually existed; for example, Morgan argues that the war 'had promoted fragmentation as much as it had fostered coherence' (1992: 23). In many policy areas, notably the introduction of the NHS[4] and attempts to modernize industry,[5] the government faced fierce political opposition. In particular, there was widespread Establishment resistance to much of the Labour Party agenda. Further, it is argued that the policies introduced by the Attlee government went well beyond those introduced by liberals such as Keynes and Beveridge during the war.

Within this account, the Attlee government was not simply the beneficent instigator of a policy consensus which developed during the war. As Hennessy argues, 'It is misleading to suggest that Labour's social programme after 1945 was merely a continuation of coalition policies with a red tinge' (1987: 33). Similarly, Morgan argues that many wartime proposals did not match the expectations which Labour might reasonably have insisted upon (1984: 22; see also, Laybourn 1988: 108).

Although many postwar policies may have owed their origins to wartime radicalism, the Labour Party was by no means an innocent bystander. Indeed, it is argued that the war had only a limited impact upon the Attlee government. In many areas Labour's proposals went much further than those developed in wartime blueprints. In particular, Nye Bevan's 1946 National Health Service Bill is cited as being much more radical than anything envisaged by the Beveridge Report. As Morgan argues, 'the National Health Service is a prime exhibit in illustrating the danger of making too much of the continuity between the social consensus of the war years and the post-war Labour welfare state' (1984: 154; see also Laybourn 1988: 115–16). Consequently, as Laybourn also suggests, 'It is far too simple to suggest that Labour's welfare state was simply a legacy of the war' (1988: 117). While in some areas, such as the National Insurance Act of 1946, the Beveridge Report clearly had an explicit influence on policy, in other areas, such as the NHS, there was little influence.

As such, within this narrative it is the political ideology of the Labour Party which is viewed as the primary variable in explaining the Attlee years. It is Labour's 1945 manifesto, *Let us Face the Future*, which is the principal source of the policy changes carried out in the immediate postwar period. For authors such as Morgan, Pelling and Cronin, the Attlee government was incredibly successful in realizing these manifesto commitments; for example, Morgan argues that 'it was without doubt the most effective of all Labour governments, perhaps amongst the most effective of any British government since the passage of the 1832 Reform Act' (1984: 503). Similarly, Cronin argues: 'Surely the most remarkable thing about the post-war Labour governments was how much they accomplished' (1991: 153).

Here, the emphasis is firmly on the achievements of the Attlee government. Despite enormous structural constraints and widespread political opposition, Labour was able to enact almost all of its manifesto commitments. Moreover, in introducing the welfare state and the mixed economy it transformed the role of the state and laid the foundations of a social democratic settlement which was to dominate British politics for the next twenty years.

The neo-liberal thesis

Neo-liberal authors such as Weiner (1981) and C. Barnett (1986) also emphasize the role of the Attlee government in introducing the welfare state. However, unlike the mainstream historiography which emphasizes the success of Labour's policies, here it is argued that they were a consummate failure. In particular, there was a complete neglect of Britain's widespread economic difficulties. Despite an acute awareness of British industries' shortcomings, the Attlee government prioritized welfare provision over long-term industrial regeneration. It is argued that this had disastrous consequences for Britain's postwar economic development.

Barnett argues that the Second World War brutally underlined the inefficiency of British industry. Outdated machinery, amateurish management, obstructive trade unions, a lack of skilled workers and low levels of investment in research and development all contributed to Britain's industrial malaise. This was the sorry 'audit of war' of which the political elite were all too well aware. Barnett argues that the Attlee government should have prioritized the reconstruction of British industry in the immediate aftermath of the war. However, instead the emphasis was on the creation of the New Jerusalem.

Both Barnett and Weiner locate this disastrous choice of priorities within the context of the cultural backwardness of a paternalistic liberal elite. They argue that Britain's wartime and postwar legislators had inherited the same cultural idealism which had stifled economic development since the Victorian period. Armed with a pompous religious belief in their moral duty to help those less fortunate than themselves, the liberal establishment embraced the prospect of a much fairer society; a New Jerusalem. Barnett attacks these New Jerusalemers as idealistic utopians who failed to address the practical realities of the modern world: 'not one of the leading New Jerusalemers was an engineer, an industrialist or a trade unionist; not one of them had ever had any experience of running any kind of operation in the real world' (1986: 18). Rather than wasting limited economic resources on welfare provision, Barnett claims that industrial restructuring should have been a priority. In this vein, he argued for the development of a Bismarckian state. As such, in contrast to the zealous, free-market nostrums of many neo-liberals, Barnett advocated the development of a vigorously interventionist state, ruthlessly geared towards achieving national efficiency (see chapter 2).

Beyond an agency-centred narrative

The most striking factor in all of these accounts is the extent to which the Labour Party is viewed as being largely responsible for its own fate. Despite the enormous constraints which the 1945 government faced, the main focus within the literature is upon the political and ideological will of the Labour Party. For, as Tiratsoo argues, the performance of the Attlee government is variously attributed to its ' "class-collaborationist ideology", or its "realistic democratic socialism" or its "unrealistic new Jerusalemism" ' (1991: 2). As such, there is a tendency to privilege the political in explaining change.

This emphasis on the political leads to an instrumentalist view of the state in which the actions of state personnel are given causal primacy over the institutional structures which they inhabit. According to the above explanations of the Attlee government, power lies not in the existing structures of the state but in the personnel of the state. As Hay argues, there is an 'implicit instrumentalist conception of the state in which control over the apparatuses of government and not the structures thus inherited are seen to hold the key to understanding political, economic and social change' (1994: 33). There is a failure to locate the decision-making process within the broader structural and strategic context by political actors. Crucially, there is a failure to recognize structural constraints.

In both the neo-liberal and betrayal theses the adoption of an agency-centred approach is clearly influenced by an inherent ideological opposition to Labourism. As I argued in chapter 2, there are both neo-liberal and Marxist authors who blame Britain's contemporary economic difficulties primarily on the failings of postwar governments. In particular, both narratives blame the policy priorities of the Attlee government. However, again, as Tiratsoo argues: 'Labour is evaluated not in terms of real possibilities, but against various sets of either left-wing or right-wing a priori and ahistorical standards' (1991: 1).

On the one hand, neo-liberalism is underpinned by an instinctive conservative dislike of big government; a normative position, eloquently summed up by Barnett's attack on the New Jerusalem: 'a dream turned to a dank reality of a segregated, subliterate, unskilled, unhealthy and institutionalised proletariat hanging on the nipple of state maternalism' (1936: 304). On the other hand, Marxist analyses are driven by a normative critique of parliamentary democracy. Marxists have always been sceptical of the possibility of achieving radical change through the existing state. In particular, they doubt the commitment of mainstream Labourism to achieving genuine socialist reforms. Consequently, in both accounts the Attlee government is seen as a failure within the context of a political agenda which, in reality, is not compatible with the dominant strands of Labour's ideology.

The inherent intentionalism within mainstream historiography

In response to these overtly ideological and theory-driven analyses of the Attlee government, mainstream historiographers argue for a less impassioned and more empirically informed narrative. As Hennessy

contends, 'the best antidote to the poison of ideological distortion distilled from prejudice and hindsight is an abundance of primary evidence' (1987: 50). In particular, he praises studies such as those by
Morgan and Pelling which draw upon political biographies and archival
material in the Public Records Office. However, while the evidence
which such an approach provides is certainly an invaluable asset in our
attempts to understand the postwar period, arguably it provides only a
partial view of the overall picture. Further, despite alluding to a more
sober detachment, the mainstream historiographer, in adopting a positivist methodology, reinforces an essentially pluralistic view of British
politics. As such, there is a tendency to contextualize the postwar
period within a theoretical framework which remains unrecognized.

Within the philosophy of social sciences literature it is now almost a
truism that explanations of social change which privilege either structure or agency are wholly inadequate. As Rajeev Bhargava contends,
'the more seasoned views on methodology in the social sciences see that
neither the individual nor the social can be given absolute explanatory
priority at all levels' (1992: 11). Individuals are neither passive bearers
of structures nor fully autonomous actors. However, here I argue that
mainstream political science continues to be dominated by essentially
agency-centred accounts of political change.

Through a detailed examination and cross-reference of the political
memoirs and governmental archives, mainstream historiography aims
to develop a reasonably accurate picture of the historical political
process. However, in emphasizing the empirical validity of their
research, the discerning historiographer (often unwittingly) adopts an
essentially positivistic epistemology which leads to an overly intentionalist account of political change.

The format of government documents and, especially, political
memoirs, focuses attention on the role of political actors. Whereas such
data offers a lucid snapshot of the intricacies of micro-level elite political conflict, it is less useful in encapsulating the wider picture. Through
this approach, political history is pieced together from the day-to-day
mechanics of the governmental process. Consequently, it is the institutions of government and the leading personnel within those institutions
which are prioritized as the principal sites of political science investigation. In drawing on the recollections of elite actors and minutes of
government meetings it is inevitable that the personalities of the main
protagonists on the historical stage will be prioritized over the prevailing political, economic and social environment in which decisions were
made. As Hay argues, while archival data may be useful for extrapolating the principle conflicts among the major players within the political
arena, they cannot 'be used so easily to depict the constraints imposed

by inherited state and economic structures, nor indeed public opinion' (1994: 33). Consequently, policy outcomes are viewed as the result of conflict among relatively autonomous political actors.

However, at the same time, the subject-matter of the social sciences cannot be treated as independent and objective sets of pre-established facts. Because people are skilled and knowledgeable, they cannot be viewed as mere bearers of social structures. Social structures are reproduced every day in people's ordinary activities. Individuals are not simply driven by external forces; they do not act mechanically as if compelled by laws of nature.

Towards a dialectical explanation of change

I suggest the need for a more sophisticated understanding of the structure / agency problem in order to improve our understanding of the policy priorities of the Attlee government. Action only takes place within a pre-existing structured context which is strategically selective. As Hay argues, the range of options open to political actors is dependent on a 'complex interplay of structure, strategy and action through which events unfold and action settings are reconstituted' (1994: 35). It is necessary to view the structure / agency relationship as a complex interplay of intentions and constraints rather than as a simple dualism. As Marsh argues in the Introduction, we need to develop an inherently relational and dialectical notion of structure. Structures are seen both as enabling and constraining, depending on the vantage point of each individual. Constraints may also be viewed as resources.

In recent years a number of authors have questioned the extent to which the Attlee government was a master of its own destiny (see, especially Tiratsoo 1991; Tiratsoo and Tomlinson 1993; Hay 1994; Tomlinson 1995, 1997). In contrast to agency-centred accounts, these authors aim to contextualize the performance of the Attlee government within the wider social, economic and political environment which it inherited. In doing so they argue that, while it was successful in realizing many of its manifesto commitments, it also faced a variety of structural constraints. In particular, they question the extent to which a real political space had opened up in 1945 for a zealous and radical reforming government to exploit.

It is argued that much of the existing literature both overstates the extent to which a wartime consensus existed and ignores the widespread opposition to much of the Labour Party agenda among key groups such as industrialists and civil servants. As Tiratsoo argues,

'Labour's room for manoeuvre was more tightly constrained than many have subsequently allowed' (1991: 5). For example, Taylor and Johnman challenge the idea that Labour was the fortunate beneficiary of a cosy consensus which developed during the war. Taylor (1991: 26) argues that the opportunities for radical change appeared much greater than they actually were, while Johnman (1991: 48) identifies increasing opposition, among key groups, to Labour's industrial and wider economic policies from mid-1944 onwards.

Additionally, Mason and Thompson argue for a more cautionary analysis of the leftwards shift in public opinion during the war. They suggest that although the political mood did shift to the left during the wartime period, 'it is the limit of that shift rather than its extent which seems so remarkable' (1991: 66–7). Many people's vision of change was blurred, with no definite idea of what they would like postwar society to look like.

Finally, Mercer (1991) emphasizes the opposition of peak industrial groups, such as the Federation of British Industries (FBI), to Labour's modernization proposals (see also chapter 2). After the war, a majority of industrialists were deeply concerned about the prospects of a Labour government. The FBI sought a close alliance with the Conservative Party and other business organizations, such as the newly formed Aims of Industry, in order to strengthen its lobby against much of Labour's economic agenda.

Hay also argues that the Attlee government was constrained by the need to implement the New Jerusalem. In contrast to agency-centred narrative which emphasize the role of the Labour Party in introducing the welfare state, Hay suggests that the legitimacy of any postwar government was dependent on realizing the promises made by the wartime coalition. As such, the realization of the New Jerusalem provided an enormous constraint on the autonomy of the Attlee government. After the defeat of France in 1940, any prospect of a British victory necessitated a total mobilization of the war effort for which the state, following the class conflicts of the interwar years, was entirely unprepared. The state in its prewar form was distinctly ill-equipped to co-ordinate a total war effort. Drawing on Gramscian thought, Hay argues that there was a need for a 'passive revolution'[6] from above with which to legitimize a much expanded role for the state. This essentially involved unifying a fractured civil society by promising all citizens a much improved quality of life in the aftermath of war. Although other factors, such as the threat to freedom and democracy, did provide a powerful ideological motivation for the war effort, it was the promise of 'something worth fighting for' which was the real source of national unity: 'This extension of social citizenship obligations during the war was to be rewarded by the extension of social citizenship rights in the post-war period' (Hay 1994: 39).

There are also a number of authors who emphasize the need to locate Britain's postwar reconstruction within an international context (Jessop 1980; Hall 1986; Taylor 1989b; Burnham 1990; Overbeek 1990). In particular, the growing dominance of America as a hegemonic power within the West and the emergence of the Soviet bloc in Eastern Europe had an enormous impact on the political space within which the Attlee government operated.

Britain's 'financial Dunkirk'[7] at the end of the Second World War left it particularly reliant on American financial aid; a position which was dramatically emphasized by the sudden end of Lend-Lease aid on 21 August 1945 (Overbeek 1990: 89). This forced the newly elected Labour government to dispatch Keynes to the USA in order to negoti-ate a new American loan. However, as Britain was effectively finan-cially dependent on the USA, the latter was able largely to dictate the terms of the loan. In particular, Britain, despite its financial fragility, was expected to retain its global defence commitments. Further, sterling was to remain a global reserve currency; a specific condition of the loan was a promise to return to full convertibility in July 1947 (Cronin 1991: 162). More generally, Britain's reliance on US aid meant that it was tacitly committed to America's postwar vision of a liberal, free trade global order. However, its continued global military role and sterling's position as an international reserve currency made it particularly vulnerable to international economic conditions. More worryingly, it could not realistically afford to build the New Jerusalem and sustain its global commitments. Therefore, in these accounts it is argued that any analyses of the performance of the Attlee government must account for the enormous structural constraints which Labour faced.

What about political constraints?

The implication of a more structural analysis of the Attlee government is that Labour was blocked in its attempts to implement a more radical agenda. In particular, it is argued that it was prevented from creating a more interventionist state. Although I agree that the Attlee govern-ment undoubtedly faced a number of constraints in implementing its manifesto commitments, I suggest that most structural narratives, in focusing on the economic difficulties which Labour inherited, fail ade-quately to account for political constraints.

Primarily, I suggest that in analysing the performance of the Attlee government we need to account for the impact of a dominant political paradigm (the British political tradition) on the development of Labour's policy priorities. However, we also need to conceptualize these constraints historically. As such, as well as identifying the impact of these constraints, we also need to account for how Labour has historically responded to Britain's distinctive political culture. In emphasizing the impact of the British political tradition, I argue for the need to identify a hierarchy of constraints, and I agree with Layder that there is a 'depth ontology' to society (1994: 142). Layder argues that, as societies develop over time, complex institutional structures emerge which have a degree of autonomy from human action. This is not to suggest that structures exist independently of agency, but that their continued existence over a prolonged period of time suggests a degree of autonomy from agency. Therefore, we need to develop a layered view of society in which some structures are seen as more durable than others.

Here, I argue that a dominant political paradigm privileges some strategies over others. Hay argues that the state is an 'uneven playing field' which is strategically selective; certain types of strategy are more likely to succeed than others. While not suggesting that this dominant paradigm has remained unaltered, I agree with Norton that change has been gradual and piecemeal (1991: 38). Furthermore, the fundamental basis of Britain's political tradition has been remarkably stable. Indeed, there are a number of historical continuities within the system: first, a strong allegiance to the existing political system and a reverential admiration for the British state, especially the notion of parliamentary sovereignty; second, a belief in top-down politics and the natural supremacy of an intellectual elite; and, third, a distinct anti-intellectualism – in particular, a distrust of abstract theory and a belief in an empirical and technocratic approach to government.

Labourism and the British political tradition

Historically, a conservative Labour leadership has sought political legitimacy within this dominant paradigm. In locating the achievements of the Attlee government within the context of Labour's historical development, I reject the notion of a radical social democratic government being frustrated in its primary aims. Much of the existing literature argues that the Attlee government failed to implement a number of radical policies, including widespread institutional change. However, here, I suggest that such policies were never seriously considered by the Labour leadership.

Labour's electability owed as much to its commitment to political stability and continuity as it did to its radicalism. As Morgan argues, 'In the pursuit of the New Jerusalem, Labour looked to the past, through the eyes of relatively conservative, conventional leaders ... Amidst the very euphoria of victory in 1945, the nation offered not a triumph of the will but a suspicion of change and the paralysis of self-doubt' (1984: 28). The corollary of the Labour leadership's acceptance of the dominant political paradigm was that the ruling class was able to absorb the threat of working-class radicalism with only minor changes in the basic structures of the state. The success of this strategy is clearly illustrated by the essentially conservative character of the Attlee leadership. However, whereas sympathetic commentators on the Attlee era such as Morgan implicitly approve of this new realism as a necessary precondition to electoral success, I argue that it also meant a failure adequately to ground social democratic policies. Arguably, this failure to construct the pillars of New Jerusalem on a concrete political and ideological base left the achievements of the Attlee government particularly vulnerable to dismantlement by a future government.

Having failed to unearth the foundations of the existing political system, Labour's electability became inherently dependent on its ability to function within that system. Consequently, rather than forging a new postwar settlement, Labour could only add a modern extension onto the existing institutions of the British state. While the Attlee government may have prioritized the construction of this new extension, it was also careful to ensure that it blended in with the traditional edifice. In a number of key policy areas, Labour was keen to ensure a continuity with the past, rather than creating a brave new world.

In reality, a Fabian-dominated leadership has sought to maximize Labour's electability through developing a political strategy which was compatible with the dominant political tradition. First, it has remained vehemently committed to achieving change through the existing state. Second, it has eschewed abstract political theories and adopted an empirical approach to problem-solving. Third, it has acquiesced with the top-down, elitist and centralized form of British democracy. Consequently, the cost of victory was a high one and effectively ruled out the modernization of the British state.

Institutional continuity

Despite the widely differing interpretations of the Attlee government which exist within the literature, there is a remarkable degree of consensus over the extent of institutional continuity which exists between the postwar period and the interwar years. Even enthusiastic exponents of the Attlee administration such as Morgan accept that there was no 'significant institutional reform' during the 1945–51 period (1992: 107). He argues that Labour's radical welfare programme was 'superimposed on a class and institutional structure which closely resembled pre-war years' (ibid.: 108). Similarly, Hutton argues that successive postwar governments have 'left the wider social and political order intact, together with its value system. In effect social democracy has been bolted on to a fundamentally conservative constitution and wider institutional structure which has blocked Labour's objectives' (1995: 46). Further, accounts as diverse as those of Middlemas (1986: 114), Anderson (1987: 56), Davies (1992: 169) and Gamble (1994: 116) all agree on the failure of the Attlee government to implement significant institutional change. In particular, there is a recognition that there was a failure to implement constitutional change.

Labour's commitment to the constitution was epitomized in its decision to rebuild the bombed House of Commons exactly as it had been before the war, thus symbolizing continuity and a resolute belief in the supremacy of the British state. The voting system, the civil service, the House of Lords, the monarchy, the armed forces, the City, the Bank of England and the public schools all remained largely unaltered. Despite a huge parliamentary majority and opinion polls showing the electorate to be in favour of radical action,[8] the instinctively conservative nature of the Labour leadership prevailed; for example, Morgan argues that reform of the House of Lords was abandoned partly as a consequence of the reluctance of Herbert Morrison to tamper with Britain's ancient institutions. Morrison is said to have told the Liberal leader, Clement Davies, that: 'We should not set up something new and different from the past' (quoted in Morgan 1992: 108).

Jones and Keating argue that Labour's constitutional conservatism is symptomatic of a historical reverence for the state within British radical movements: 'Rooted in persistent and pervasive native traditions, political radicals in Britain exhibited a cautious conservatism in their dealings with the state, rarely confronting it and seeking incremental reform of its institutions' (1985: 10). Even radical groups such as the Levellers and the Diggers remained committed to the existing state institutions. The advancement of universal rights was to be achieved through the application of universal suffrage to the existing parliamentary system. Chartist political demands also focused on an extension of the franchise. Implicitly, they also accepted the legitimacy of the parliamentary system and simply wanted to make it more representative. The abolition of the existing state was rejected in favour of implementing reforms which would return sovereignty to the people. Therefore, within British political history there is a strong tradition of pragmatic and constitutional reform which is markedly different from the revolutionary nature of much European politics. Jones and Keating argue that this constitutionalism is integral to the British political tradition.

Labourism, and especially Fabianism, remain firmly rooted within this tradition. A strong belief in the possibility of radical change through the existing parliamentary channels has been central to the Labour Party's ideology since its formation. As Nairn argues, 'It was only rarely that the political leaders of "British Socialism" perceived a new state and constitution as the precondition of achieving class demands. Normally, the perception was that *the* state could be bent in the direction of these demands' (1976: 30). From the outset Labour has been a reformist rather than a revolutionary party; the aim has been to socialize capitalism as opposed to creating socialism (Hutton 1995: 47).

The principal theoretical influence on Labour's view of the state was Fabianism. Rejecting the Marxist emphasis on class conflict as the driving force behind historical change, leading Fabians, such as Sidney and Beatrice Webb, argued for an incremental approach to social change. Citing recent advances which the working class had achieved in its social and economic conditions, they expressed a belief in the possibility of gradual change through the existing parliamentary channels: 'Whilst mistrust of the state was widespread amongst socialists, at the time the Fabian Society perceived it as the institutional expression of the public interest, staffed by public-spirited, enlightened and capable administrative elite' (Shaw 1996: 4). Consequently, they rejected any revolutionary notions of the radical overthrow of the state and argued for a democratic and peaceful road to socialism.

The commitment to parliamentary democracy emphasized Labour's credentials as a politically respectable and responsible party of government. This position was further strengthened during the 1920s and 1930s as Labour sought to distance itself from the ideological extremities of communism and fascism. As Tomlinson argues, 'The rise of these antiparliamentary ideologies reinforced the commitment to parliamentary norms' (1995: 92). However, in emphasizing its commitment to democracy, Labour has tended to construct a narrow defence of existing forms of parliamentary democracy. Although there was a commitment to some constitutional reforms, there remained a fundamental belief that only limited reforms were needed to make Parliament an instrument of the people's will. As Hutton argues, 'Neither Shaw nor Keynes nor even Bevin doubted that the state would do their bidding' (1995: 48).

This belief in the efficacy of the present system precluded any real discussion of institutional change. For example, Tomlinson argues that Labour's commitment to the doctrine of parliamentary sovereignty ruled out the possibility of creating a separate planning department outwith the 'normal administrative machinery' (1995: 95). Rather than creating a planning department with some autonomy from other government departments, it was subsumed within existing parliamentary channels. The convention of parliamentary sovereignty ruled out the possibility of taking away power from the executive. Consequently, this lack of 'institutional distance' meant that as Britain's short-term economic problems worsened in the immediate postwar period, planning fell victim to more pressing concerns.

A pragmatic approach to government

Norton argues that an empirical approach to problem-solving is the most significant aspect of British political culture: 'Empiricism seems appropriate to the English consciousness. Instinct, trial and error, and incremental change are the essence of the English approach to problem solving' (1991: 34). Again, the Labour Party has been quite content to embrace this culture. In particular, the basis of Fabian reforms was not abstract political theory but an appeal to empirical logic. As Desai argues, 'the sheer weight of evidence was expected to convince the public of the suitability of proposed reforms' (1994: 48).

Within mainstream Labourism, any expansion of the state has always been justified in terms of empirical claims to increased efficiency. There has been no attempt to develop a theoretical justification of the need for an expanded role for the state which could be reconciled with individual liberty. For example, nationalization was justified in terms of economic efficiency, not as a stepping stone to socialism. The basis for nationalization, like all other areas of the Attlee government's policy agenda, was its practical feasibility rather than its theoretical purity. For example, as Herbert Morrison, the minister responsible for nationalization, argued at the 1945 Party Conference:

> In our electoral arguments it is no good saying that we are going to socialise electricity, fuel and power because it is in accordance with Labour Party principles so to do ... you must spend substantial time in arguing the case for the socialisation of these industries on the merits of their specific cases. That is how the British mind works. It does not work in a vacuum or in abstract theories. (quoted in Miliband 1972: 279)

Such a strategy was clearly influenced by the Fabian wing of the party, which 'eschewed revolutionary rhetoric in favour of detailed investigation of the facts' (Davies 1992: 35). As nationalization remained, in typically Fabian fashion, a largely technical exercise, there was no question of altering the balance of class forces or of altering the distribution of economic power.

An intellectual elite and top-down government

A defining characteristic of the British state is the centralization of power which the political process allows. As Marsh and Tant argue, 'The British political tradition ... stresses strong decisive leadership; responsible government meaning strong, rather than responsive, government. It is this view of democracy, an elitist or top-down view, which underpins the institutions and processes of British government' (1989: 4). As was noted above, the Attlee government did little in the way of constitutional change to decentralize power. The ancient institutions of the British state remained largely untouched. However, here I argue that the lack of institutional change during the Attlee government was primarily a consequence of a Fabian belief in the efficacy of top-down government. As Kavanagh and Morris, despite their belief in the existence of a social democratic consensus, concede, 'It is fair to claim that many of the ruling ideas on which the consensus rested were elitist. Like the Fabians, Beveridge and Keynes were paternalistic and technocratic, believing in the rule of expertise and the importance of basing policy on evidence and research' (1989: 6). Similarly, Addison argues: 'A prominent feature of wartime political thought was elitism: the belief that society was divided into leaders and followers' (1987: 24). Both Keynes and Beveridge believed in the inevitability of top-down government and the efficacy of allowing elites to run the state. None of their reforms presupposed a greater democratization or decentralization of the British state. This is a view which sat easily with the dominant beliefs of the Labour leadership.

It is, therefore, no historical accident that the main protagonists within the unfolding drama of the postwar period should share such similar social backgrounds. Attlee (Haileybury and University College, Oxford), Beveridge (Charterhouse and Balliol College, Oxford) and Keynes (Eton and King's College, Cambridge) all possessed the archetypal pedigree necessary to enter the elite cadre of the traditional British Establishment. By the end of the Second World War the political leadership of Labourism was dominated by men with the 'right' credentials to govern the country (Nairn 1976: 31). They represented the enduring impact of what Morgan terms an Edwardian, pre-1914 new liberalism (1992: 111).

Conclusion

Although mainstream historiography acknowledges the influence of structures on political actors their methodological approach inevitably leads to analyses which understate structural constraints. The empirical nature of the methodology means that they are primarily concerned with observable behaviour. This ignores the impact of unobservable structural constraints, such as ideology and hegemonic value-systems. I have argued here that, crucially, it ignores the impact of the British political tradition on the policy process.

The British political tradition is based upon a theoretically conservative view of political change. As such, there is a tendency towards gradual and piecemeal change which is based on an appeal to empiricism rather than abstract theory. Additionally, there is a strong belief in realizing pragmatic change within existing state institutions. The Attlee government can be firmly placed within this tradition. I also suggest that mainstream political science continues to be dominated by a similar view of the political process.

In adopting a critical realist position within this book we recognize the problem of 'reflexivity' within the social sciences. While inanimate objects remain blissfully unaware of the natural scientist, the social scientist must account for the impact which he or she has on his or her subject-matter. Whereas the publication of a physical theory has no impact on its subject-matter, the publication of a social theory can be highly influential; for example, as Kerr suggests in chapter 3, the 'consensus thesis' had a strong impact on the emergence of Thatcherism. Similarly, as Watson demonstrates in chapter 6, the notion of globalization has a strong political resonance. Equally, in this chapter I have argued that, in adopting a positivist methodology, mainstream historiographers implicitly reinforce the efficacy of the British political tradition and provide an essentially agency-centred view of the Attlee government.

Notes

1   For example, Pelling argues that the public's admiration for the heroic struggles of the Red Army led to a wider sympathy for socialist ideas. Home Intelligence reports suggested that there was an almost 'unanimous belief that the success of the Russian armies is due to the political system of that country' (quoted in Pelling 1986: 143). Similarly, despite a wartime electoral truce banning it from almost all political activity outwith Parliament, membership of the Labour Party rose markedly from 2,633,000 in 1939 to 3,039,000 in 1945 (Morgan 1984: 32), while membership of the Communist Party also rose substantially during this period to between 50,000 and 60,000, three times its prewar peak (Mason and Thompson 1991: 56).

2   The Common Wealth Party was founded by Sir Richard Acland to challenge Conservative candidates at by-elections and was mainly comprised

of middle-class intellectuals, disgruntled with the wartime electoral truce between the mainstream parties.

3   A savage indictment of the politicians involved in the appeasement of Nazi Germany. Published in 1940, it sold almost a quarter of a million copies.

4   An excellent account of the opposition which Bevan faced, especially from the BMA, in implementing his proposals for a National Health Service can be found in Morgan 1992: 151–63; see also Hennessy 1987: 36–7; and Laybourn 1988: 115–17.

5   See, especially, Mercer 1991.

6   This concept originates in Gramsci's 'Prison Notebooks' to denote how the ruling class absorbs a radical threat to its hegemonic position through the implementation of political and economic concessions to more moderate factions within opposition groups.

7   A famous comment by Keynes, warning of the economic difficulties which Britain faced in the immediate postwar period (Hennessy 1987: 35).

8   For example, Davies cites a Mass Observation poll in 1947 which 'suggested that people were "ready for radical action" but were disappointed by the lack of "spectacular appeals" and "wider explanation" from the government' (1992: 169–70).

8

Explaining Thatcherism: Towards a Multidimensional Approach

The election of the Conservatives in 1979 led to a veritable academic industry analysing Thatcherism. However, as several authors have pointed out, the myriad of interpretations which emerged out of the debate over Thatcherism reveal an underlying weakness of political science explanations in coming to terms with the multidimensional processes and mechanisms which shaped the development of the Conservatives' unfolding strategy. Most authors tended to talk past one another: state theorists emphasized Thatcherism as an attempt to re-regulate patterns of economic growth in response to the wider trajectory of the world system; cultural theorists insisted that Thatcherism was an attempt to engage in a form of hegemonic politics; and most political scientists preferred to see the Thatcherite strategy in the context of a reassertion of governing competence after the breakdown of the postwar consensus. The only thing that united these authors was a belief that Thatcherism represented a distinctive strategy which signalled a significant break with past practice. However, beyond this often undefended assertion, few could agree about the specific development and content of the Thatcherite strategy.

In this chapter we will briefly consider some of the main problems in existing explanations of Thatcherism. In our view, we need to develop an evolutionary account of change which is sensitive both to the processes of selection and adaptation that generate governmental strategy and to the temporal dimension of political change, in order to produce a multidimensional account of the Thatcher project. This allows us to suggest a novel interpretation of Thatcherism which emphasizes that the Conservatives' strategy was a constantly changing dynamic process, driven by political learning, adaptation and strategic selection in response to the constraints of the global political and economic system. Overall, we will argue that the Thatcherite project is best conceived of as an inherently flawed evolutionary process, aimed at redressing Britain's perceived long-term economic and institutional decline, which was hampered by the Conservatives' dogmatic attachment to a narrow, neo-liberal anti-statist discourse. Our analysis is located at a theoretical rather than an empirical level given that our main aim is to introduce concepts which may be utilized to inform future explanations of Thatcherism.

The Thatcherite chameleon

Few authors agree on what 'Thatcherism' actually entailed.[1] To most, the term implies a purely political phenomenon, driven by such factors as the personality and style of Mrs Thatcher (King 1985; Jenkins 1987; Minogue and Biddiss 1987), an attack upon the postwar policy consensus (Kavanagh 1990; Kavanagh and Morris 1994) and traditional forms of Conservative Party statecraft (Bulpitt 1986). Others, however, highlight the ideological and discursive dimensions of Thatcherism (Hall, S. 1979; O'Shea 1984; Hay 1996c). To these authors, the Thatcher project represented an alternative ideological vision to social democracy, constructed around a predominantly New Right discourse. For a smaller number, Thatcherism is interpreted in economic terms; as a national response to wider international crises in capitalist profitability brought about by the exhaustion of Fordism (Jessop et al. 1988; Overbeek 1990; Taylor, P. J. 1992). Overall, given this diversity, the term Thatcherism has become chameleon-like; lacking any precise definition, it means different things to different analysts.

This eclecticism in the approaches to defining and explaining Thatcherism could, of course, be attributed to the depth of the Conservatives' strategy itself. After all, the Conservatives argued that they were engaged in a radical restructuring of a multitude of political, economic and ideological practices. They espoused political conviction rather than consultation and consensus, individualism rather than collectivism and, on an economic front, competition and market forces rather than state intervention. Certainly, the Conservatives spent much time and energy reminding us of the diversity of their objectives. It could therefore be argued that the sheer scope and complexity of the Conservatives' project made the academic confusion which characterized the study of Thatcherism almost inevitable.

Such an interpretation is unsatisfactory. It is certainly true, as several authors have pointed out (Jessop et al. 1988; Marsh and Rhodes 1992, 1995; Marsh 1995; Hay 1996c; Kerr et al. 1997), that the literature on Thatcherism fails to develop explanatory frameworks which can incorporate the diversity and complexity of the Thatcher years. However, in our view, it is possible to remedy this failure and this is our intention here.

Before developing our own perspective, it is crucial to deal with some of the limitations of the existing literature at more length. Here, we shall concentrate on four weaknesses. First, by failing to acknowledge the crucial temporal dimension of Thatcherism, most authors do not recognize the essentially contingent, and often changing, development of the Conservatives' strategy over time. Second, the fact that most literature is based on a cursory and often false reading of the historical antecedents of Thatcherism means that it fails to provide an adequate analysis of the longer-term conflicts and institutional compromises which both shaped and constrained the Conservatives' strategy. Third, in emphasizing unidimensional explanation, by focusing almost exclusively on political or ideological or economic variables, most authors fail to provide a rounded approach which can incorporate the complex range of dynamics which generated the Thatcherite project and contributed to its uneven temporal development. Fourth, most analysis of Thatcherism is ethnocentric; it fails to examine British developments in the context of wider international changes.

Problems with current explanations

Taking time out

A central theme of the Thatcher governments' rhetoric was the idea that the Conservatives had a coherent, developed strategy for reducing the size and scope of the state through the introduction of market forces. However, beyond vague pledges to recharacterize the role of government, the Conservatives were unclear about both the extent to which this strategy should be implemented and, indeed, the means by which it could be achieved.[2] This suggests that Thatcherism emerged as an open-ended strategy which had to be worked out and redefined over time. Yet this point has rarely been acknowledged within the literature. As a result, most authors have failed to consider one of the defining features of Thatcherism: its inherent dynamism and elasticity, as the Conservatives continually experimented with, and reworked, the parameters of their own strategic objectives.

Several studies of Thatcherite policies have demonstrated that the Conservatives' strategic interventions were far more pragmatic and incoherent than suggested by ideological rhetoric (Riddell 1991; Marsh and Rhodes 1992). Thus, although the Thatcher governments were adept at articulating a relatively consistent vision of the direction in which they wanted to go, many of their attempts to translate this vision into actual practice were much more haphazard. It was only over the course of a considerable time, specifically into their third term in office, that they were able to achieve the consistency and coherence which has been generally associated with Thatcherism as a whole. Thus, it is possible to detect a heightened radicalism and sophistication in the Conservatives' reforms as their strategy evolved (Gamble 1988; Jessop et al. 1988; Hay 1996c; Kerr et al. 1997). Unfortunately, this evolutionary process of reform has received only a limited acknowledgement within the literature. Many authors have been content to view Thatcherism as a singular, static and unified phenomenon, failing to recognize its uneven development through a series of interventions, which were often *ad hoc* and which changed over time.

There has been a consequent failure to develop a sophisticated assessment of the Conservatives' strategy under John Major (Kerr et al. 1997). Whereas the Thatcher years gave rise to an industry of theoretically informed academic debate, the Major government merely evoked a strange mixture of indifference and indecision as to its precise relationship with earlier post-1979 Conservative strategy (see chapter 9). The few authors who have analysed the Major period are uncertain whether post-1990 Conservative reforms reflected a continuation of previous Thatcherite strategy, or whether 'Majorism' represented a distinct political phenomenon. Most have merely concluded, in a manner which can only be described as theoretically agnostic, that there was some continuity and a limited amount of change.

This is a truism, but the key point here is the absence of any real conceptual link between the strategy pursued by John Major and the evolution of Thatcherism as a whole (although, see Hay 1996c). When we consider that Major was the Conservatives' Prime Minister during more than a third of his party's term in office, this represents a significant gap in our understanding of how Thatcherism has developed over time. Most importantly, the failure to focus upon the evolution of Thatcherism negates any real understanding of the processes of institutional change which occurred in the Major years, and which will undoubtedly influence the development of the policies and strategies of New Labour.

Dislocating post-1979 Conservatism from its past

There is also a failure to place Thatcherism in proper historical perspective. Few serious attempts have been made to link the post-1979 period to the historical conflicts and institutional compromises which both shaped and constrained the development of the Conservatives' strategic choices. Of course, most authors do pay at least a partial lip-service to the historical background to Thatcherism, by emphasizing that it was a reaction to the period of postwar consensus. However, it would be misleading to assume that these, often passing, references to the earlier postwar period constitute a proper consideration of the links between Thatcherism and its past. On the contrary, this type of analysis merely detaches Thatcherism from its ancestry and ignores the lines of continuity which have characterized the postwar period as a whole.

Throughout their term in office, the Conservatives sought to distance themselves from the practices of their predecessors by emphasizing their opposition to almost every aspect of the earlier postwar era. This led them discursively to construct an image of radicalism based upon a manufactured, and often false, dichotomy between the pre-1979 and post-1979 eras (Kerr and Marsh 1996). In particular, they presented themselves as overturning the consensual commitment to state intervention which they argued had dominated the earlier postwar period. Unfortunately, many political scientists have usually accepted the Thatcherites' own attempt to contrast their strategy with past practice, because these political scientists wished to assert that 1979 marked a decisive break with the past.

As chapters 2 and 3 suggest, we need to remain cautious when assessing the extent to which Thatcherism can be judged radical in relation to past practice. The seeming discontinuity between Keynesianism and monetarism has been overstated by most authors, whilst the commitment by earlier postwar administrations to state intervention has been greatly exaggerated. The result is that, by explaining Thatcherism in terms of a single 'opposition' between it and its presumed historical 'others', there has been a failure to develop a proper conception of the processes and mechanisms which have guided the evolution of the state in the postwar period.

The prevalence of partial explanations

Marsh (1995) points out that the majority of interpretations of Thatcherism are unidimensional, rather than multidimensional, and have focused upon political or ideological or economic explanatory variables.

Little attempt has been made to provide an explanatory framework which can integrate these different dimensions.[3] Moreover, in terms of the relationship between structure and agency, most accounts emphasize either structuralist or intentionalist explanations, without giving due attention to the complex and dialectical interplay between both sets of variables.

Political explanations Most unidimensional explanations of Thatcherism are political, emphasizing the importance of Mrs Thatcher's personality or political style. So, King argues, 'She seeks to control the context of public policy and through it Britain's destiny' (1988: 57). In this view, the key political context of Thatcherism was a widespread belief that Britain in the postwar period, and particularly in the late-1970s, had suffered from over-government and weak government. This provided the political space into which Mrs Thatcher, as a strong, decisive personality, entered.

Considerable attention is also paid to the electoral imperative. In this vein, Jim Bulpitt offers the most interesting and politicist explanation of Thatcherism, arguing that the key concern of political parties is to win elections and that to do this they search for a successful statecraft. The major dimensions of this statecraft are party management, a winning electoral strategy, victory in elite debate about political problems and an image of governing competence, especially in relation to policy implementation (1986: 21–2). To Bulpitt, the ideology and policies of the 1979–83 Thatcher government were not particularly consistent; rather, they were involved in a, largely successful, search for 'a governing competence, through a reconstruction of . . . traditional central autonomy' (ibid.: 34).

The key problem with the politicist interpretation is that it over-emphasizes the role of Mrs Thatcher and, more generally, of agents as against structures. As such, it pays little attention to the way in which broad economic forces constrained and facilitated the Conservative government's actions.

Ideological explanations A number of authors argue that it was New Right thinking which provided the sense of direction, the route-map which the strong decisive leader followed (see Kavanagh 1987: 11; Benyon 1989: 170–1). Here, political and ideological explanations are linked. However, other authors focus almost exclusively on ideological explanation. So, for example, O'Shea (1984) argues that Thatcherism was not just a set of policies but a series of discursive strategies which were politically effective. They were effective both because they built upon existing popular common sense and because they provided the framework, the terms and the boundaries within which people discussed politics. In O'Shea's view, Thatcherism was a coherent, and largely successful, hegemonic project (ibid.: 22–3).

Again, this unidimensional explanation has weaknesses. It over-emphasizes the coherence and consistency of the Thatcher government's ideological position. In fact, it utilized different ideological elements at different times to forward its political and electoral ends (see Jessop et al. 1988: 45). Second, there were significant ideological divisions in the Conservative Party up to, and indeed beyond, 1979, and it was only a political event, the 'Winter of Discontent', which helped resolve some of these ideological disputes. Third, there is considerable doubt as to the success of the hegemonic project. So, for example, the Major government's emphasis on 'Back to Basics' suggests that, in their view at least, the ideological battle had not been won by 1990 but rather needed to be constantly waged.

Economic explanations   Most economic explanations of Thatcherism view it as a response to economic crisis. The majority of this material is Marxist and offers a strong, structuralist explanation of Thatcherism and Thatcherite policies. So, for example, Coates (1989) sees industrial relations policy as a key element in the Thatcherite response to a deepening economic crisis. In this view, the crisis of capitalism, given the fundamental incompatibility of the interests of capital and labour, led to the collapse of corporatist strategies, the pursuit of market solutions and, in particular, the attack on trade unions. To Coates, New Right ideology, and its attack on trade unions as a crucial constraint on the operation of the market, was a tool used by a government intent on shifting the balance between class forces in the interests of capital (ibid.: 118).

The problems with this reading of Thatcherism are the problems of economism generally: the mechanisms through which the government forwards the interests of capital are not specified; the emphasis is almost totally upon structural at the expense of intentional explanation; both theoretical discussions and empirical evidence about the auto-nomy of the state are ignored; and it fails to specify or examine the articulation between the economic, the political and the ideological, merely asserting the dominance of economic relations.

Clearly, the Conservatives' strategy was propelled by a whole series of different inputs, ranging from the particular personality and style of Mrs Thatcher to the more generic institutional crises which provoked it. It was shaped by electoral and political concerns as much as by ideo-logical conviction. Economically, the Conservatives had to deal with a key contradiction. They wanted, on the one hand, to encourage processes of market liberalization, whilst, on the other, strengthening the ability of the state to oversee and encourage these processes. Yet, the complexity of these types of dynamics remains under-theorized within the literature.

Beware of ethnocentric analysis

One related problem is worth emphasizing here. The literature is ethnocentric. It largely ignores comparative evidence and for that reason overemphasizes British exceptionalism,[4] neglecting the external factors which shaped and constrained the development of the Conservatives' strategy. This also helps explain why there have been few serious attempts to characterize Thatcherism as part of a wider, international, response to political and economic crises within the world system. Once again, this means that the focus has been upon the role of the Thatcherites and their ideological commitments. So, the majority of analysts appear happy to conclude that the combination of Mrs Thatcher's dominant personality and New Right ideas converged to provoke an 'exceptional' conjuncture in British politics; the fact that similar policies were introduced across the globe was largely ignored.

Restating the problem of Thatcherism

Overall then, Thatcherism is most often presented as a singular, static, snapshot in time, dislocated from its historical antecedents, whilst explanatory emphasis has often been upon either agency-centred accounts of change or structural determinism. Such analyses fail to provide a proper examination of the processes of change through the dynamic and dialectical interplay between structure, agency and strategy which would elucidate the true complexity behind the Conservatives' strategic interventions (see chapter 1). How can we construct an alternative approach to explaining Thatcherism which can overcome such problems?

In our view, such an approach needs to include:

- an appreciation of the temporal dimension of Thatcherism and a recognition that Conservative reforms evolved and gained coherence over time;
- an appreciation of the historical forces which shaped the development of Conservative strategy;
- a sensitivity to the complex interplay between the political, ideological and economic dimensions of Thatcherism;
- an appreciation of the importance of both the structural and intentional factors in the process of Conservative reforms;

- a commitment to analysing both the domestic and external contexts which constrained and enabled the Conservatives' strategic choices.

Of course, this is no small challenge. Yet, to us it is crucial if we are to gain a proper insight into the complex and dynamic processes which contributed to Thatcherism and, in addition, to understand the types of processes which are likely to influence future government strategy. The major problem, however, is that current explanations provide us with few guidelines. The gulf which separates existing approaches represents a profound obstacle which cannot simply be overcome through a vague commitment to greater holism. As Jessop et al. point out: '[whilst] all would probably agree that a rounded account must be sensitive to each dimension ... *the central question is how this can be achieved without simply presenting a more or less random mix of factors*' (1988: 154; emphasis added).

In the following sections, we suggest that one way to develop a multi-dimensional perspective that really articulates all the major dimensions is to utilize an evolutionary conception of political change which emphasizes the temporal unfolding of change through a constant and dynamic process of strategic learning and adaptation in response to wider environmental pressures. We need a theoretically informed narrative, rather than the abstracted redescription which is usually on offer.

Towards an evolutionary conception of Thatcherism

In recent years the utility of evolutionary conceptions of change within a variety of social science subdisciplines has been reaffirmed. In particular, neo-institutional economists[5] and organizational theorists[6] have developed theoretical models built upon insights derived from Darwinian and Lamarckian biology. Meanwhile, less formalized conceptions of evolutionary change have been employed within the field of historical sociology.[7] Some of the most sophisticated theoretical work has come from attempts by state theorists[8] and historical institutionalists to incorporate an evolutionary conception of change into political science discourse.[9]

Of course, these approaches differ markedly in the extent to which they employ evolutionary concepts. This is hardly surprising, given the diverse range of theoretical projects underpinning each approach; however, it does demonstrate that an evolutionary perspective provides us with a general framework for explaining change which can have specific applications in a number of different research areas (Nelson 1995: 54). An evolutionary approach does not represent a unified theory of change; rather, it reflects an overall research paradigm, or heuristic device, used to focus our attention on certain types of variables or processes governing change (De Bresson 1987).

This is not the place to review these developments. However, we can identify some of the general insights which may be used to illuminate a study of political change. There are four main elements central to any evolutionary explanation in social science:

1 A concern with the temporal dimensions of change. An evolutionary approach focuses our attention upon a variable, such as Thatcherism, which is changing over time (Nelson 1995: 54). It diverts us away from a preoccupation with static phenomena and directs us towards viewing change as a dynamic and ongoing process (see chapter 1).

2 A concern with the factors which generate change. The theoretical quest behind an evolutionary approach is to examine the complex interaction of variables which contribute to making evolution occur (Nelson 1995: 5). Primary emphasis is placed upon 'explaining' change, rather than merely 'describing' it.

3 Change is perceived as occurring through a combination of both selective and adaptive processes. In this sense, evolutionary theory emphasizes that the environment in which variables evolve imposes selective pressures which favour certain types of change over others. In turn, however, the variables which are evolving can often adapt both themselves and, to a lesser extent, their environment, in order to increase their chance of survival.

4 Change is seen as both path-dependent and contingent. It is path-dependent in the sense that a combination of environmental constraints and past adaptations shape the direction of future changes. In this sense, the changes which occur must inevitably display certain continuities with past adaptations. However, because of the crucial input which goal-oriented and purposeful actors bring to bear upon their environment, there is also a large degree of contingency involved in the process of change. Thus, the environment does not simply determine the direction of change; rather, it provides the context in which actors can learn to adapt strategies in order to negotiate the constraints which they face.

These then are the main features of an evolutionary approach. In our view, the advantages of utilizing such an approach in order to elucidate the multidimensional nature of the Thatcher project are numerous (see table 8.1). First, an evolutionary account allows us to move beyond a static conception of Thatcherism, thereby enabling us to view it as a series of contingent interventions which unfolded and evolved over time. Second, by focusing our attention on the path-dependency of change, an evolutionary perspective focuses upon the historical factors which shaped the development of Conservative strategy. Third, an

Table 8.1 An evolutionary approach to explaining Thatcherism

Problems of current explanations	Advantages of an evolutionary approach	Applications to Thatcherism
Neglect of the temporal dimensions to the Conservatives' strategy. Thatcherism seen as a singular, unified snapshot in time.	Draws specific attention to the time-span through which the development of the variable under scrutiny occurs. Thus, directs our focus to change rather than stasis and to the temporal compass along which this takes place.	Thatcherism viewed as a constantly changing and evolving phenomenon. Allows us to chart the development of Thatcherism from its early, tentative stages of reform to its maturation during the Conservatives' third and fourth terms.
Absence of an historical perspective. Thatcherism viewed as a reaction to previous government strategy. No analysis of the lines of continuity between the post-1979 era and the earlier postwar experience.	Views change as path-dependent; i.e., past changes affect future adaptations. This directs our focus to the fact that change will exhibit a crucial element of continuity with the past.	Thatcherism considered in the context of the historical forces and institutional compromises which constrained, enabled and provoked its development. Thus, viewed in the context of the crisis of social democracy and the failure of Fordism.
Failure conceptually to link the political, ideological and economic dimensions of Thatcherism.	Evolution seen as the product of a multiplicity of different factors. The theoretical quest is to examine the complex interaction of dynamics which generate change.	Thatcherism viewed as evolving in response to a diffuse number of inputs, including the personality traits of key actors, New Right ideology, Conservative Party statecraft and crises in capitalist profitability.

Unequal consideration given to structural and intentional factors. Failure to view change as the product of the dialectal interplay between structure, agency and strategy.	Equal consideration given to the interaction between purposeful human agents and the selective environment, or context, within which these operate. Thus, change is seen as both contingent and path-dependent; i.e. as the product of agents developing strategies to negotiate their structural environments.	Thatcherism viewed as the outcome of an evolving process in which the Conservatives attempted to implement their political, ideological and economic objectives within an environment which both constrained and enabled their strategic choices. Thus, consideration given to the ability of the Conservatives to adapt their strategic interventions and learn how to implement these over time.
Prevalence of ethnocentric approaches. Thatcherism seen as an exceptional phenomenon. Little attention given to the spread of similar policies across the globe and to the factors which provoked these similarities.	Attention given to the full range of environmental factors which shape evolution. Thus, directs our attention to the global as well as the domestic structures which influenced the development of Conservative strategy.	Thatcherism seen within the context of both the national-specific institutional environment in which it emerged as well as the global factors which influenced its development. Thus, viewed as a response both to generic crises within the international system and to the specific articulation of these on the domestic front.

evolutionary account necessarily entails a proper appreciation of the complex range of dynamics – political, ideological, economic, structural, intentional, domestic and external – which governed both the selection and adaptation of Conservative strategy over time. Overall then, an evolutionary approach provides us with an explanatory device which would, *a priori*, preclude the type of static, ahistorical, ethnocentric and reductionist accounts which have so far dominated the literature by directing our focus to the inherent dynamism of the Conservatives' strategy and to the multilayered processes which generated, facilitated and constrained it.

How can we develop an evolutionary approach through which to elucidate the multidimensional nature of Thatcherism? In the following section, we outline three key factors which need to be considered: first, the strategic selectivity of the environment in which Conservative strategy was implemented; second, the subjective inputs which the Conservatives' brought to bear upon their own selection of strategic choices; and, third, the ability of the Conservatives to learn how to adapt their strategy in order to renegotiate the environmental constraints which they faced. Our aim is not to theorize the relationship between these factors but, rather, to begin to develop a conceptual framework which can inform future, more developed, accounts.

Factors governing the evolution of Thatcherism

Strategic selectivity

Any informed analysis of Thatcherism must account for the inherent biases in both the global and domestic environments within which Conservative strategy was implemented. Thus, we need to recognize that Thatcherism evolved within a structured context which was itself the product of previous strategies and historical processes and which necessarily favoured certain interventions over others. In other words, Thatcherism was subject to a variety of selective pressures which both constrained and facilitated its strategic development over time.

The most notable factor conditioning the development of Thatcherism was the political and economic crises of the 1970s. Any analysis of Conservative reforms must account for the pressures which these crises brought to bear upon all governments to implement appropriate forms of strategic response. This necessarily entails an awareness of wider evolutionary movements within the global system of economic and interstate relations. The global environment exerts pressures upon all nation-states to accommodate themselves to the wider trajectories and crises of the world economy. As a result, co-evolutionary tendencies emerge between global economic patterns and national-specific strategic responses (Ward 1997). This then should direct our attention to the constraints imposed upon the Conservatives' responses to crises and remind us of the path-dependent nature of change incurred by the selective environmental pressures to which they were subject. Most authors agree that the Thatcher governments were forced to engage in the strategic readjustment of Britain's socio-economic and political structures in response to two key pressures within their external environment: the weakening of US hegemony and the global economic crisis. Whilst the former squeezed the UK into a readjustment of its international political and economic alliances, the latter has forced domestic economic restructuring to accommodate more flexible forms of economic growth. This has brought about the introduction of appropriate forms of institutional organization, including the recomposition of welfare delivery, as part of a transition towards what Jessop (1994b) has termed a 'Schumpeterian workfare state'.

However, although these external pressures are crucial, they are mediated by pressures which are nation-specific. So, in analysing the strategic interventions brought about by the Thatcher governments, we need to consider the historical specificity of Britain's own position with the world system. This entails an assessment of the pressures upon the Conservatives' strategic calculations as a result of Britain's decline from its previous hegemonic position within the international and interstate environment.[10] Here, Thatcherism must be viewed as a conditioned response to UK decline, whilst, at the same time, the weakened structures of the UK economy can be seen as conditioning the Conservatives' ability to respond effectively. Moreover, consideration must also be given to the constraints imposed by previous failures to halt Britain's decline and to the factors which contributed to these failures (see chapter 2).

The Conservatives' selection of their strategic objectives

Any analysis which merely emphasizes the external and internal environmental context of Thatcherism would run the risk of reductionism. For, although strategies evolve partly in response to these contexts, they are the result of interventions by social and political actors. Thus, the Conservatives were never passive bearers of the structural context; rather, their strategic interventions also reflected their own sets of meanings and objectives. We need to recognize that the Conservatives were actively involved in both extrapolating meaning from the information they received from their environment and injecting their own intentionality about their strategic responses.

There are three key considerations here. First, although the environment may exert pressures for particular types of solutions to crises, the actors' bounded rationality will invariably prevent them from gaining full knowledge of what these might be. As a result, the actors' limited awareness will inevitably force them both to develop and to insert their own interpretations of the types of strategic intervention which are appropriate to the environmental crises with which they are faced. Second, and relatedly, actors carry their own sets of goals and strategic heuristics. Thus, governments are not merely bounded actors; they are also intentional, motivated agents who have their own objectives. As a result, responses to crises are mediated, filtered and, thus, selected through the ideational and subjective processes of purposeful human beings. Third, 'crises' themselves cannot be conceived narrowly as objective properties of the system; rather, they are essentially contested constructs which reflect the subjectivity and intentionality of the actors who narrate them (see chapter 6).

Certainly, we can detect inherent flaws within the Conservatives' strategic interventions. So, although the Thatcher governments appeared to acknowledge and, indeed, embrace the economic pressure for the liberalization and deregulation of market forces, much of their energies were spent in adapting their strategic interventions to suit narrower political and ideological objectives; in particular, the pursuit of an electoral strategy which could provide material gains to key categories of Conservative voters. Even a cursory examination of the Conservatives' privatization programme in the 1980s illustrates this process (Marsh 1991). This programme was, to an extent, a response to global pressures for privatization, but it was adapted to achieve short-term political and electoral gains, particularly providing material benefits for key sections of the electorate (see Marsh 1995).

A second, but no less important, factor which shaped the essentially flawed interventions which the Conservatives made was their dogmatic reliance upon a narrow, anti-statist, neo-liberal ideology. This influenced them to abandon the active use of state mechanisms in order to ensure the successful re-regulation of Britain's failing economy. Instead, much of their energies went into a succession of attempts to reduce the role of the state in economic regulation, whilst strengthening the state's power in areas such as law and order, thereby allowing them to deal with the increased problems and contradictions which emerged from their failure to implement strategic adaptations which could halt Britain's continuing failure to compete within the global economic environment.

Overall then, although the selective pressures imposed by environmental exigencies are crucial to explaining the development of Thatcherism, the trajectory of Conservative strategy was also shaped by the Conservatives' own narrower interests, objectives and ideas. Thus, we need to focus attention upon the Conservatives' particular ideological and discursive articulation of environmental crises and the ways in which they inserted their own political aims and objectives into their longer-term strategic responses. This allows us to view the Conservatives' strategy as a process, which was often *ad hoc*, and which was both shaped and constrained as much by the government's desire to achieve short-term political goals, as by any longer-term ideological aims.

Strategic learning and adaptation

The idea of strategic, or political, learning must be considered central to any evolutionary schema, since actors are involved in a continual process of reflexively monitoring both their actions and the effects of those actions and, indeed, of the evolving environment in which they are located. Thus, a developing strategy is affected by the agents' perception of the relative success of previous interventions. However, we also need to acknowledge the inherent inertia which exists within institutional structures and the rigidity of organizational routines and institutional practices. Thus, initial strategic interventions will invariably prove unsuccessful in meeting desired outcomes. This means that the evolution of state structures and practices is heavily dependent upon a government's persistence and its ability to respond and adapt to previous failures. For this reason, if we are to explain the evolution of the state under the Conservatives, then it is crucial to focus upon both the evolution of Conservative strategy and its adaptive potential. This entails a recognition that the evolution of organizational structures is, in many ways, dependent upon the ability of strategic actors to engage in adaptive learning over time, in order to steer strategic responses towards optimal solutions to environmental crises.

We also need to acknowledge that, over time, both agents and the environment which they seek to affect are open to transformation. Thus, agents are transformed through action, as they become more strategically aware of their relationship with their evolving environment.[11] In time, this constant process of adaptive learning within a structured environment will inevitably allow agents to become more informed of the type of strategic interventions which are appropriate to achieve the bounded, and narrowly conceived, strategic objectives which they seek; such learning will almost inevitably be cumulative.

Turning our attention once again to Thatcherism, it is clear that the Conservatives' strategic interventions gained some form of unity and, hence, a coherence, and indeed a radical momentum, through time. Of course, they were able to achieve this because of the length of time they were in office, a fact that is too often neglected. Throughout the 1980s, a stream of solutions to the crisis of the state were thrown into the political marketplace. These included monetarism, denationalization, contracting-out and management reform. Whilst these initial responses to environmental demands appear to have been relatively inconsistent and random, by the Conservatives' third and fourth terms such strategic adaptations were beginning to display a greater degree of consistency and sophistication. Whilst selective pressures were brought to bear through the evolving environment which they inhabited and, indeed, through the Conservatives' own extrapolation and interpolation of their strategic objectives, this evolutionary process also reflects the government's capacity, and indeed willingness, to adapt and respond to previous failures.

Thus, if we reflect upon the temporal dimension of the Conservatives' strategy, we can see that the contours of Thatcherism were progressively worked out over time. Although they were initially formulated around a discursive commitment to reduce the role of the state through monetarist strategies, these responses were consistently redefined. When analysing Thatcherism, therefore, it is important not to treat the Conservatives' strategy as though it was coherent and consistent over time. Rather, we need to recognize that from the mid-1970s the strategy went through various stages; it had a contingent, evolutionary trajectory. As such, we need to 'periodize' Thatcherism and, thus, to acknowledge that Conservative interventions under John Major differed markedly from those during Mrs Thatcher's first two terms in office.

The evolution of Thatcherite state strategy

Here, we develop a periodization of the evolution of the Conservatives' strategy which builds upon the previous theoretical work of Jessop et al. (1988) and Hay (1996c), as well as upon the previous discussion (see table 8.1). It is crucial to recognize that Thatcherism evolved out of the political and economic crises of the 1970s. On an international level, the ascendancy of New Right ideas across the globe has to be placed within the context of the weakening of US hegemony and the crisis of Fordist modes of economic regulation. This point remains relatively uncontested, if largely ignored, within the literature. However, more controversially, we would argue that any analysis of the domestic conditions which shaped the Conservatives' strategy must acknowledge the failure of the postwar Keynesian, social democratic, domestic consensus to translate itself into an institutionalized state settlement. In this respect, Thatcherism, as well as representing a response to wider evolutionary trajectories within the world system, must also be read in the context of the flawed evolutionary trajectory of the postwar British state. This previous, failed evolutionary process was crucial in laying the foundations for the later emergence of Thatcherism, because crucial elements of the Thatcherite strategy were already present within the institutional architecture of the postwar British state. The key point here is that we must acknowledge the crucial constraints placed upon the domestic Keynesian consensus by the existence of a more durable, longer-term, previously institutionalized consensus on the need to secure the interests of financial capital and the value of sterling and to sacrifice active, interventionist strategies in favour of short-term fiscal prudence (see chapter 2). Thus, as well as viewing Thatcherism as a paradigmatic break with the ideological rhetoric of the postwar period, it is equally important to emphasize the crucial continuity of post-1979 Conservatism with previous political and economic institutionalized routines.

In our view, the period between 1975 and 1976 was a crucial conjunctural moment for the emergence of Thatcherism as an active state project. It is important to highlight the decisive effect of the Labour government's failure to enact its domestic economic strategies and its consequent appeal to the IMF, as more evidence of the impossibility of maintaining both a domestic commitment to Keynesian demand management (which, as Kerr argued in chapter 3, was always limited if it existed) and support for the City of London's position as a leading player in the international financial markets. Thus, the attempts by Labour to conduct the first real experiment with a Keynesian budgetary deficit revealed many of the contradictions of the postwar settlement, and contributed, together with the events of the 'Winter of Discontent', to the delegitimization of social democratic and corporatist strategies. The crisis of the British state in the late 1970s allowed the New Right to reinterpret Britain's postwar decline as a crisis of social democracy and state intervention. Thus, Thatcherism emerged initially as a determined critique of the, largely mythical, practices of the postwar period; a critique which political scientists, as well as the public at large, have been all too willing to accept.

The Thatcherites' successful interpretation of the deleterious effects of socialism throughout the postwar period enabled the Conservatives to lay the foundations for a hegemonic, anti-statist discourse based around the false notion that social democracy had been successfully implemented and failed. However, it is important to emphasize that Thatcherism emerged out of the Conservatives' electoral victory in 1979 as an ill-defined, and in some senses poorly articulated, strategy. Thus, early Thatcherite policies reveal an overall lack of strategic coherence, even though they were held together by a fairly coherent ideological discourse. It is this ideological discourse, or strategic vision, together with a cleverly constructed electoral strategy, which enabled the Conservatives to gain the space to adapt to, and learn from, the environmental pressures which formed their strategic context. As a result, their policies became more consistent and developed through their successive terms in office. However, the narrow articulation of a non-regulatory, neo-liberal discourse, together with the emphasis upon short-term political aims, also proved damaging to the Conservatives' ability to formulate successful adaptations which could improve Britain's performance in the overall, changing, global environment. This created longer-term problems for the Conservatives which ultimately damaged their electoral fortunes under John Major. As Hay (1996c) and Jessop (1994b) argue, this revealed latent contradictions in the state settlement emerging out of the periods of radical and late Thatcherism.

Although throughout both the Thatcher and Major periods the Conservatives adapted their strategy to cope with the exigencies imposed by selective environmental pressures, they were learning the wrong lessons. Whilst crises and contradictions within their environment pointed towards the re-regulation of the UK economy in order to cope with its strategic readjustment to changing global political and economic relations, the Conservatives consistently failed to respond effectively. Therefore, Thatcherism, although a dynamic and evolving process, was essentially flawed. In large part, this resulted from the narrow conceptions the Conservatives had of the types of problem which they faced and, indeed, of the optimal solutions required to solve these problems. This, in turn, resulted from their dogmatic attachment to an anti-statist, neo-liberal, ideological paradigm which meant they ignored any lessons about how state mechanisms might be used to generate economic growth and successful accumulation. In an evolutionary schema, it could argue that this type of naked, aggressive neo-liberalism was neolithic.

Conclusion

Most existing interpretations of Thatcherism are flawed because: they cannot explain the changes which occurred between the mid-1970s and 1997; they reinterpret the past, particularly the so-called postwar consensus, in order to emphasize the distinctiveness of the post-1979 era; they offer a unidimensional rather than a multidimensional explanation; and they are ethnocentric, emphasizing British exceptionalism.

In contrast, we have offered an evolutionary perspective which is sensitive to the temporal dimension; which recognizes that both structures and agents, and, most importantly, the dialectical relationship between the two, affect outcomes; and which is multi-dimensional. Using that approach, we argue that Thatcherism was an evolving process which changed significantly over the eighteen years the Conservatives were in office, in the process becoming more coherent and more radical, ultimately culminating in the reforms which characterized the party's third and fourth terms.

Notes

[1] The literature on Thatcherism has been reviewed by a number of authors. See, for example, Jessop et al. 1988: 22–51; Douglas 1989; Marsh 1995; Evans and Taylor 1996: 219–46. For summaries of the legacy of the Thatcher governments, see Gamble 1990b; Crewe 1993. More extensive surveys are provided by Riddell 1991; Cloke 1992; Marsh and Rhodes 1992; Ludlam and Smith 1996.

[2] For a detailed discussion of this issue in relation to industrial relations policy, see Marsh 1992: chapter 2.

[3] For partial exceptions see Hall, S. 1979; Gamble 1988; Jessop et al. 1988; Taylor, P. J. 1992; Hay 1996c. As Marsh has highlighted, however, although these analyses do succeed in providing more holistic approaches to Thatcherism, each fails in different ways to provide an adequate multidimensional theoretical perspective which is elastic enough to pay sufficient weight to the range of political, economic and ideological inputs to the Conservatives' strategy. Thus, Gamble affords a primacy of explanation to the political dimensions to Thatcherism, Hall and Hay emphasize ideational factors, while Jessop et al. ultimately rely upon analyses which are, at times, strictly economistic.

[4] This is a common problem with analyses of British politics; see Rose 1991.

[5] For a review, see Hodgson 1993; Nelson 1995.

[6] See, for example, the various contributions to Singh 1990.

[7] For a review, see Sztompka 1993: 113–25.

[8] See, for example, Jessop 1990; Ward 1997, 1997b; Hay 1996c, 1997b.

9 For a review of the broad promise which historical institutionalism has to offer an evolutionary conception of political change, see Hay 1997b. Meanwhile, for a review of the relationship between historical institutionalism and neo-institutionalism more broadly, see Hall and Taylor 1996.

10 For an analysis of Britain's 'post-hegemonic trauma', see Taylor, P. J. 1989, 1992.

11 In this way, as Margaret Archer (1995) has pointed out, the morphogenesis of agency coincides with the process of environmental elaboration as the outcome of strategic interventions impacts upon both the agents themselves and the context which they inhabit.

9

The Post-Thatcher Era

In political science it is common to designate periods of government and political eras by reference to leading politicians of the time. So, for example, authors talk of 'the Thatcher era', 'the Heath government' or 'the Attlee administration'. In the same way, when speaking of British government since 1990 it is second nature to come up with designations such as 'the post-Thatcher era', 'the Major period' or, since 1 May 1997, 'the Blair government'. Generally speaking, such categories provide us with a useful shorthand way of denoting a period of political time. However, there is an unfortunate underside to this nominal habit, because it awards an implicit importance to the actor invoked; a prejudice which all too often skews our interpretation of the period. For example, to speak of 'the Major period' tempts us to differentiate it somehow from 'the Thatcher period' and even to suggest a significant break between the two eras. In contrast, I shall argue that the experience of the 1990s and its juxtaposition with events of the 1980s demonstrate the significant limitations, indeed possible dangers of categorizing governments or periods of political change according to the careers of key political actors. The biggest risk is that political ideas, policies and changes become excessively identified with actors, leading us to strongly intentionalist, voluntarist and contingent forms of political analysis (see the Introduction and chapter 1).

However, we must not seek to downplay the role of key actors and agents. Indeed, it is not only the actual importance of actors which we must stress but also the importance actors are believed to have, which, in turn, affects both perceptions of a period and political outcomes. This chapter seeks to show that it is through evaluating the role of agency in relation to the pre-existing and emergent structural and ideational contexts that we can properly evaluate the efficacy of agents and actors (see the Introduction and chapter 1). Necessarily, then, an evaluation of the Major government must be built on an understanding of the structural and ideational legacies of the Thatcher government. For this reason, whilst the main focus of this chapter is upon change under the Major government, it will also seek to place this in the context of the post-1979 period as a whole. In this context, I will also seek to explain why the Conservatives' electoral and ideological dominance during this era came to a dramatic end in the 1997 election.

I shall develop four main arguments:

1   That a categorical distinction between the Thatcher and Major governments has, despite limitations, a considerable utility. It is useful in two main ways. First, it can help us to periodize post-1979 Conservatism, with the Major period forming a stage we may see as 'late-Thatcherism', an advanced stage in the development of what is usually termed Thatcherism. Second, it can also helpfully denote a break with the Thatcher period as far as the discursive articulation and public reception of Thatcherism are concerned.
2   The above distinction also has interpretative limitations. In many senses, the strong continuities between the periods in terms of structural trends, government actors, policy and ideology make it more useful to think of post-1979 Conservatism more holistically.
3   The perceptions of the Major government as crisis-ridden, grey and incompetent can be explained in two main ways. First, the roots of this view lie in perceptions of the Thatcher government which are often nostalgic and fictitious. Second, changes in forms of opposition and resistances to Thatcherism, particularly from New Labour, have exposed the failures of Conservative government.
4   In the post-Thatcher era, the leadership of both main parties has invested great energies in party management and image-making. In part, this results from recent developments in each party. However, such developments are also, in part, the product of longer-term structural changes in the conduct of public politics which have important implications for the nature of British democracy.

Overall, this chapter has three main aims. First, it places the Major government in context. It outlines the type of strategic circumstances, both political and economic, which conditioned the actions of the Major government. In addition, it seeks to portray the ideational context within which the Major government worked. As such, it identifies the types of constraints and legacies with which the government was faced. Second, it seeks to evaluate the agency of the Major administration; an evaluation which presages an explanation of the fate of Thatcherism during this period and within the post-1979 period as a whole. This will

involve reviewing the discourse, style and policies of the Major government, as well as showing how they relate to the approach of the
Thatcher governments. Third, this chapter analyses the importance of
party management and image-making to the practice of contemporary
politics. In particular, this involves looking at the forms of leadership,
discipline and ideology adopted within the main parties, as well as
tracing the development of relations between the media, politicians and
political parties during this era. The chapter concludes with some initial
appraisals of the New Labour government and the likely fate of British
politics as we enter the twenty-first century.

Placing the Major government in context

Strategic context: hard times, great expectations?

The Major government had to confront a number of difficult circumstances, both political and economic. Unfortunately for John Major, by
the time he took over as leader of the Conservatives, Mrs Thatcher and
her governments' policies had succeeded in alienating much of the
party's popular support. As a result, Major found himself bequeathed
with a legacy of discontent. The Conservatives' election win in 1992 was
widely thought to be more a reflection of electoral mistrust of the
alternatives rather than a ringing endorsement of their political agenda
(Dorey 1995: 231). The majority of twenty-one gained at the 1992 election was in itself much smaller than any the Thatcher governments of
the 1980s had achieved. Subsequently, defeats at local and European
elections and by-elections became commonplace. However, even more
problematic were the persistent splits within the parliamentary party.
The central focus of intra-party division was the issue of European integration. As Buller explains in chapter 5, the Major government had to
face the reignition of the process of European integration which
emerged following German reunification. So, as Evans and Taylor
(1996) note, the Major years witnessed the division of Conservative
opinion into two main 'factions': mainstream (centrist) and lollards
(right-wing). Thus, in 1993 the votes on the Maastricht Treaty resulted
in what Ludlam calls 'the most serious defeat sustained in Parliament
by any Conservative government in the twentieth century' (1996: 101).

Similarly, Seldon (1994b) argues that two other kinds of emergent
division were also crucial. First, there was a reformer versus consolida-
tor division in which the reformers sought to continue the Thatcherite
policy momentum and agenda-setting, while the consolidators opposed

too much further change. Second, there was a division between traditionalists and modernizers. Traditionalists sought to maintain postwar
values, such as support for the welfare state, whereas modernizers
attempted to promote the neo-liberal agenda of reducing the role of the
state. Such divisions were also reflected at Cabinet level.

However, the Major government's political problems were not only
at a parliamentary and electoral level. The Conservative grassroots
became increasingly demoralized during the Major years and, to some
extent, alienated from the national party. Ordinary members showed
considerable sympathy with Thatcherite pressure groups such as the
'92' or 'No Turning Back' groups. The party's long-term membership
decline continued under Major, and financial contributions from local
associations fell.

One of the decisive factors in the Thatcher governments' electoral
successes was the fact that throughout the 1980s the Conservative Party
exuded an image of economic competence. This meant that the Major
government faced popular expectations regarding the economy which
were simply impossible to meet, given the emergent economic context
following Thatcher's departure. Dorey (1995: 242) argues that three
main factors severely constrained the Conservatives' economic strategy
under Major. First, the protracted period of economic recession largely
inherited from the Thatcher years created a sustained period of economic hardship. This produced unemployment and economic discontent among groups largely untouched by the harsh effects of
Thatcherism during the 1980s. Second, the Major government had to
cope with a burgeoning Public Sector Borrowing Requirement. By
1993, this had reached £50 billion, with little evidence of the possibility
of a recovery. Third, this led directly to an unpopular budget in which
the Chancellor, Kenneth Clarke, was forced to raise levels of indirect
taxation and announce cuts in public spending of £10 billion over three
years.

Perhaps the most devastating economic constraints acting upon the
Major government were the structural developments at an international
level. The most outstanding economic problem arose as a result of the
collapse of Britain's membership of the European Exchange Rate
Mechanism (ERM) in September 1992. Throughout its first eighteen
months of ERM membership, sterling had no difficulty staying within
the target bands. This owed much to the fact that during this period
German interest rates were the lowest in Europe, as the Bundesbank
attempted to ease the transition to unification by operating an unusually lax monetary policy. However, given the outbreak of inflationary
pressures in Germany in the summer of 1992, this monetary stance was
tightened significantly. As a result, the interest rate differential between

Britain and Germany suddenly became much less pronounced, thus removing the main reason why the pound had previously had no difficulties maintaining its parity. This immediately reduced the attractiveness of holding sterling. International currency speculators undertook a so-called 'flight to strength', moving to buy Deutschmarks *en masse*, whilst liquidating their assets denominated in sterling and some other European currencies. Consequently, sterling, along with the Italian lira, the Spanish peseta, the Portuguese escudo and the Irish punt, plummeted to their ERM floor at a speed which no central bank intervention could resist. On 'Black Wednesday', 16 September 1992, the government's efforts to save sterling's ERM membership failed in the face of rampant financial speculation over devaluation. This event in itself was enough to shatter the government's reputation for economic competence and allowed the Labour Party quickly to become the more trusted party on economic management (Crewe 1994). Furthermore, consequent devaluation injected fresh inflationary impulses into an economy still suffering the inflationary effects of the credit-expansion, 'Lawson' boom of the late 1980s. As a result, there was no respite from the austerity brought about by a high interest rate policy, even though such a policy was no longer necessary to keep the pound within its ERM bands.

Ideational context: ghosts around but few 'others'

Each political era is influenced both by 'ghosts' of the past and by 'spectres' of the present or future (Derrida 1994). The Major era was no exception. Indeed, we can identify three such spirits which were to haunt the Major government over several years.

Ghost 1 – Mrs Thatcher After Michael Heseltine's act of political regicide, it was inevitable that Thatcher's 'ghost' would, in some way, cast a shadow over the party; particularly given her expressed wish to be a 'back-seat driver' (Junor 1996: 265). Initially, Major's strongest political suit was that he was 'not Thatcher'. However, contrasts between his style and that of his predecessor were to haunt him through most of his premiership. The thrice victorious Thatcher was a heroine to the party at large and to most of the parliamentary party. Her perceived strength of ideological conviction and dominance of the government was contrasted with Major's supposed consensual, pragmatic approach. Major's 'niceness' came to be seen as weakness, and his preference for consultation to be seen as dithering. Many of the comparisons were based on Thatcher mythology (see chapter 8) and sheer nostalgia or, as Major himself put it, 'harking back to a golden age which never existed'. Thatcher's interventions from 'beyond the grave' were also unhelpful as she whipped up support for the Euro-rebels and threw scorn on Major's leadership style, even expressing admiration for Tony Blair and New Labour.

Ghost 2 – the spectre haunting Europe (Ludlam 1996)   It is easy to overlook the fact that, for all her posturing in her political afterlife, it was Mrs Thatcher who signed the Single European Act, an action which surrendered far more British sovereignty than Major's latest signature of the Maastricht Treaty. This perhaps illustrates the extent of the Conservatives' difficulties in dealing with the issues around European integration. It has often been commented that the Conservative Party's great historical asset has been a membership which is basically pragmatic in disposition and whose beliefs extend little beyond a traditional type of British patriotism. Yet, it is precisely such core notions of British patriotism and sovereignty which the issue of Europe throws into question. The option of simple national-istic opposition to any move towards European integration presaged by the adoption of a single currency is unavailable given the party's close historical ties with sections of capital, many of which are pro-moting an integrated European currency. Thus, the party finds its nationalist and capitalist interests in conflict. Evans and Taylor argue that reconciling such positions is impossible (1996: 269). Therefore, this issue throws into question the identity and purpose of the Conservative Party, threatening its very future. In recent years the Conservatives have been unable to exorcise the European spectre, despite many elaborate attempts to do so.

Ghost 3 – the Grim Reaper   Faced with a small parliamentary majority after the 1992 election, the government knew it would have the continual threat of backbench rebellion with which to contend. There was the additional likelihood of high-profile by-election losses and the possible consequent removal of the Conservative majority.

These three ghosts were each important to the Tory mind-set during the Major years. However, even more important than the political ghost of Thatcher was the fate of Thatcherism as a project. It is widely accepted that much of the success of the Thatcher governments came because they won the 'battle of ideas' (Hall 1979). Understanding how they achieved this is crucial to evaluating and explaining the Major government's fortunes at a discursive or ideational level. The Thatcher era achieved significant political change at a symbolic level; a level which we may in abstract terms distinguish from short-term, or even medium-term, material change. To name a period as radical is always a relative judgement, as such notions of radicalism will, to some extent, depend on the role of the 'other'.

For a politician who famously declared that 'There Is No Altern-ative', Mrs Thatcher spent a lot of time identifying alternatives. Frequently, she drew upon images and experiences of preceding gov-ernments, most particularly the Labour administration of 1974–9. The purpose of this was, as Hay argues (see chapter 4), to present a radically different conception of the political 'good' from that of previous gov-ernments by presenting the ideas and practices associated with them as obsolescent. In particular, the 'Winter of Discontent' was regularly por-trayed as the 'other' of Thatcherism. The media presentation of this period of industrial strife frequently distorted, or fictionalized, events. Thatcher and her government were adept, with the complicity of the media, at 'speaking' the past in such a manner as to legitimize Thatch-erism's use of state power. To a large extent, the Thatcherite version of the 'Winter of Discontent' was bound up with a critique of the history of postwar British politics. This invoked the idea that the postwar con-sensus, Keynesian demand management, social democracy and corporatism had all failed (see chapter 8).

The past was not the only 'other' recruited by Thatcherism; it was also able to sustain its radicalism throughout the 1980s through refer-ence to the malign presence of assorted 'others'. This involved con-structing various different political groupings either as a threat to the national interest, or as somehow acting against common sense. Thus, they would justify the centralization of power away from local authori-ties by invoking the dangers posed by 'loony left' Labour councils. Closure of much of the coal industry was justified partly through refer-ences to the threat of 'the enemy within', identified as the National Union of Mineworkers.

There is little doubt that the Conservatives' privatization initiatives became central to people's understanding of Thatcherism. To a large extent, privatization was promoted through delegitimizing its 'other': namely, state-ownership or nationalization. Indeed, the phrase 'privati-zation' was scarcely heard in popular discourse prior to the Thatcher era, since previously such reforms were called 'denationalization'. Labour was put firmly on the defensive on an issue very much seen as both anti-Labour and a complete break with the postwar period. Perhaps more than any other issue, the privatization question invoked in the public mind the discursive dichotomies of individualism (share-owning) / collectivism (state-owning) and market choice / state-control.

The presence of such 'others' were crucially absent from Major's ideational context. During his government, trade-union militancy was minimal and union leaders tended to be political moderates. Little political radicalism emerged from local government, even though the Conservatives themselves were virtually wiped out in this arena. Most importantly perhaps, New Labour sought, with great success, to avoid being constructed as Thatcherism's 'other'. Labour's long modernization process, as continued by John Smith and Tony Blair, can be understood as an attempt to evade the right's discursive tactics, which were employed to such effect in the 1980s. When Kinnock moved Labour to the political centre, the Conservatives were still able to argue that, at heart, Labour was a pro-nationalization, anti-business and high-taxation party. Smith and Blair pursued reforming measures of great symbolic importance for public consumption. The Blair strategy may be seen as attempting to avoid being drawn into the types of binary oppositions mentioned earlier, such as public/private and individual/collective. Thus, the aim was to evade or usurp attempts to narrate Labour as the Conservatives' 'other' on unfavourable political terrains. This can quite clearly be seen in the construction of many key watchwords of New Labour. Phrases such as the communitarian-inspired 'the rights we enjoy reflect the duties we owe' and 'individual achievement, backed up by a strong community' were designed to emphasize the importance of both individualism and community to Labour's basic philosophy (see Blair 1996: 13). Thus, Labour hoped to avoid being seen as still 'against' the principle of individual achievement and choice as it was in the 1980s. In this sense, then, the Major government faced a much less convenient ideational context than the Thatcher governments, since there were few 'others' against which it could symbolically articulate its beliefs.

The agency of the Major government

Having reviewed the type of contexts within which the Major government had to work, it is now necessary to look at how government actors coped within these broadly unfavourable conditions. This involves looking at the type of discourse, governing style and policy direction that were adopted. In doing so, it is instructive to compare the Major government's strategy with that of the preceding Thatcher governments in each of these respects. It is also important to reflect on what exactly happened to the phenomenon of Thatcherism during the Major era.

Discourse

In the wake of Thatcher's departure, John Major played adeptly to the anti-Thatcher mood of the early 1990s. He rhetorically qualified

Thatcherism, speaking of his desire for a 'classless society' and 'a nation at ease with itself' (Evans and Taylor 1996: 247). He hoped to present a more caring face of Conservatism, by sporadically injecting 'one nation' epithets into a generally Thatcherite discourse. Yet, Major and his government ministers' public pronouncements and initiatives were, for the most part, strongly Thatcherite in tone. However, they failed to project an image that resonated with the public in the way achieved by some of Thatcher's pronouncements. Numerous public 'relaunches' failed; most notably, perhaps, Major's 'Back to Basics' initiative, which stressed the need for traditional morality and standards in matters such as education, law and order and the family. For various reasons, the initiative failed to resonate. Its presentation left something to be desired, as, for a long time, it was unclear in which areas the government wished to see a return to 'basics' and what the practical implications of such a move might be. In addition, the call for traditional morality and standards drastically backfired when several ministers became entangled in 'sleaze' incidents involving extra-marital affairs and 'cash for questions'. Both the Labour Party and media critics of the government were able effectively to use the unifying signifier 'sleaze' to draw various government embarrassments together into one overall issue.

The public's waning enthusiasm for privatization during the Major years created a disincentive for the government rhetorically to promote initiatives such as rail privatization. In essence, Major was unable to engage in the type of symbolic politics which sustained the Thatcher governments' appearance of radicalism.

Style

John Major was widely interpreted as adopting a consensual style of government. Certainly, he conducted Cabinet meetings in such a vein, believing that his greatest political skill was to produce agreement amongst people with differing views (Junor 1996: 210). Such skills proved necessary as he filled his Cabinet with people from different wings of the party, hoping to keep those respective wings sufficiently happy in order to keep the party together. Major proved particularly adept at humouring the various factions of the party, often with great cynicism and duplicity. These skills, together with his pragmatic image (see Crewe 1994) enabled him to achieve the remarkable feat of leading the party for a full term after 1992 – a fourth straight election victory for the Conservatives – in spite of the divisions over Europe and his own unpopularity with both the public and the party. However, over the longer term, his understated style meant he was a figure who, according to Young, 'at best, people couldn't give a damn about' (1994: 21). Perceptions of Major's weakness as a leader were reinforced by incidents in which he seemed to prevaricate, or do a partial U-turn, in the face of public or party pressure, such as in the handling of pit closures or the imposition of VAT on fuel bills.

As Buller explains (see chapter 5), Thatcher's replacement by Major gave the Conservative Party a somewhat more Euro-enthusiastic leadership. In as much as the Major administration had a European strategy, this consisted of seeking to be more co-operative than the Thatcher government, whilst resisting further moves to greater centralization. As we have seen, however, the leadership faced an intractable problem; the party was split internally, yet there was a strong momentum within Europe for greater integration. In view of this, the leadership was forced to concentrate on the narrow political need to sustain some kind of veneer of unity regarding the party's position on Europe. I argue below that Major had considerable success in this regard. Yet, the issue of Economic and Monetary Union (EMU) proved so unmanageable that in the 1997 election the leadership gave up trying to impose any kind of unity, giving candidates carte blanche to issue their own statements to the electorate.

Despite Major's preference for the rhetoric of consultation above confrontation, his government's record can sustain a different reading. For example, research by Baggot (1995: 501) into policy initiatives under Major portrays a picture of a government which was anything but keen to consult widely, or at length, with interest groups. In fact, Baggot argues that the Thatcher style of eschewing proper consultation over policy change continued under Major. In introducing changes to local government, police conditions and law and order, Major allowed a similarly limited time for consultation with interest groups to that generally allotted by the Thatcher governments. Indeed, as the next section explains, the policy style of the Major government may generally be characterized as aggressive, rather than consultative or conciliatory.

Policy

A review of policy change under the Major government does much to challenge the popular myth of an uncommitted, non-ideological leader leading a directionless, crisis-ridden party. Moreover, it dispels any notion that the project of Thatcherism somehow became exhausted following the departure of Mrs Thatcher. For example, Barker argues that over a broad sweep of policy fields the Major government pursued 'trouble seeking, ideologically aggressive policies' (1995: 128). Similarly, Ludlam and Smith argue that: 'It has been in precisely those areas where Thatcherism was incomplete that Major has remained most faithful to the Thatcher project' (1996: 278).

If Thatcherism's flagship policy of the 1980s was its sell-off of public utilities, then the ship was to continue sailing into the 1990s, however choppy the political waters. The privatization of rail and the sell-off of coal and parts of the prison service were deeply unpopular moves which many argue that Thatcher would have shirked had she still been leader. The government backed down over plans to sell the Royal Mail only when it was clear that a backbench rebellion would sink the proposal. What is perhaps most important to consider is the manner in which the Major government handled policy implementation burdens inherited from Thatcher, most significantly in the areas of social policy and civil service reform. In areas such as health, social security, education and the civil service, the Major government was bequeathed a massive programme of radical policy implementation which, rather than shirk, it pursued vigorously. (A rare exception was, of course, the poll tax, which was quickly abandoned by Major in the face of trenchant public opposition.) Far from merely consolidating such change, the Major government reinforced and extended the processes of reform with new legislative moves, most particularly perhaps in the civil service and social security fields (Kerr et al. 1997). Of course, the Major government also faced serious implementation problems and sometimes had to backtrack over issues in order to secure its key objectives (for example, see the review of education policy in Kerr et al. 1997: 12). Such implementation problems may also be taken as evidence of continuity with the experience of the Thatcher governments. Marsh and Rhodes (1992) argue that large implementation gaps between policy aims and policy outcomes characterized the Thatcher experience. Such gaps emerged under the Major government for similar reasons; sometimes there is a lack of consultation with interest groups and sometimes a lack of clarity surrounding policy goals. However, as we have seen, the policy initiatives pursued under Major tended to be more radical in scope than those under Thatcher, certainly than those of the first two Thatcher terms. As such, the policy experience was in many senses qualitatively different.

The pursuit of late-Thatcherism

Some of the more persuasive accounts of the Thatcher period have emphasized that Thatcherism as a phenomenon must be periodized into different stages of development (Gamble 1988; Jessop et al. 1988; Hay 1996c: ch. 7; and see chapter 8). Gamble notes that Thatcherism had the continuing capacity to renew its radical purpose, with the post-1987 period forming the most radical phase, as it sought to dismantle social democratic relations between state and civil society. The notion of the post-1987 phase as 'radical' Thatcherism gives us a useful starting point for evaluating the Major period in theoretical terms.

As chapter 8 shows, the literature on Thatcherism can be classified according to the emphases authors variously put on economic, political and ideological explanatory factors. It is clear from a review both of policy developments under Major and of their economic, ideological and political motivations that it makes no sense to speak of Thatcherism as somehow ending in 1990. Indeed, it can be argued that it is precisely in the post-Thatcher era that Thatcherism achieved its most significant success in penetrating large sections of the public sector with market-oriented reforms. In some respects, one can view the post-1992 period as one in which the ambitions of 'radical' Thatcherism (1987–92) were more fully to be realized, as a result of further legislation and effective implementation.

Kerr et al. (1997: 26) argue that we should designate this period as 'late Thatcherism'. This characterization has two aspects. First, it denotes Thatcherism's evolution into a more coherent, mature and sophisticated set of strategies for state reform. However, second, it refers to the way in which the Conservatives have struggled at a discursive level to win popular support for their programmes and ideas. It is at this discursive level of analysis that it is most useful to think of the Major period as involving a break in the progress of Thatcherism. But rather than explaining this break through reference to a change of Prime Minister and a resultant change in the style of government, it is much more convincing to emphasize the highly unfavourable strategic and ideational contexts within which the Major government had to operate. In such an unfavourable economic and political context, it was difficult for the Major government to project its ideas in a way which could resonate with the public. Overall, however, the continuities in policy, ideology and political outlook between the Thatcher and Major governments encourage us to think of the post-1979 period in a holistic way.

Partycraft – the discipline of the new democracy?

Having looked at the fate of Thatcherism during the 1990s, it is necessary to examine what changes may have occurred in the make-up of

British politics more generally during this period. Of crucial importance are changes in the conduct of the political parties and their respective leaderships.

As we saw in chapter 9, one of the most influential explanations of Thatcherite change centres round Jim Bulpitt's notion of statecraft (1986). In Bulpitt's view, a party will seek to gain an image of governing competence and to win and retain power. This is, in part, achieved through successful party management. Certainly, the 1990s has seen both main parties place an absolute premium on issues of party management and image-making. One could argue that 'partycraft' has, in many ways, become the dominant concern of party leaders. A review of the recent fortunes of Conservative and Labour leaders demonstrates that some causes of this are contingent and specific to the individual parties. However, there are other factors which suggest that partycraft concerns may remain of central importance in the longer term. Of particular importance are both the development of post-ideological politics and the transformations in the relationship between political parties and the media.

Major's partycraft

As we have seen, John Major encountered a host of difficulties during his leadership of the Conservative Party. However, he demonstrated considerable partycraft abilities in working within almost intolerable conditions for a leader throughout most of his premiership.

Despite the volatile divisions over Europe, Major generally managed to maintain a successful balancing act between the pro-European and anti-European wings of the party. In negotiations over the Maastricht Treaty, the government secured an outcome which, at least in the short term, placated each wing of the party. Major secured a UK opt-out from the social protocol of the Treaty, a coup which enabled him to reinforce a right-wing neo-liberal stance for the Conservatives within the domestic political battlefield. Crucially, Major also gained the right for the UK to opt out of later moves towards creating a single European currency, conveniently delaying a decision on the issue which, more than any other, split the party. From this point on, Major engaged in a highly cynical, yet effective and necessary, strategy of holding his party together by sending out sympathetic signals to each camp in turn. Major in fact would privately assure supporters on each side that he was at heart 'One of Them' (as suggested by both Edwina Currie and Teddy Taylor in *Bye Bye Blues*, Channel 4, 18 October 97). He would publicly appease the Europhobes through expressing hostility to the notion of a federal Europe. Yet, he would frequently strike a more pro-European note, stressing Britain's continued involvement at the heart of Europe. The numerical strength of the Euro-sceptics in Parliament put particular pressure on Major to play up his Euro-sceptic credentials. He did this to great effect with his one-man rejection of the Belgian pro-federalist, Jean Luc Dehane, as the new European Community President. However, Major had to keep pro-European cabinet colleagues such as Chancellor Kenneth Clarke on board. He continued to walk this tightrope up to and during the 1997 election.

As we have seen, various factors conspired to undermine Major's leadership credibility. Yet, despite massive external and internal unpopularity, he was continually tactically adept at persuading sufficient sections of the party that he was their best option as leader. He appealed to the party's one-nation left wing as the best available candidate to tame the Thatcherite right wing, whilst maintaining enough Euro-sceptic credibility to maintain right-wing support against alternative leaders such as Clarke or Heseltine. Major's success in provoking a leadership election in 1995 was considered a political masterstroke. He was able to defeat John Redwood's challenge after forcing the hand of his enemies at a time which suited him rather than his opponent (Garnett 1996: 155).

Labour's partycraft

Defeat in the 1992 election persuaded Labour leaders that the party had to do more to convince voters that it was worthy of trust and was capable of governing competently. In their view, this required an acceleration of the modernization process begun by Neil Kinnock in order to demonstrate that changes in Labour party policy and attitude were sincere. John Smith won the argument for 'One Member One Vote', indicating that Labour was distancing itself from trade-union influence. Tony Blair's leadership of Labour can be read as an extraordinary exercise in partycraft. The title 'New Labour' was coined almost as soon as he gained the leadership, enabling modernizers discursively to construct that which they wished to change as 'Old' Labour. Blair dramatically provoked the Clause IV debate in order to purge from both the party and the public any notion that it might still, in some latent way, oppose the market and wish to extend public ownership of the economy. In doing so, he argued that it was insufficient for party members merely to support him pragmatically, arguing that he wanted people 'with me, heart and mind'. The notion of a genuinely transformed 'new' party was reinforced by a mass membership campaign which proved hugely successful. Broadly speaking, Blair gained great popularity with members and support for his strategy (Young et al. 1997: 507). The unity and discipline shown by the Labour Party enabled it to fight an election campaign over several years. These internal party changes played a central role in creating the image of competence and unity which led to Labour's landslide win in May 1997.

A new discipline?

It is possible to review the Conservative Party's recent attempts to cope with its internal split over Europe as a necessary response to the medium-term problem of formulating a clear stance on the issue of European integration. Changes in the Labour Party can be explained through reference to the party's need for discipline to bring a long period of opposition to an end. However, we should not seek to overlook trends which may be working at a more general level to make partycraft considerations a dominant issue of the age. Two developments may be of significance in this regard; namely, changes both in the ideological content of British politics and the nature of relations between politicians and the media.

The development of post-ideological politics   Many have argued that in the wake of the collapse of Communism we now live in a post-ideological age. In Britain, this means that the main political parties are all liberal democratic and agree on the fundamentals of how government should operate. Although such perspectives exaggerate the degree of political consensus in Britain and elsewhere, the view has some validity. There is, perhaps, particular resonance in the notion that old categorizations such as left and right, labour and capital no longer have the same import or meaning as in previous eras (Giddens 1994: 251). As such, political parties increasingly confront issues over which they have no 'natural' role to adopt. Thus, both Labour and the Conservatives face the threat of divisions, and even irreversible splits, over Europe – an issue which challenges and displaces traditional UK-centred political and ideological orthodoxies within each party. Without any natural position to adopt, the pressure is on party leaderships to impose a line and quell dissent. Alternatively, there may be many issues upon which the main parties are essentially agreed. This leaves political actors with little option but to compete on the basis of image and notions of governing competence, rather than in terms of substantive ideological differences. This creates another pressure for the appearance of unity, making the centralization of party structures ever more attractive to party leaders.

The media–party politics relationship Indeed, these trends toward centralization and discipline within political parties create a reinforcing ratchet effect. As the parties become more disciplined, the media search for interesting stories becomes ever more intensified. If the media cannot find big debates, the search will be on to find division or controversy over less substantial issues. When the party sees where the media spotlight is placed, then it is exactly there that the party will face pressure to show that it is not divided, or at least to show that the leadership's will comfortably prevails. Party conferences are a particular case in point where, as Semetko et al. (1991) argue, the media play an active value-laden role in constructing coverage of these 'pseudo-events' (McNair 1995). Paradoxically, as parties come to place an ever greater premium on creating an image of competence, the means of achieving it are becoming all the more problematic. It can be argued that transformations in the media, in both their penetration and their presentation of public life, make it increasingly difficult for politicians to appear effective. Derrida (1994: 81) argues that, at present, no matter how competent political leaders are, they tend to be seen as structurally incompetent. John Major may have some sympathy with such a view, since it was historically unprecedented journalistic endeavour which helped bring 'sleaze' incidents to public attention. However laudable Major's decision to hold inquiries such as the Committee on Standards in Public Life, chaired by Lord Nolan, in media terms they were ineffective responses. The need for parties to be able to respond almost instantaneously to stories portraying the party negatively places even more responsibility and hence power, in the hands of party apparatchiks and 'spin-doctors' to present, and perhaps even establish, the party line quickly and effectively.

New Labour's success since its election in 1997 may be interpreted as owing much to the partycraft skills it has developed. Many are alarmed by the sheer extent to which the party has centralized decision-making and placed power in the hands of a few who may be neither internally nor externally elected. Yet, whatever the democratic fears, the trend seems to be towards more of the same, as William Hague puts internal party reform and the improved use of media at the heart of his project to revive the Conservative Party.

The post-That-jor era: first appraisals

Labour into power – blueprint, redprint or no print?

Some commentators thought the term 'landslide' to be too weak a description of Labour's historic election win in May 1997. Anthony King argued that the result was the political equivalent of 'an asteroid hitting the planet, practically destroying all life' (BBC Election 97, 1 May 97). Such a sea change in voting behaviour inevitably provoked comparisons with Labour's win in 1945 and the Conservatives' win in 1979. The early experience of the new government can be read in different ways. Here, I shall briefly review three types of interpretation. In turn, these approaches can be seen to have economic, democratic and cultural foci.

New era or new consensus? Following Labour's win, speculation began as to whether the new government would bring a period of radical and exceptional political change, as many argue was the case with the Attlee and Thatcher governments. Such views are, of course, often challenged within this volume. Johnston argues in chapter 7 that, despite its 'radical socialist' agenda, the post-war Labour government never realized its vision of a social democratic state and, indeed, in practice tended to work within the parameters of a historically conservative polity. Similarly, Kerr and Marsh argue in chapter 8 that the radicalism of the Thatcher administrations only evolved over time. Thus, if we are to absorb the lessons of this volume, it is clear that Labour's historic win in May 1997 should not lead us *a priori* either to infer or expect an ensuing period of radical political change.

Many academic commentators have no such expectations of political change. Indeed, a fashionable view within academia has been to reject any such predictions out of hand. It has been argued that New Labour, far from offering the prospect of significant political change, is part of a new consensus in British politics, in which there is fundamental agreement between the main parties on most key political issues (Dorey 1995: Garnett 1996; Hay 1996g; Hay and Watson 1998). Labour's modernization process is read by some as essentially involving the party's accommodation of the key principles of Thatcherism. These accounts emphasize changes in Labour's economic policy: its embrace of the market economy, privatization, fiscal prudence and the shedding of the party's 'tax and spend' image. Perhaps the strongest argument put forward by those promoting the new consensus thesis concerns macroeconomic policy. It is argued that Labour, at least thus far, is committed to working within a broadly monetarist, neo-liberal, economic framework. One can interpret Chancellor Gordon Brown's decision to cede operational responsibility for the control of interest rates to the Bank of England as reflecting this consensus, in the sense that it depoliticizes the setting of interest rates (Hay and Watson 1998). The new consensus is also taken to extend to other policy areas, such as industrial relations, law and order and welfare 'retrenchment'. For example, Labour's new 'welfare to work' programme may be taken as emulating the neo-liberal 'workfare' system found in the United States, which aims to reduce the burden of welfare costs for the state and the taxpayer (Dolowitz 1998).

Alternative interpretations are viable. Kerr's discussion of the postwar consensus in chapter 3 indicates that we should be wary of attempts to resurrect the notion of consensus as a descriptive or explanatory concept. The arguments to date for a new consensus can be seen, like their historic predecessors, to be superficial readings which violate a more complex reality. In my view, there are two key criticisms of this position. First, such a view is too economistic in focus. Second, the analysis misunderstands recent Labour Party strategies and tactics.

Towards a renewed democracy and state?   Some supporters of the new consensus thesis cite Labour's lack of bold and specific policy commitments in its election manifesto and, more broadly, its 'safety-first' approach as evidence of a party with anything but radical ambitions. Yet, as the previous chapter points out, the Conservatives were elected in 1979 without a blueprint for power. The fact that the Conservatives' vision was to a large extent vague and non-specific did not prevent them from later pursuing radical changes. Thus, it may be a mistake to interpret Labour's cautious political campaigning tactics as indicative of an intention to be cautious in power. Indeed, arguably, whilst Labour's 1997 manifesto was by no means a 'redprint' for power, it was also not the anodyne document commonly portrayed. There were radical commitments to constitutional changes and, certainly, the early experience of the Blair government indicates a clear commitment to pursuing a 'rolling' agenda of democratic reform. The new government quickly called, and subsequently won, devolution referenda in Scotland and Wales, with plans to set up a London assembly in the pipeline. In addition, the new government soon launched a White Paper regarding freedom of information which aims significantly to extend the type of government information available to the public. The notion of a new style of politics was further developed as Labour invited prominent Liberal Democrats on to a Cabinet subcommittee on the constitution.

As such, these changes can be read as marking a significant break with aspects of the centralizing tradition of British politics. Arguably, the Labour government has a quite different vision of the role of the state from that of its neo-liberal predecessor. In contrast to the above interpretation, the 'welfare to work' programme may be taken as an example of an enabling state redistributing resources to create opportunities, in this case through taxing profits of the privatized utilities in order to ensure that young people enter employment or training.

New Britain: a cultural 'revolution'? Some commentators saw the New Labour government as both cause and effect of a political / cultural change in Britain towards a more inclusive and compassionate society (Hall, S. 1997). Labour's win brought more than a hundred new female MPs into Parliament and openly gay Labour candidates were successful. The public reaction to the death of Diana, Princess of Wales, and Tony Blair's personal response, were seen as symbolic of a shift away from both Thatcherite individualism and subservient monarchism. Strong recognition of Labour's capture of the public mood came at the Conservative Party Conference, at which the new leader William Hague called for the party to become inclusive of people regardless of race, culture or sexual orientation. However, it may be, as Howe suggests, that cultural shifts in broader society present Blair with more expectations and demands from the public than he bargained for (Howe 1997: 13). As such, contemporary culture may also present a problem for New Labour, which may lack the political ideas and / or the institutional apparatus required to meet public aspirations for change.

Given that, at the time of writing, the new administration is barely a year old, each of the above interpretations must be counted as tentative. The experience of the Thatcher governments should act to caution us against making strong interpretative claims about the new government while it is still in its political infancy. Ultimately, then, the effect of New Labour, as with Thatcherism, will only be known over the longer term.

Conclusion

The Major government should primarily be thought of in terms of its place within the post-1979 era as a whole. In terms of policy, ideas and political purpose, the Major period demonstrated overwhelming continuity with the Thatcher era. Thatcherism continued under Major, but entered a distinctive period in its development, gaining new coherence at a policy level and effecting radical institutional reform. The ideas informing government action remained largely those which had informed Thatcherism from its earliest days in the mid- to late 1970s. Yet, the popular base of support for such ideas, so important during the 1980s, crumbled under Major. His government had to confront severe constraints emerging both from the international economy and the longer-term effects of the Thatcher governments' policies. In a sense, the Major government had to deal with a number of Thatcherite chickens coming home to roost. The prolonged economic recession of the early 1990s took the shine off Thatcherism's claim to economic competence and the ERM exit damaged this reputation irreparably. Lacking the presence of ideational 'others', the Major government was unable discursively to articulate its programme in a manner which resonated with the public. Thus, the image of an incompetent, indecisive and crisis-prone government gained salience. Yet, beneath the surface, the Major government pursued a strongly ideological policy agenda in a resolute manner. However, its colossal defeat in the 1997 election highlights the importance of perceptions of a political period. In particular, it reinforces the point that the construction of image is central to political success or failure. This is perhaps the key lesson Labour learned from its electoral and intellectual defeats over the four previous elections. New Labour's capture of the discursive and electoral ground from the Conservatives gives it the opportunity to effect political change. Yet, Thatcherism's profound transformation of British politics – institutionally, ideologically and politically – ensures that its legacy will condition governments of whatever political hue for many years to come. Adequate reflection upon how the New Labour government is wrestling with this legacy will only become possible over time.

Conclusion

Analysing and Explaining Postwar British Political Development

When we began this book, we had a clear aim: to provide a theoretically informed account of postwar British political development. This is no easy task. The problem results in part from the difficulty of analysing a period of more than fifty years. However, it is compounded by the fact that few analysts of the postwar era are explicit about their theoretical, analytical and interpretative positions. In our view, this is a, indeed perhaps *the*, major weakness of the existing literature. As such, one of our major tasks has been to assess and evaluate critically the range of existing approaches in order to identify the positions that analysts take up on a set of broader questions crucial to any consideration of political change or development over this time-frame.

This may seem an abstract point, but it is a very important one and one which is all too often understated. It is simply illustrated. It should came as no surprise that analysts are divided over particular issues. Within the voluminous literature on the postwar period these might include: the degree of autonomy that the Attlee government enjoyed; the extent of the break with the past that Thatcherism marked; the scale, scope and likely duration of the Thatcherite legacy; or the nature of the relationship of Major and Blair to this Thatcherite inheritance. Of course, these are important themes which have been dealt with in the text, but the point being made here is more fundamental. Our answers to these specific questions reflect positions on a series of broader theoretical, conceptual and epistemological issues which most authors fail to address but which nonetheless underpin and shape their analysis. Amongst these, we might usefully identify the following:

- How should we conceptualize change? More specifically, is it evolutionary or punctuated by crisis?
- How important are political, economic and ideological factors in any explanation of change and what is the relationship between these factors?
- How important are structural factors and agency factors in explaining change and how should we conceptualize their relationship?
- How important are material and ideational factors in explaining change and what is the relationship between the two?
- What is the relative importance of the international and domestic contexts within which political development takes place and how should we conceptualize the relationship between these factors?

Of course, these are the issues we raised in the introduction and these concerns will structure much of this conclusion. However, the crucial point here is that the authors' positions on these broader questions and issues, which are most often implicit, inform and perhaps even constrain their answers to the more familiar and more substantive questions which have divided and continue to divide historians, political scientists and commentators on British political development.

In contrast, our aims have been to make explicit our position(s) on these issues, to urge others to do likewise and to entreat readers to read the existing literature with such questions in mind, seeking to tease out different authors' positions with respect to these issues. Indeed, our book should mainly be judged in terms of the extent to which it has fulfilled this third aim.

One other point needs to be made before we readdress these questions directly. Given the scope and significance of these issues in both theoretical and substantive terms, it is not surprising that, in our attempts to develop our theoretical positions, we have more clearly identified some of the existing differences between us, whilst uncovering others. That such differences remain is testimony, at least in part, to the nature of the questions we have posed. After all, what could be more significant to a social scientist than the question of whether social and political change is evolutionary or punctuated? Similarly, what could be more fundamental to a political scientist analysing contemporary Britain than the question of the extent of the Thatcherite legacy? Moreover, these two issues are essentially related. In our view, the fact that we present an account, or a series of accounts, which is unified more by the questions it poses than by the answers it offers is not only defensible, but in some sense essential. We have not attempted to present a definitive, nor for that matter necessarily consistent, overview of the period. Rather, our aim has been to reveal the nature and significance of the issues which underlie *any* attempt to assess the extent, timing and duration of social and political development in postwar Britain. In that sense, our divisions, which we will acknowledge in this conclusion, highlight some of the key issues involved in developing such an account. These are issues which would need to be resolved were one to pursue a definitive and fully integrated account. More fundamentally, of course, we would find such a pursuit problematic given our epistemological position; in our view, there will always be a struggle to establish a dominant discourse about, or interpretation of, the postwar period.

This suggests at least one context with respect to which our contribution might be assessed. In what follows, we will focus upon these fundamental issues. Our aim is to highlight and recapitulate both the large areas of agreement among us and the few bases of continuing disagreement and controversy. This will also allow us to identify yet more forcefully the weaknesses of existing approaches and analyses and, perhaps more importantly, avenues for future consideration (both theoretical and empirical).

Analysing and explaining change

The key conceptual issues dealt with in this book concern the analysis and explanation of change. Of course, much work on the postwar period focuses on the consequences of change rather than on its causes (far less the processes which underpin it). In this way, much of the material on the initial postwar period is concerned with the origins, content and effects of the so-called postwar consensus. Similarly, a veritable industry has developed in recent years examining the effects of Thatcherism, spawning a vigorous debate between 'radicals' (for instance, Kavanagh 1990; Moon 1994) and 'sceptics' (for instance, Marsh and Rhodes 1992) about the extent to which the Conservatives transformed policy outcomes, particularly between 1979 and 1987. In our view, this concentration on the outcome of, rather than the broader process of, change is partial in both these senses of the term. Authors who focus solely on outcomes only deal with part of the process. More importantly, their interpretation of those outcomes and the extent of change are shaped by their usually unstated positions on the nature of change itself. This, perhaps above all else, is an issue we have sought to render problematic in the present volume.

This latter point is important enough to be developed at some length. There is a strong tendency in the literature to adopt a simplistic conception of change in which the postwar period is simply bisected. In this view, the late 1940s, the 1950s and the 1960s are seen as decades in which a postwar consensus first developed around the ideas of

Keynesianism and social democracy became entrenched and institutionalized. This consensus, it is argued, became increasingly questioned
from the mid-1970s and was finally undermined by Thatcherism. This
singular project, in the view of many, transformed the institutions,
processes and hence the outcomes of British politics and, some authors
claim, produced a new consensus, based on a bipartisan commitment to
market solutions. As we saw in chapter 8, to a large extent this analysis
involves a reinterpretation of the past from the perspective of the
present, or, as Pimlott (1988) puts it in rather more provocative terms, a
'reading of history backwards'. So, as Kerr and Marsh argue, the
literature emphasizing the existence of the postwar consensus
developed almost parasitically on the literature on Thatcherite transformation; the transformative nature of Thatcherism was defined in terms
of the undermining and replacement of the postwar consensus.
Although this is not in itself a problem, it is rarely, if ever, explicitly
acknowledged.

Our view is that such an approach is inadequate because it assumes
that political change is a stepwise and inevitable process; that stasis is
undermined by crisis, which leads to a new stasis, which is undermined
by crisis, and so on. As Hay shows in Chapter 1, this is a very simplistic
conception of change. Of course, there might be something to be said
for such a simplistic conception if it provided a parsimonious, but
broadly accurate, account of 'reality'. Unfortunately, this is not the case
for three major reasons. First, there has been significant continuity in
some areas throughout the postwar period. Second, the extent and
depth of the postwar consensus has tended to be somewhat exaggerated; the period was characterized by disagreement as well as agreement. Accordingly, the abruptness and extent of the break with the past
that Thatcherism marked has often been overstressed (at least in conventional accounts). Third and consequently, any analysis of the
postwar period needs to recognize that the process of change was
complex and, as such, evolutionary rather than stepwise. Each of these
points deserves brief consideration.

The entire postwar period has been marked by some continuities as
well as much change. Two continuities are particularly striking. First, as
Buller demonstrates in chapter 5, Britain continued to claim and indeed
attempt to play a world role long after its status as a first-class power
had declined. This attempt was partly responsible for the fact that its
foreign policy was based on historical links to the Commonwealth and
the 'special' relationship with the USA, rather than on developing a
qualitatively new (and perhaps rather more appropriate) international
role from within Europe. At the same time, the cost of such pretensions
clearly contributed to Britain's economic decline. Second and much

more significant, the defence of the exchange rate and the interests of the City dominated economic policy-making throughout the period under review. As shown in Chapter 2, this was perhaps the major reason for sustained and accelerating economic decline. At the same time, this policy persisted throughout the period of putative postwar consensus, remained unquestioned in the Thatcher years and appears once again as a seemingly unassailable assumption of New Labour economic strategy.

As argued in Chapter 3, the period between 1945 and the mid-1970s was marked by conflict as well as consensus, and the key pillars of the so-called postwar consensus – Keynesianism and social democracy – were not only challenged but in certain respects also defeated. Thus, Kerr argues, it was only in the area of social policy that there was general agreement on a broadly (if grudgingly) social democratic 'settlement'. In the field of economic policy, the interests of the City continued to shape policy to the detriment of the manufacturing sector and the general population alike. At the same time, key elements of the political elite opposed the frequently mouthed doctrine of voluntarism, with the judges in particular consistently attempting to restrict trade-union immunities (Marsh 1992, ch. 1).

As a result, we must be sceptical about the extent and depth of the postwar consensus and, consequently, about the degree to which Thatcherism marked a break with that consensus. Not only did Thatcherism itself evolve significantly over time; it also built upon developments predating 1979 (see also Jessop et al. 1988: 11–20, 59–65). For example, the Thatcher government's trade-union reforms owed at least something to the continuing opposition by the judges to voluntarism and perhaps more to the Health government's attempted reform of industrial relations in the 1971 Industrial Relations Act. Similarly, its commitment to monetarism and the market owed a great deal to the gathering influence of such ideas in the Treasury and the Bank of England from the mid-1960s. By 1975, significant players within the Treasury (if not the Cabinet) were converts to monetarism; a commitment which was strengthened, not initiated, by the conditions of the International Monetary Fund loan in 1976.

As we have argued, many existing accounts exhibit a certain tendency to rationalize change after the event (by, for example, reinterpreting the past to show the present in a particular light) and/or to establish change by counterposing static snapshots (such as postwar consensus versus Thatcherism). Such approaches, we contend, are dubious, since they assume, almost as an article of faith, that development is stepwise. Accordingly, they resolve the crucial question of whether change is evolutionary or more punctuated by definitial (almost ontological) fiat. This is obviously unsatisfactory. In contrast, our aim has been to consider, to concentrate upon, and to interrogate the processes of change themselves.

Over the postwar period, we suggest, change is usefully conceptualized in evolutionary terms. This perspective is most directly outlined in Chapter 8 by Kerr and Marsh. They suggest that an evolutionary approach to change in the postwar period generally – and the Thatcher years specifically – has four key features: it is sensitive to temporality, emphasizing a dynamic conception of change over time; it focuses on explaining, rather than describing, change; it emphasizes that change occurs through a combination of selective and adaptive processes; and it argues that change is both path-dependent and contingent.

We all share this broad perspective. However, we remain divided over the extent to which this evolutionary process can be regarded as directional, cumulative and progressive, or punctuated and periodically interrupted. Again, we all acknowledge that the pace of evolution is not even; some moments are more significant than others. We nonetheless differ over the extent to which crisis plays a crucial mediating role in this process. In Hay's view, developed at length in chapter 4, moments of crisis are crucial because they may result in a fundamental change in the very goals and aspirations informing policy and institutional development – in the form of a paradigm shift (see also Hall, P. A. 1993). This shift interrupts the incremental process of evolution and may precipitate a change in the evolutionary trajectory as policy and institutions are refashioned (however incrementally) in line with the new paradigm. To Hay, then, any dualism between evolution and transformation is highly suspect since, as in contemporary biological theory, evolution is a punctuated process (Eldredge 1989; Gould 1989). More substantively, such a view would suggest that certain watersheds or punctuating moments (in particular, the period 1942–8 and the period of the late 1970s) can be identified and used to develop a simple periodization of postwar British political development (for a full elaboration, see Hay 1996c: chs 2 and 6). Two further points need immediately to be noted, however. First, to posit punctuating moments of crisis in the course of complex institutional change is not necessarily to downplay the significance of incremental change in the phases between moments of crisis. It is merely to suggest that such evolution takes place within, and is to some extent circumscribed by, an institutional and ideational (or 'paradigmatic') environment which may prove to be more decisively reshaped in moments of crisis. Second, as previous chapters will have made clear, such a conception of 'punctuated evolution' is not a view (nor does it give rise to a periodization of British political development) shared by all the authors in this collection. As we have seen, Kerr and

Marsh in particular emphasize a more incremental, cumulative and (classically) evolutionary conception of change. This places considerably less focus on moments of punctuation. It would, in turn, seek to problematize any simple periodization of social and political development couched in terms of watersheds.

For example, in Hay's view Thatcherism cannot be understood outside of its historical context; the evolutionary trajectory of the postwar British state. However, it was the crisis of the 'Winter of Discontent' in 1978 / 9 (occurring in the wake of the global economic recession precipitated by consecutive 'oil shocks') which led to a paradigm shift. For it provided the discursive space which allowed the Thatcher governments to build (over time) a political project based (at least rhetorically) on the contradictory combination of a 'free economy and a strong state' (Gamble 1988). The 'Thatcherite instinct' then became the basis of a new evolutionary trajectory (Hay 1996c: 135, 147). In contrast, although Kerr and Marsh accept that evolution is punctuated, and would acknowledge that the Thatcher period was one in which the process of change was accelerated, they place more emphasis upon the continuities between the periods before and after 1979.

This is largely a matter of emphasis, but such disagreements do suggest a number of questions which might be examined in more detail.

- To what extent does an evolutionary perspective involve a notion of progress? If so, what was the postwar British state evolving towards?
- If crisis is the key cause of punctuated evolution, how do we identify a crisis?
- Which crises proved transformative in the postwar period (the 1973 oil crisis, the 'three-day week', the 'Winter of Discontent') and how? How can such claims be adjudicated?

Explaining change: the relationship between economic, political and ideological explanation

As we have argued throughout, there is a tendency in the literature to give primacy to either economic, political or ideological factors when explaining change. In contrast, our analysis illustrates the need to develop a multidimensional approach.

In this vein, for example, in chapter 2 Johnston demonstrates how much of the existing literature on Britain's relative economic decline is dominated by accounts which stress either economic or ideological factors. He argues that this leads to deterministic explanations of change in which decline is explained as the inevitable consequence of an anti-industrial culture or the dominance of the interests of the financial sector. As such, most analysis understates the political and, in particular, fails to address the postwar policy initiatives taken by the Attlee and Wilson governments to improve industrial productivity. An adequate explanation of decline has to integrate all three sets of explanatory factors.

Kerr and Marsh also make this point forcibly in their analysis of the literature on Thatcherism in chapter 8. In this literature some authors stress the role of economic crisis, while others focus upon the role and style of Mrs Thatcher and some emphasize the importance of New Right ideology (see Marsh 1995). In contrast, Kerr and Marsh argue for a multidimensional approach, advocating an evolutionary perspective. Such a perspective recognizes the strategic selectivity of any environment in which an agent operates, the agent's own strategic objectives and the process of strategic learning and adaptation in which the agent is involved. This approach obviously involves a view on the relationship between structure and agency, and we shall return to this issue below. However, it also takes a clear position on how to integrate (and, indeed, more fundamentally, on the need to integrate) economic, political and ideological explanations of change. More specifically, in explaining the development of Thatcherism, they argue that it evolved within a structured strategic context which was the product of the political and economic crisis of the 1970s. But, although the strategies which the Conservatives adopted evolved partly in response to those contexts, their strategic interventions also reflected their own set of meanings and objectives. Indeed, they reflected the Conservatives' desire to present an image of governing competence and to win elections and their growing commitment to free market-based economic strategy. This, in turn, reflected the influence of New Right ideology. Obviously this approach requires further development, but it has the advantage of directly attempting to produce an integrated, multidimensional explanation.

In contrast, Buller is more sceptical about the nature of a multidimensional analysis. His analysis of Britain's relations with Europe in chapter 5 places greater emphasis on political explanation than any other contributor to the book. He suggests that there was significant continuity in Britain's foreign policy, despite the fact that Britain's move towards Europe marked a break with the past. In his view, faced with growing constraints on domestic economic policy, British governments throughout the twentieth century have attempted to find external solutions to domestic policy problems. Their chief aim has been to retain as much autonomy as possible, to create an image of governing competence and to win elections. This is a broadly politicist interpretation which owes much to the work of Bulpitt on statecraft (1986, 1992). Here, the emphasis is upon the strategic decisions of politicians, although it is acknowledged that these decisions are taken within a context which reflects economic and social relations and is imbued with a dominant ideology. In essence, Buller suggests that any empirical analysis will inevitably give priority to one set of explanatory variables, while acknowledging a role for all, to avoid getting buried under a mass of often contradictory material.

As such, while we are all agreed that a multidimensional approach is essential, two key issues remain:

- How can we develop a multidimensional approach? Does this evolutionary perspective offer a fruitful way forward?
- In empirical analysis, is it inevitable that we give priority to one particular set of explanatory variables? In so far as this is so, which set should that be?

Beyond structural versus intentional explanation

A further common theme of the volume is the need to take a more sophisticated approach to the relationship between structure and agency than is usually found in the literature on the postwar period. As Johnston argues in chapter 7, the methodology adopted by most political scientists and historians often, indeed usually, results in a narrowly intentionalist analysis of the political process. In drawing on the recollections of elite actors, or the minutes (and minutiae) of government meetings, it is inevitably drawn to the personalities and principal protagonists of the historical drama. Accordingly, the political, social and economic context within which actors take strategic decisions tends to be downplayed. This means that policy outcomes are often explained in terms of the personal characteristics of leaders.

This is perhaps most clear in the literature on Thatcherism. There is a great deal of analysis of Mrs Thatcher's personality and political style (see, for example, King 1988; Kavanagh 1990), much of which suggests that these were crucial in producing strong, decisive leadership, resulting in fundamental changes in various policy areas, especially in the fields of industrial relations and the welfare state. However, this orientation is by no means restricted to the literature on the Thatcher years. Thus, for instance, Attlee's inability to project himself in the same light as the 'physically imposing and temperamentally aggressive' Bevin (Morgan 1984: 49) becomes a metaphor for the former's perceived pragmatism and political caution. Correspondingly, Britain's 'forceful' foreign policy during this period is attributed to the Foreign Secretary's physical stature and robustness.

McAnulla's treatment of the Major period in chapter 9 clearly demonstrates the limitations of an intentionalist or voluntarist approach. He shows that most accounts of the Major government explain political outcomes primarily in terms of the actions of politicians. As a result, the former's perceived failures are often simply attributed to Major's supposedly (indeed, notoriously) weak leadership. In contrast, McAnulla argues that a far more convincing account is provided if we identify the structural and ideological constraints with which the Major government was faced and trace its attempts to negotiate those constraints.

What is required is an approach which recognizes that the relationship between structure and agency is dialectical. Although structures constrain and facilitate agents, it is agents who interpret those structures and who attempt to reconstruct, change or, indeed, accommodate themselves to it. Moreover, it is the actions of agents which affect outcomes. Whilst this truism leads some analysts to privilege agents, this only gives us part of the story. For we cannot explain why agents take strategic actions without understanding how structures simultaneously constrain and facilitate them.

Obviously, even if we agree on the need for a dialectical approach, this leaves a key question which deserves further attention:

* How do we develop a dialectical conceptualization of the structure–agency relationship? (for different views see: Giddens 1984; Hay 1995b and Archer 1995).

The relationship between the material and the ideational

All the authors here acknowledge that the relationship between the material and ideational is also dialectical and, more specifically, that the ideational sphere does have direct, and in a sense independent, effect on political outcomes. This point is clear throughout the book but is perhaps clearest in the chapters by McAnulla and Watson. McAnulla makes the point quite succinctly in his treatment of the post-Thatcher period. He argues that as material problems, both economic (such as 'Black Wednesday') and political (such as divisions over Europe and Major's perceived weakness), mounted in the 1990s, the discourses of Thatcherism began to lose resonance. The two processes fed off one another and created the discursive space into which New Labour expanded, building up public appeal at the ideational level and winning the opportunity to initiate material political change.

It is Watson's chapter, however, on globalization which most directly addresses the question of the relationship between the material and the ideational. He argues that it is not globalization *per se* which is driving change in contemporary Britain; the image of inexorable forces demanding necessary political responses is a misleading one. Rather, it is the distinctively neo-liberal interpretation of globalization which explains much of the revision of economic policy priorities in recent years by both parties. The particular associations and connotations conjured by this neo-liberal discourse of globalization in turn produce material effects. These are reflected in the redefinition (and attendant downsizing) of the claimed responsibilities and competencies of the state (in Britain as elsewhere). In this vein, Watson highlights the most common misunderstanding of the whole globalization debate – that globalization heralds the end of the nation-state. Instead, he argues that the rhetoric of globalization is in fact being used to recast the role of the state as an active facilitator of globalizing tendencies. Whilst some globalizing tendencies undoubtedly exist, then, their extent and their inevitability have both tended to be over-emphasized significantly. More interestingly still, it is state actors who are authoring, or at least orchestrating, these processes in response to their often inaccurate understanding of the structural 'necessities' globalization is seen to imply.

Consequently, Watson's analysis of the processes of globalization draws on a dialectical approach to the relationship between the material and the ideational. In his view, globalization has both material and ideational or discursive properties: the former relating to 'real' tangible processes of economic change (such as financial liberalization, deregulation and the growth of derivatives markets), the latter to the hold of neo-liberal assumptions over our understanding of such processes. We must examine not one nor the other but both and their dynamic and changing relationship.

The broad agreement between the authors on this issue reflects a common epistemological position. While acknowledging the role of the ideational, they reject the view of discourse analysts and other post-modernists that the 'real' is a free-floating discursive construct bearing no relationship to the material. In our critical realist view, there *is* an external, 'real' world which is independent of its social construction, but the social or discursive construction of that world has an effect on outcomes and, thus, an effect on the material world. To continue with the globalization example, there are 'real' material processes of globalization but their effect on outcomes is mediated by and through their discursive construction.

However, once again there are also significant differences between the authors on this issue. Hay, Watson and McAnulla place more emphasis upon the independent explanatory power of the ideational: that is, upon the significance of the ideas that political actors hold about the environment in which they act, for both the nature of that action and its consequences. In contrast, Kerr, Marsh and Johnston point to what they see as the dangers of overstressing the significance of the ideational / ideological realm. These are twofold. First, they emphasize not only that the ideational realm does not exist independently of the material realm, but also that the material constrains and facilitates the ideational. The material establishes limits to the likely 'success' of a discursive construction; the discourse is unlikely to become dominant or hegemonic unless it has resonances in the material world. Second, they argue that there is an unfortunate tendency to suggest that a diverse phenomenon or group of practices, for example Thatcherism, is coherent in practice if it is unified by a fairly coherent rhetoric, discourse or ideology. In the view of these authors, ideas are often used to legitimize political action that is taken to promote economic or political interests rather than being the cause of such action. Thus, Kerr and Marsh argue that for the Thatcher governments New Right ideology was a tool used to forward or justify policy initiatives, rather than a cause of, or blueprint for, those objectives. Similarly, Watson refers to globalization as a *post hoc* rationalization of a process of change already under way. Such examples perhaps indicate, once again, the utility of a more dialectical understanding of the relationship between the ideational and the material.

These differences in emphasis suggest two questions which deserve further attention:

- To what extent and in what way does the material constrain the ideational?
- To what extent does the ideational sphere have an effect independently of the material sphere?

The relationship between the domestic and the international

The main focus of this book has been on British domestic politics, but it is crucial to recognize how domestic politics are shaped by the international context. Johnston's chapter on the Attlee years, Kerr and Marsh's on Thatcherism and McAnulla's on post-Thatcherism focus on the specificity of domestic political dynamics. This approach is based upon the view that, because the processes of change are principally national, we cannot identify, let alone explain, national dynamics merely by pointing to international tendencies. The international context may affect the domestic, but it clearly does not determine it.

The relationship between the international and the domestic is most directly explored in Buller's and Watson's chapters. Buller's chapter illustrates that the development of the British state cannot be understood adequately unless it is set within an international context. He emphasizes that traditional accounts of Britain's relationship with Europe see Britain as an 'awkward partner' (George 1994). Of course, this view emphasizes the (at least relative) autonomy of domestic political actors from external constraints and, more specifically, the supposedly more important role played by domestic political constraints. In contrast, Buller points out that it is crucial not to neglect the external institutional constraints which faced those British policy-makers trying to resist moves towards EMU after 1988. The momentum towards a single currency had its origin in powerful geopolitical forces (the collapse of communism in Eastern Europe and the reunification of Germany). Moreover, this policy is supported by a powerful coalition of member states worried about a revival of German strategic interests in the East. In attempting to resist this 'Euro-ratchet', British politicians and diplomats were simply not operating on a level external playing-field.

Buller goes on to emphasize that the relationship between the domestic and the international field is dialectical. So, the EU constrains British political actors but it can also provide opportunities for them, as they attempt to achieve their objectives. In addition, domestic actors' conduct can affect the structure and operation of the EU; in other words, they have some space to renegotiate the constraint.

Watson's chapter on globalization also emphasizes the importance of the international context, while recognizing that this context does not 'play' in the same way in different countries. The globalization discourse has become increasingly international – or, at least, almost hegemonic across what is often known as the Triad: Europe, North America and South East Asia. However, while the idea of globalization has penetrated political debates throughout the Triad, its articulation, particularly in terms of what are regarded as the necessary policy responses, is different in different national contexts. As such, we have seen the development of a 'multi-speed' globalization process across different countries. In Britain, the extent of globalization has been exaggerated by domestic politicians for their own aims. Nevertheless, there can be little doubt that globalization is an international (or transnational) phenomenon which influences domestic policy, albeit as mediated through the interests of domestic politicians and the discursive representation of the processes that sustain it.

Although there is broad agreement between the book's authors in this area, at least two questions deserve more consideration.

- How are the domestic and the international articulated?
- What autonomy do domestic actors have?

This latter question is particularly crucial in a world in which many observers suggest that the dual processes of globalization and the 'hollowing out of the state' mean that the autonomy of the nation-state is withering away or, more graphically, that the nation-state is in terminal decline.

Conclusion

Our aim has been twofold: to offer a theoretically informed account of postwar British political development and to highlight and explore the key issues and questions which any attempt to explain, rather than merely to describe, change must address.

As we stated in the introduction, our aim has not been to produce parsimonious explanatory / predictive models of the sort beloved by rational choice theorists. In our analysis, the role of theory is very different. We have not sought to construct a model, to make predictions or to generate and test hypotheses. Rather, in our approach, theory informs enquiry, suggests questions and renders problematic taken-for-granted assumptions; it does not provide definitive answers or predictions. As indicated at the outset, this book is a reflection of our conception of critical political enquiry.

In our view, we have advanced the debate in two key respects. First, we have highlighted and interrogated the key conceptual questions which must underpin any attempt to explain change over time. Second, we have offered an alternative model of change in the postwar period, replacing the dominant conceptualization with one stressing a process of punctuated evolution.

Of course, many questions remain unresolved, some of which divide the authors of this volume and many of which have been discussed in this conclusion. However, here we wish to highlight two areas where further research is clearly needed: the period from the 1950s to the 1970s and the post-Thatcher period.

The neglect of the 1950s, 1960s and 1970s

In this book, we have concentrated on the Attlee, Thatcher and post-Thatcher eras. This emphasis reflects the biases of existing accounts and can be justified only in so far as our principal concern has been to open a dialogue with this literature, assessing and evaluating prominent narratives and understandings of the period. Nevertheless, as such it remains a weakness. More theoretically informed research is clearly required on the 1950s, 1960s and 1970s if we are to adjudicate adequately arguments made about the development, duration and disintegration of the so-called postwar consensus. These are issues which we intend to take up in future research.

Two examples should help to clarify this point. First, although many people emphasize the existence of a consensus in the 1950s and the 1960s, others stress that this was a period in which policy in a range of areas was characterized by inconsistency. The nationalization, denationalization and renationalization of the steel industry is often cited in this context. Indeed, such inconsistency is, in some accounts, seen as a key factor in explaining Britain's accelerating economic decline during this period (see King 1975). This is not the place to adjudicate between these two positions. Suffice it to note that although apparently mutually inconsistent, both are frequently held by the same authors. Second, we need more analysis of the 1970s. For this is often argued (at least implicitly) to be the definitive decade of the postwar era: the period to which many of the causes of the subsequent changes of the 1980s and 1990s can be traced. Although the 1970s emerge as a crucial, even determining period in many accounts, it is rarely scrutinized in any depth.

The post-Thatcher era: is there a new consensus?

Since the mid-1990s attention has focused on the question of whether we are witnessing the emergence of a new consensus; one which developed over the Thatcher years to persist through and beyond the Major era and into the brave new world of New Labour. Here, debate has tended to concentrate on the extent of bipartisan convergence in economic policy. It is suggested the New Labour has capitulated to the view that there is and should be no alternative to market solutions to economic, industrial and even social problems. Set in this context, the rhetoric associated with the New Right has triumphed. This is reflected in the Labour Party's acceptance of Conservative expenditure limits, as it is with the view that the processes of globalization leave them with little room for manoeuvre that might allow a more radical break with the Thatcherite inheritance.

This question is likely to preoccupy students of British politics well into the 2010s, and it is not impossible that in 2030 or so a group of authors will write a book similar to this, analysing the second postwar consensus. However, while prophecy is an interesting if dangerous game, we would urge caution. There are three fairly obvious reasons for this caution.

First, we cannot predict with certainty the unfolding trajectory of Labour's policy in government. The view that the new consensus is here to stay relies on what can only be the assumption that New Labour will not move in a qualitatively different direction to that followed by the Conservatives in power. This is an issue on which the authors of this volume are split. McAnulla's view is that the Labour Party adopted Conservative expenditure limits for two years in order to win the 1997 election, but will be anxious to demonstrate its social democratic credentials – increasing social and public expenditure – once this period has elapsed. The rest of the authors are sceptical of this interpretation, partly because most argue that the Labour leadership has accepted a logic of globalization which leaves them little latitude for manoeuvre in both fiscal and monetary policy.

Second, although the Labour Party has accepted much of the Conservative legacy, it has broken significantly with the past in certain areas. A year after its election, it shows at best limited signs of breaking with the Conservative legacy on economic, industrial relations or industrial policy. What is more, arguably it has moved beyond the Conservatives in the area of welfare policy, embracing a 'workfare' system modelled on the USA. Yet, on the vexed issue of Europe, there are signs that the government will adopt a less Eurosceptic stance than its predecessor. More obviously, it has introduced radical changes on the constitutional front. There will be a Scottish Parliament with tax-raising powers and a Welsh Assembly without such fiscal responsibilities. Labour has also promised a far-reaching Freedom of Information Act to remove much of the secrecy which has become a fundamental characteristic of British democracy. In addition, there are plans for a London mayor with executive powers. This may provide a blueprint for other cities. Finally, in furthering significantly the prospects of a lasting peace in Northern Ireland, Labour raises the possibility of a constitutional settlement that can encompass the entire United Kingdom. Such plans and achievements do mark a break not only with the previous Conservative government but also with the traditions of British politics. These changes, it is argued may serve to threaten and even undermine the elitist nature of British democracy. However, only time will tell if this does indeed prove to be the case.

Third, the idea that the notion of a new consensus exhausts our understanding of political change in contemporary Britain is crass in the extreme. Apart from anything else, consensus is, like other aspects of political culture, fashioned by political actors. As such, tendencies towards convergence can be rapidly reversed. Of course, our reading of the past affects our interpretation of the present and our expectations of the future. The idea that there is a new consensus is, as we have seen, often based upon a stepwise model of change – of alternating and, in some accounts, even inevitable periods of stasis and crisis. Such a conception we have been at pains to challenge. It suggests that the postwar consensus was undermined by Thatcherism, which in turn provided the basis for a new consensus. In contrast, this book has argued that analyses of change need to be more sophisticated. We question the utility of the notion of postwar consensus widely identified within the existing literature. From such a vantage-point, prophetic talk of an inevitable, immutable and enduring new consensus may, thankfully, prove somewhat premature. The future, like the past and the present, is inherently contested.

Bibliography

Addison, P. (1975) *The Road to 1945: British Politics and the Second World War*, London: Cape.
—— (1987) 'The Road From 1945', in P. Hennessy and A. Seldon (eds), *Ruling Performance: British Governments from Attlee to Thatcher*, Oxford: Blackwell.
—— (1993) 'Consensus Revisited', *Twentieth Century British History*, 4 (1), 91–4.
Aglietta, M. (1979) *A Theory of Capitalist Regulation*, London: New Left Books.
Amin, A. (ed.) (1994) *Post-Fordism: A Reader*, Oxford: Blackwell.
Anderson, P. (1964) 'Origins of the Present Crisis', *New Left Review*, 23, 26–53.
—— (1966) 'Socialism and Pseudo-Empiricism', *New Left Review*, 35, 2–42.
—— (1987) 'The Figure of Descent', *New Left Review*, 161, 21–77.
—— (1992) *English Questions*, London: Verso.
Archer, M. S. (1995) *Realist Social Theory: The Morphogenetic Approach*, Cambridge: Cambridge University Press.
Armstrong, K. and Bulmer, S. (1996) 'United Kingdom', in D. Rometsch and W. Wessels (eds), *The European Union and Member States: Towards Institutional Fusion*, Manchester: Manchester University Press.
Ashford, N. (1992) 'The Political Parties', in S. George (ed.), *Britain and the European Community*, Oxford: Clarendon Press.
Atkins, F. (1986) 'Thatcherism, Populist Authoritarianism and the

Search for a New Left Political Strategy', *Capital and Class*, 28, 25–48.

Bacon, R. and Eltis, W. (1976) *Britain's Economic Problem: Too Few Producers*, London: Macmillan.

Baggot, R. (1995) 'From Confrontation to Consultation? Pressure Group Relations from Thatcher to Major', *Parliamentary Affairs*, 48 (3), 484–503.

Bairoch, P. (1996) 'Globalisation Myths and Realities: One Century of External Trade and Foreign Investment', in R. Boyer and D. Drache (eds), *States Against Markets: The Limits of Globalisation*, London: Routledge.

Baker, D., Gamble, A. and Ludlam, S. (1993) 'Whips or Scorpions? Conservative MPs and the Maastricht Paving Motion Vote', *Parliamentary Affairs*, 46 (2), 151–66.

Ball, S. and Seldon, A. (eds) (1996) *The Heath Government, 1970–74*, London: Longman.

Barker, A. (1995) 'Major's Government in a Major Key: Conservative Ideological Aggressiveness Since Thatcher', *New Political Science*, 33, 125–50.

Barnett, C. (1986) *Audit of War: The Illusion and Reality of Britain as a Great Nation*, London: Macmillan.

—— (1996) *The Lost Victory: British Dreams, British Realities, 1945–50*, London: Pan.

Barnett, J. (1982) *Inside the Treasury*, London: André Deutsch.

Barratt Brown, M. (1988) 'Away with All the Great Arches: Anderson's History of British Capitalism', *New Left Review*, 167, 22–51.

Baxendale, J. (1986) 'Review of Martin J. Weiner's "English Culture and the Decline of the Industrial Spirit 1850–1980" ', *History Workshop Journal*, 21, 171–4.

Bédarida, F. (1991) *A Social History of England 1851–1990*, London: Routledge.

Beer, S. (1965) *Modern British Politics*, London: Faber.

Beloff, Lord (1996) *Britain and the European Union: Dialogue of the Deaf*, Basingstoke: Macmillan.

Berger, S. and Dore, R. (eds) (1996) *National Diversity and Global Capitalism*, Ithaca, NY: Cornell University Press.

Beynon, J. (1989) 'Ten Years of Thatcherism', *Social Studies Review*, 4 (5), 170–8.

Bhargava, R. (1992) *Individualism in Social Science*, Oxford: Clarendon Press.

Bhaskar, R. (1989) *Reclaiming Reality*, London: Verso.

Blackwell, T. and Seabrook, J. (1988) *The Politics of Hope*, London: Faber.

Blair, T. (1996) *New Britain: My Vision of a Young Country*, London: Fourth Estate.

Booth, A. (1986) 'Simple Keynesianism and Whitehall 1936–44', *Economy and Society*, 15 (1), 1–22.

Boyer, R. (1990) *The Regulation School: A Critical Introduction*, New York: Columbia University Press.

—— (1996) 'State and Market: A New Engagement for the Twenty-First Century?', in R. Boyer and D. Drache (eds), *States Against Markets: The Limits of Globalisation*, London: Routledge.

Boyer, R. and Drache, D. (eds) (1996) *States Against Markets: The Limits of Globalisation*, London: Routledge.

Brittan, S. (1975) 'The Economic Contradictions of Democracy', *British Journal of Political Science*, 5 (2), 129–59.

—— (1979) *Participation Without Politics*, London: Institute for Economic Affairs.

Brooke, S. (1992) *Labour's War: The Labour Party During the Second World War*, Oxford: Oxford University Press.

Brown, C. J. F. and Sheriff, T. D. (1978) 'De-Industrialisation: A Background Paper', in F. Blackaby (ed.), *De-Industrialisation*, London: Heinemann Educational Books.

Brown, J. (1995) *The British Welfare State: A Critical History*, Oxford: Blackwell.

Budd, A. (1978) *The Politics of Economic Planning*, London: Fontana.

Buller, J. (1995a) 'Britain As An Awkward Partner: Reassessing Britain's Relations with the EU', *Politics*, 15 (1) 33–42.

—— (1995b) 'Foreign and Defence Policy', in S. Ludlam and M. J. Smith (eds), *Contemporary British Conservatism*, London: Macmillan.

Bulpitt, J. (1983) *Territory and Power in the United Kingdom*, Manchester: Manchester University Press.

—— (1986) 'The Discipline of the New Democracy: Mrs Thatcher's Domestic Statecraft', *Political Studies*, 34 (1), 19–39.

—— (1992) 'Conservative Leaders and the Euro-Ratchet: Five Doses of Scepticism', *Political Quarterly*, 63 (3), 258–75.

Burk, K. and Cairncross, A. (1992) *'Goodbye, Great Britain'. The 1976 IMF Crisis*, New Haven: Yale University Press.

Burke, E. (1790) *Reflections on the Revolution in France*, London: Pelican (1968 edition).

Burnham, P. (1990) *The Political Economy of Postwar Reconstruction*, London: Macmillan.

Busch, A. (1999) 'Unpacking the Globalization Debate: Approaches, Evidence and Data', in C. Hay and D. Marsh (eds), *Demystifying Globalization*, London: Macmillan.

Butler, A. (1993) 'The End of Post-War Consensus: Reflections on the Scholarly Uses of Political Rhetoric', *Political Quarterly*, 64 (4), 435.

Cain, P. and Hopkins, A. (1980) 'The Political Economy of British Expansion Overseas, 1750–1914', *Economic History Review*, 33 (4), 463–90.

—— (1993a) *British Imperialism: Innovation and Expansion, 1688–1914*, London: Longman.

—— (1993b) *British Imperialism: Crisis and Deconstruction, 1914–1990*, London: Longman.

Cairncross, A. (1992) *The British Economy Since 1945*, Oxford: Blackwell.

Calder, A. (1969) *The People's War*, London: Cape.

Campbell, J. (1993) *Edward Heath: A Biography*, London: Pimlico.

Cash, B. (1996) 'A Response to the Government's White Paper', *The European Journal*, 3 (6), 4–10.

Castle, B. (1984) *The Castle Diaries, 1964–70*, London: Weidenfeld and Nicolson.

Charlton, M. (1983) *The Price of Victory*, London: British Broadcasting Corporation.

Clarke, P. (1988) *The Keynesian Revolution in the Making, 1924–1936*, Oxford: Clarendon Press.

Clarke, S. (1988) *Keynesianism, Monetarism and the Crisis of the State*, London: Edward Elgar.

Cleaver, T. (1997) *Understanding the World Economy*, London: Routledge.

Cloke, P. (ed.) (1992) *Policy and Change in Thatcher's Britain*, Oxford: Pergamon.

Coakley, J. (1992) 'London as an International Financial Centre', in L. Budd and S. Whimster (eds), *Global Finance and Urban Living*, London: Routledge.

Coakley, J. and Harris, L. (1992) 'Financial Globalisation and Deregulation', in J. Michie (ed.), *The Economic Legacy 1979–1992*, London: Academic Press.

Coates, D. (1980) *Labour in Power? A Study of the Labour Government 1974–79*, London: Longman.

—— (1989) *The Crisis of Labour*, Oxford: Philip Allan.

Coates, D. and Hillard, J. (1986) *The Economic Decline of Modern Britain: The Debate Between Left and Right*, Hemel Hempstead: Harvester Wheatsheaf.

—— (1995) *UK Economic Decline: Key Texts*, Hemel Hempstead: Prentice Hall / Harvester Wheatsheaf.

Cohen, C. D. (1983) 'Growth, Stability and Employment', in C. D. Cohen (ed.), *The Common Market: Ten Years After*, Deddington: Philip Allan.

Collins, B. and Robbins, K. (eds) (1990) *British Culture and Economic Decline*, New York: St Martin's Press.

Conservative Research Department (1979) *Campaign Guide For Europe 1979*, London: Conservative Central Office.

Cox, R. (1996) 'A Perspective on Globalization', in J. Mittelman (ed.), *Globalization: Critical Reflections*, London: Lynne Rienner.

Crafts, N. and Woodward, N. (eds) (1991) *The British Economy Since 1945*, Oxford: Oxford University Press.

Crewe, I. (1988) 'Has the Electorate Become Thatcherite?', in R. Skidelsky (ed.), *Thatcherism*, London: Chatto and Windus.

—— (1993) 'The Thatcher Legacy', in A. King (ed.), *Britain at the Polls 1992*, Chatham, NJ: Chatham House.

—— (1994) 'Electoral Behaviour', in D. Kavanagh and A. Seldon (eds), *The Major Effect*, London: Macmillan.

Cronin, J. (1991) *The Politics of State Expansion: War, State and Society in Twentieth-Century Britain*, London: Routledge.

Crosland, C. A. R. (1956) *The Future of Socialism*, London: Jonathan Cape.

Crossman, R. H. S. (1963) 'British Labour Looks at Europe', *Foreign Affairs*, 41 (4), 732–43.

—— (1975) *The Diaries of a Cabinet Minister: Volume One, Minister of Housing, 1964–66*, London: Hamish Hamilton and Jonathan Cape.

Crouch, C. (ed.) (1979) *State and Economy in Contemporary Capitalism*, London: Croom Helm.

Crozier, M. (1975) 'Are European Democracies Becoming Ungovernable?', in M. Crozier, S. Huntingdon and J. Watanuki, *The Crisis of Democracy*, New York: New York University Press.

Cutler, T., Harlam, C., Williams, J. and Williams, K. (1989) *1992 – The Struggle For Europe*, Oxford: Berg.

Davies, A. J. (1992) *To Build a New Jerusalem: The Labour Movement from the 1880s to the 1990s*, London: Michael Joseph.

Davis, E., Kay, J. A., Geroski, A., Manning, A., Smales, C., Smith, S. R. and Szymanski, S. (1989) *1992: Myths and Realities*, London: London Business School.

De Bresson, C. (1987) 'The Evolutionary Paradigm and the Economics of Technical Change', *Journal of Economic Issues*, 21 (2), 751–62.

Denman, R. (1996) *Missed Chances: Britain and Europe in the Twentieth Century*, London: Indigo.

Derrida, J. (1994) *Spectres of Marx: The State of the Debt, the Work of Mourning and the New International*, London: Routledge.

Desai, R. (1994) *Intellectuals and Socialism: 'Social Democrats' and the Labour Party*, London: Lawrence and Wishart.

Dessler, D. (1989) 'What's at Stake in the Agent / Structure Debate?', *International Organization*, 43 (3), 441–74.

Dolowitz, D. (1998) *Learning From America: Policy Transfer and the Development of the British Workfare State*, Brighton: Sussex Academic Press.

Dorey, P. (1995) *British Politics Since 1945*, Oxford: Blackwell.

Dorfman, G. (1979) *Government Versus Trade Unionism in British Politics since 1968*, London: Macmillan.

Douglas, J. (1976) 'The Overloaded Crown', *British Journal of Political Science*, 6 (4), 483–505.

—— (1989) 'The Changing Tide: Some Recent Studies of Thatcherism', *British Journal of Political Science*, 19, 399–424.

DTI (1993) *Monthly Review of External Trade Statistics*, London: HMSO.

Dutton, D. (1991) *British Politics Since 1945: The Rise and Fall of Consensus*, Oxford: Blackwell.

Eatwell, R. (1979) *The 1945–51 Labour Governments*, London: Batsford.

Elbaum, B. and Lazonick, W. (eds) (1986) *The Decline of the British Economy*, Oxford: Clarendon Press.

Eldredge, N. (1989) 'Punctuated Equilibria, Rates of Change, and Large-Scale Entities in Evolutionary Systems', in A. Somit and S. Peterson (eds), *The Dynamics of Evolution: The Punctuated Equilibrium Debate in the Natural and Social Sciences*, Ithaca, NY: Cornell University Press.

Epstein, G. A. and Schor, J. B. (1990) 'Macropolicy in the Rise and Fall of the Golden Age', in S. Marglin and J. Schor (eds), *The Golden Age of Capitalism: Reinterpreting the Postwar Experience*, Oxford: Clarendon Press.

Evans, B. and Taylor, A. (1996) *From Salisbury to Major: Continuity and Change in Conservative Politics*, Manchester: Manchester University Press.

Ewing, K. D. and Gearty, C. A. (1990) *Freedom Under Thatcher: Civil Liberties in Modern Britain*, Oxford: Clarendon Press.

Fielding, S., Thompson, P. and Tiratsoo, N. (1995) *England Arise! The Labour Party and Popular Politics in the 1940s*, Manchester: Manchester University Press.

Fine, B. and Harris, L. (1985) *The Peculiarities of the British Economy*, London: Lawrence and Wishart.

Finer, S. (1975) 'Adversary Politics and Electoral Reform', in S. Finer (ed.), *Adversary Politics and Electoral Reform*, London: Anthony Wigram.

—— (1987) 'Thatcherism and British Political History', in K. Minogue and M. Biddiss (eds), *Thatcherism: Personality and Politics*, London: Macmillan.

Fyrth, J. (ed.) (1995) *Labour's Promised Land? Culture and Society in Labour Britain 1945–51*, London: Lawrence and Wishart.

Gamble, A. (1988) *The Free Economy and the Strong State: The Politics of Thatcherism*, London: Macmillan.

—— (1990a) *Britain in Decline (3rd Edition)*, Basingstoke: Macmillan.

—— (1990b) 'The Thatcher Decade in Perspective', in P. Dunleavy, A. Gamble and G. Peele (eds), *Developments in British Politics 3*, London: Macmillan.

—— (1990c) 'Theories of British Politics', *Political Studies*, XXXVIII, 404–20.

—— (1994) *Britain in Decline (4th Edition)*, London: Macmillan.

Garnett, M. (1996) *Principles and Politics in Contemporary Britain*, London: Longman.

George, S. (ed.) (1992) *Britain and the European Community*, Oxford: Clarendon Press.

—— (1994) *An Awkward Partner (2nd Edition)*, Oxford: Oxford University Press.

—— (1995) 'A Reply To Buller', *Politics*, 15 (1), 43–7.

Gerschenkron, A. (1962) *Economic Backwardness in Historical Perspective*, Cambridge, MA: Harvard University Press.

Giddens, A. (1984) *The Constitution of Society*, Cambridge: Polity.

—— (1994) *Beyond Left and Right: The Future of Radical Politics*, Cambridge: Polity.

Gill, S. (1992) 'The Emerging World Order and European Change', in R. Miliband and L. Panitch (eds), *New World Order? The Socialist Register 1992*, London: Merlin.

—— (1996) 'Globalization, Democratization, and the Politics of Indifference', in J. Mittelman (ed.) *Globalization: Critical Reflections*, London: Lynne Rienner.

Gilmour, I. (1977) *Inside Right*, London: Hutchinson.

Glyn, A. and Harrison, J. (1980) *The British Economic Disaster*, London: Pluto Press.

Glyn, A., Hughes, A., Lipietz, A. and Singh, A. (1990) 'The Rise and Fall of the Golden Age', in S. Marglin and J. Schor (eds), *The Golden Age of Capitalism: Reinterpreting the Postwar Experience*, Oxford: Clarendon Press.

Gould, S. J. (1989) 'Punctuated Equilibrium in Fact and Theory', in A. Somit and S. Peterson (eds), *The Dynamics of Evolution: The Punctuated Equilibrium Debate in the Natural and Social Sciences*, Ithaca, NY: Cornell University Press.

Gramsci, A. (1971) *Selections From Prison Notebooks*, London: Lawrence and Wishart.

Grant, W. (1987) *Business and Politics in Britain*, London: Macmillan.

—— (1997) 'BSE and the Politics of Food', in P. Dunleavy, A. Gamble, I. Holliday and G. Peele, *Developments in British Politics 5*, Basingstoke: Macmillan.

Hall, P. A. (1986a) *Governing the Economy: The Politics of State Intervention in Britain and France*, New York: Oxford University Press.

—— (1986b) 'The State and Economic Decline', in B. Elbaum and W. Lazonick (eds), *The Decline of the British Economy*. Oxford: Oxford University Press.

—— (1993) 'Policy Paradigms, Social Learning and the State: The Case of Economic Policy-Making in Britain', *Comparative Politics*, 25 (3), 185–96.

—— (1995) 'The State and Economic Decline', in D. Coates and J. Hillard (eds), *UK Economic Decline: Key Texts*, Hemel Hempstead: Prentice Hall / Harvester Wheatsheaf.

—— (ed.) (1989) *The Political Power of Economic Ideas: Keynesianism Across Nations*, Ithaca, NY: Cornell University Press.

Hall, P. A. and Taylor, R. (1996) 'Political Science and the Three New Institutionalisms', *Political Studies*, 44 (5), 936–57.

Hall, S. (1979) 'The Great Moving Right Show', *Marxism Today*, January, reprinted in S. Hall and M. Jacques (eds) (1983) *The Politics of Thatcherism*, London: Lawrence and Wishart.

—— (1997) interviewed by M. Jacques, 'Cultural Revolutions', *New Statesman*, 5 December, 24–6.

Hall, S., Critcher, C., Jefferson, T., Clarke, J. and Roberts, B. (1978) *Policing the Crisis: Mugging, the State and Law and Order*, London: Macmillan.

Harris, J. (1986) 'Political Ideas and the Debate on State Welfare, 1940–45', in H. Smith (ed.), *War and Social Change*, Manchester: Manchester University Press.

Harvey, D. (1989) 'From Managerialism to Entrepreneurialism: The Transformation in Urban Governance in Late Capitalism', *Geografiska Annaler*, 71B (1), 3–17.

Hay, C. (1994) 'The Structural and Ideological Contradictions of Britain's Post-War Reconstruction', *Capital and Class*, 54, 25–59.

—— (1995a) 'Rethinking Crisis: Narratives of the New Right and Constructions of Crisis', *Rethinking Marxism*, 8 (2), 60–76.

—— (1995b) 'Structure and Agency', in D. Marsh and G. Stoker (eds), *Theory and Methods in Political Science*, London: Macmillan.

—— (1995c) 'Re-Stating the Problem of Regulation and Re-Regulating the Local State', *Economy and Society*, 24 (3), 387–407.

—— (1996a) 'From Crisis to Catastrophe? The Ecological Pathologies of the Liberal-Democratic State Form', *Innovation: The European Journal of the Social Sciences*, 9 (4), 421–34.

—— (1996b) 'Narrating Crisis: The Discursive Construction of the "Winter of Discontent" ', *Sociology*, 30 (2), 253–77.

—— (1996c) *Re-Stating Social and Political Change*, Buckingham: Open University Press.

—— (1997a) 'Divided by a Common Language: Political Theory and the Concept of Power', *Politics*, 7 (1), 45–52.

—— (1997b) 'Political Time and the Temporality of Crisis: On Institutional Change as Punctuated Evolution', paper presented at the *Conference on Institutional Analysis*, Copenhagen, 21–4 August.

—— (1997c) 'A Sorry State? Diagnosing the British Affliction', *Socialism and Democracy*, 11 (1), 87–104.

—— (1997d) 'The Tangled Webs We Weave: The Discourse, Strategy and Practice of Networking', in D. Marsh (ed.), *Policy Networks in Theoretical and Comparative Perspective*, Buckingham: Open University Press.

—— (1997e) 'Marxism and the State: Flogging a Dead Horse?', in A. Gamble et al. (eds), *Marxism and Social Science*, London: Macmillan.

—— (1997f) 'Anticipating Accommodations, Accommodating Anticipations: The Appeasement of Capital in the Modernisation of the British Labour Party, 1987–1992', *Politics and Society*, 25 (2), 234–56.

—— (1997g) 'Blaijorism: Towards a One-Vision Polity', *Political Quarterly*, 68 (4), 372–78.

—— (1998) 'That Was Then, This Is Now: The Revision of Policy in the Modernisation of the British Labour Party, 1992–97', *New Political Science*, 20 (1), 7–33.

Hay, C. and Jessop, B. (1998) 'The Governance of Local Economic Development and the Development of Local Economic Governance', *Urban Affairs Review*, forthcoming.

Hay, C. and Watson, M. (1998) *Rendering the Contingent Necessary: New Labour's Neo-Liberal Conversion and the Discourse of Globalisation*, Center for European Studies Program for the Study of Germany and Europe Working Paper 8.4, Cambridge, MA: Harvard University Press.

Heffernan, R. (1996) 'Accounting for New Labour: The Impact of Thatcherism, 1979–1995', in I. Hampsher-Monk and J. Stanyer (eds), *Contemporary Political Studies 1996, Volume 2*, Belfast: PSA.

Helleiner, E. (1996) 'Post-Globalisation: Is the Financial Liberalisation Trend Ever Likely to be Reversed?', in R. Boyer and D. Drache (eds), *States Against Markets: The Limits of Globalisation*, London: Routledge.

Hennessy, P. (1987) 'The Attlee Governments 1945–51', in P. Hennessy and A. Seldon (eds), *Ruling Performance: British Governments from Attlee to Thatcher*, Oxford: Blackwell.

Heraclitus (1979) *Heraclitus on the Universe*, Cambridge: Cambridge University Press.

Hirsch, J. (1991) 'From the Fordist to the Post-Fordist State', in B. Jessop, H. Kastandiek, K. Nielsen and O. K. Pedersen (eds), *The Politics of Flexibility: Restructuring State and Industry in Britain, Germany and Scandinavia*, London: Edward Elgar.

Hirschman, A. O. (1970) *Exit, Voice and Loyalty: Responses to Decline in Firms, Organisations and States*, Cambridge, MA: Harvard University Press.

Hirschman, A. O. (1986) 'Exit and Voice: An Expanding Sphere of Influence', in *Rival Views of Market Society and Other Essays*, Cambridge, MA: Harvard University Press.

Hirst, P. (1997) 'The Global Market and the Possibilities of Governance', paper presented at the conference, *Globalisation: Critical Perspectives*, University of Birmingham, 14–16 March.

Hirst, P. and Thompson, G. (1996) *Globalisation in Question*, Cambridge: Polity.

HM Treasury (1993) *Public Expenditure Analysis to 1995–96: Statistical Supplement to the 1992 Autumn Statement*, London: HMSO.

—— (1997) *Overseas Investment and the UK – Explanations, Policy Implications, Facts and Figures*, London: HMSO.

Hobsbawm, E. J. (1969) *Industry and Empire*, Harmondsworth: Penguin.

Hodgson, G. (1993) 'Theories of Economic Evolution: A Preliminary Toxonomy', *Manchester School of Economic and Social Studies*, LXI (2), 125–43.

Holland, R. (1991) *The Pursuit of Greatness: Britain and the World Role, 1900–70*, London: Fontana.

Holmes, M. (1982) *Political Pressure and Economic Policy*, London: Butterworths.

Horne, A. (1989) *Macmillan, Volume 2: 1957–98*, London: Pan.

Howarth, D. (1995) 'Discourse Theory', in D. Marsh and G. Stoker (eds), *Theory and Methods in Political Science*, Basingstoke: Macmillan.

Howe, D. (1997) 'After Diana', *New Statesman*, 12 September, 13.

Howe, G. (1982) *Conservatism in the Eighties*, London: Conservative Political Centre.

—— (1988) *The Conservative Revival of Britain*, London: Conservative Political Centre.

—— (1990) 'Sovereignty and Interdependence: Britain's Place in the World', *International Affairs*, 66 (4), 675–95.

—— (1994) *Conflict of Loyalty*, London: Macmillan.

Hübner, K. (1991) 'Flexibilisation and Autonomisation of World Money Markets: Obstacles for a New Long Expansion?', in B. Jessop, H. Kastandiek, K. Nielsen and O. K. Pedersen (eds), *The Politics of Flexibility: Restructuring State and Industry in Britain, Germany and Scandinavia*, London: Edward Elgar.

Hutton, W. (1995) *The State We're In*, London: Jonathan Cape.

—— (1996) *The State We're In*, revised edition, London: Viking.

—— (1997) *The State to Come*, London: Viking.

Ingham, G. (1984) *Capitalism Divided*, London: Macmillan.

Isaac, J. C. (1987) *Power and Marxist Theory: A Realist View*, Ithaca, NY: Cornell University Press.

Jacquemin, A. and Sapir, A. (eds) (1989) *The European Internal Market: Trade and Competition*, Oxford: Oxford University Press.

Jay, D. (1980) *Change and Fortune*, London: Hutchinson.

Jay, P. (1977) 'Englanditis', in R. E. Tyrell (ed.), *The Future That Doesn't Work*, New York: Doubleday.

Jefferys, K. (1991) *The Churchill Coalition and Wartime Politics 1940–45*, Manchester: Manchester University Press.

Jenkins, P. (1987) *Mrs Thatcher's Revolution*, London: Jonathan Cape.

—— (1988) *The Thatcher Revolution: The Post-Socialist Era*, London: Jonathan Cape.

Jessop, B. (1980) 'The Transformation of the State in Postwar Britain', in R. Scase (ed.), *The State in Western Europe*, London: Croom Helm.

—— (1990) *State Theory: Putting Capitalist States in their Place*, Cambridge: Polity.

—— (1993) 'Towards a Schumpeterian Workfare State? Preliminary Remarks on Post-Fordist Political Economy', *Studies in Political Economy*, 21, 355–96.

—— (1994a) 'Post-Fordism and the State', in A. Amin (ed.), *Post-Fordism: A Reader*, Oxford: Blackwell.

—— (1994b) 'The Transition to Post-Fordism and the Schumpeterian Workfare State', in R. Burrows and B. Loader (eds), *Towards a Post-Fordist Welfare State?*, London: Routledge.

Jessop, B., Bonnet, K., Bromley, S. and Ling, T. (1988) *Thatcherism: A Tale of Two Nations*, Cambridge: Polity.

Jessop, B., Kastandiek, H., Nielsen, K. and Pedersen, O. K. (eds) (1991) *The Politics of Flexibility: Restructuring State and Industry in Britain, Germany and Scandinavia*, London: Edward Elgar.

Johnman, L. (1991) 'The Labour Party and Industrial Policy, 1940–45', in N. Tiratsoo (ed.), *The Attlee Years*, London: Pinter.

Johnson, B. and Lundvall, B.-Å. (1991) 'Flexibility and Institutional Learning', in B. Jessop, H. Kastandiek, K. Nielsen and O. K. Pedersen (eds), *The Politics of Flexibility: Restructuring State and Industry in Britain, Germany and Scandinavia*, London: Edward Elgar.

Jones, B. and Keating, M. (1985) *Labour and the British State*, Oxford: Clarendon Press.

Junor, P. (1996) *John Major: From Brixton to Downing Street*, Harmondsworth: Penguin.

Kavanagh, D. (1987) *Thatcherism and British Politics: The End of Consensus?*, Oxford: Oxford University Press.

—— (1990) *Thatcherism and British Politics*, 2nd edition, Oxford: Oxford University Press.

—— (1992) 'The Postwar Consensus', *Twentieth Century British History*, 3 (2), 175–90.

—— (1996) 'The Fatal Choice: The Calling of the February 1974 Election', in S. Ball and A. Seldon (eds), *The Heath Government, 1970–74*, London: Longman.

Kavanagh, D. and Morris P. (1989) *Consensus Politics from Attlee to Thatcher*, Oxford: Blackwell.

—— (1994) *Consensus Politics from Attlee to Major*, Oxford: Blackwell.

Kavanagh, D. and Seldon, A. (eds) (1994) *The Major Effect*, London: Macmillan.

Kearns, G. and Philo, C. (eds) (1993) *Selling Places: The City as Cultural Capital, Past and Present*, Oxford: Pergamon Press.

Keegan, W. (1984) *Mrs Thatcher's Economic Experiment*, London: Allen Lane.

Kerr, P. (1995) 'Why the Conservatives are Heading Towards the Goal with No-one Marking Them', paper presented at the Political Studies Association annual conference, University of York, April.

Kerr, P. and Marsh, D. (1996) 'False Dichotomies and Failed Assumptions: Revisiting and Revising the Consensus Debate', in I. Hampsher-Monk and J. Stanyer (eds), *Contemporary Political Studies, 1996: Volume 2*, Oxford: Blackwell / PSA.

Kerr, P., McAnulla, S. and Marsh, D. (1997) 'Charting Late-Thatcherism: British Politics Under Major', in S. Lancaster (ed.), *Developments in Politics*, Ormskirk: Causeway.

Kilpatrick, A. and Lawson, T. (1980) 'On the Nature of Industrial Decline in the UK', *Cambridge Journal of Economics*, 4 (1), 85–102.

King, A. (1975) 'Overload: Problems of Governing in the 1970s', *Political Studies*, 23 (2 / 3), 284–96.

—— (1985) 'Margaret Thatcher: The Style of a Prime Minister, in A. King (ed.), *The British Prime Minister*, London: Macmillan.

—— (1988) 'Margaret Thatcher as a Political Leader', in R. Skidelsky (ed.), *Thatcherism*, London: Chatto and Windus.

King, D. S. (1987) *The New Right: Politics, Markets and Citizenship*, London: Macmillan.

Kotler, P., Haider, D. and Rein, I. (1993) *Marketing Places: Attracting Investment, Industry and Tourism to Cities, States and Nations*, Oxford: Macmillan.

Krasner, S. D. (1984) 'Approaches to the State: Alternative Conceptions and Historical Dynamics', *Comparative Politics*, 16 (1), 223–46.

Krieger, J. (1986) *Reagan, Thatcher and the Politics of Decline*, Cambridge: Polity.

Krugman, P. (1994) 'Competitiveness: A Dangerous Obsession', *Foreign Affairs*, 73, 28–44.

Laclau, E. and Mouffe, C. (1985) *Hegemony and Socialist Strategy*, London: Verso.

Lawson, N. (1992) *The View From Number Eleven*, London: Bantam.

Laybourn, K. (1988) *The Rise of Labour: The British Labour Party 1890–1979*, London: Edward Arnold.

Layder, D. (1994) *Understanding Social Theory*, London: Sage.

Lee, S. (1996) 'Finance for Industry', in J. Michie and J. Grieve Smith (eds), *Creating Industrial Capacity: Towards Full Employment*, Oxford: Oxford University Press.

Levitas, R. (ed.) (1986) *The Ideology of the New Right*, Cambridge: Polity.

Leys, C. (1983) *Politics in Britain*, London: Heinemann.

—— (1986) 'The Formation of British Capital', *New Left Review*, 160, 114–20.

Lipietz, A. (1985) *The Enchanted World: Inflation, Credit and the World Crisis*, London: Verso.

Lord, C. (1993) *British Entry to the European Community under the Heath Government, 1970–74*, Aldershot: Dartmouth.

Ludlam, S. (1996) 'The Spectre Haunting Conservatism: Europe and Backbench Rebellion', in S. Ludlam and M. J. Smith (eds), *Contemporary British Conservatism*, London: Macmillan.

Ludlam, S. and Smith, M. J. (eds) (1996) *Contemporary British Conservatism*, London: Macmillan.

Lukes, S. (1974) *Power: A Radical View*, London: Macmillan.

McKenzie, R. (1955) *British Political Parties*, London: Heinemann.

McNair, B. (1995) *An Introduction to Political Communications*, London: Routledge.

Macmillan, H. (1972) *Pointing the Way, 1959–61*, London: Macmillan.

Maddison, A. (1982) *Phases of Capitalist Development*, Oxford: Oxford University Press.

—— (1991) *Dynamic Forces in Capitalist Development: A Long-Run Comparative View*, Oxford: Oxford University Press.

Major, J. (1993) 'Raise Your Eyes, There Is a Land Beyond', *The Economist*, 25 September, 23–7.

Marglin, S. and Schor, J. (eds) (1990) *The Golden Age of Capitalism: Reinterpreting the Postwar Experience*, Oxford: Clarendon Press.

Marlow, J. D. (1995) 'Metaphor, Intertextuality and the Postwar Consensus', *Politics*, 17 (2), 127–34.

—— (1996) *Questioning the Postwar Consensus Thesis: Towards an Alternative Account*, Aldershot: Dartmouth.

Marquand, D. (1988) *The Unprincipled Society*, London: Jonathan Cape.

—— (1989) 'The Decline of Postwar Consensus', in A. Gorst, L. Johnman and W. Lucas (eds), *Post-War Britain, 1945–64: Themes and Perspectives*, London: Pinter.

Marsh, D. (1992) *The New Politics of British Trade Unionism*, Ithaca: ILR Press.

—— (1995) 'Explaining "Thatcherite" Policies: Beyond Uni-Dimensional Explanation', *Political Studies*, 43 (4), 595–613.

Marsh, D. and Rhodes, R. A. W. (eds) (1992) *Implementing Thatcherite Policies: Audit of an Era*, Buckingham: Open University Press.

—— (1995) 'Evaluating Thatcherism: Over the Moon or Sick as a Parrot?', *Politics*, 15 (1), 49–54.

Marsh, D. and Tant, T. (1989) 'There is No Alternative: Mrs Thatcher and the British Political Tradition', *Essex Papers in Politics and Government*, 69.

Mason, T. and Thompson, P. (1991) 'Reflections on a Revolution? The Political Mood in Wartime Britain', in N. Tiratsoo (ed.), *The Attlee Years*, London: Pinter.

Martin, A. (1997) 'What Does Globalisation Have To Do With the Erosion of Welfare States? Sorting Out the Issues', *Zentrum für Sozialpolitik, Universität Bremen, Arbeitspapier Nr. 1 / 1997*.

Marwick, A. (1968) *Britain in the Century of Total War*, London: The Bodley Head.

Matthews, R. C. O. (1968) 'Why Has Britain Had Full Employment Since the War?', *The Economic Journal*, 78, 555–69.

Mercer, H. (1991) 'The Labour Government of 1945–51 and Private Industry', in N. Tiratsoo (ed.), *The Attlee Years*, London: Pinter.

Middlemas, K. (1986) *Power, Competition and the State, Volume 1: Britain in Search of Balance, 1940–61*, London: Macmillan.

—— (1990) *Power, Competition and the State, Volume 2: Threats to the Postwar Settlement, 1961–74*, London: Macmillan.

—— (1991) *Power, Competition and the State, Volume 3: The End of the Postwar Era*, London: Macmillan.

—— (1994) 'The Party, the Industry and the City', in A. Seldon and S. Ball (eds), *Conservative Century: The Conservative Party Since 1900*, Oxford: Oxford University Press.

Middleton, R. (1985) *Towards the Managed Economy: Keynes, the Treasury and the Fiscal Debate of the 1930s*, London: Methuen.

—— (1996) 'The Size and Scope of the Public Sector', in S. Green and R. Whiting (eds), *The Boundaries of the State in Modern Britain*, Cambridge: Cambridge University Press.

Miliband, R. (1970) *Parliamentary Socialism*, 2nd edition, London: Merlin.

—— (1972) *Parliamentary Socialism: A Study in the Politics of Labour*, London: Merlin.

Minogue, K. and Biddiss, M. (eds) (1987) *Thatcherism: Personality and Politics*, London: Macmillan.

Mittelman, J. (ed.) (1996) *Globalization: Critical Reflections*, London: Lynne Rienner.

Mooers, C. (1991) *The Making of Bourgeois Europe*, London: Verso.

Moon, J. (1994) 'Evaluating Thatcherism: Sceptical Versus Synthetic Approaches', *Politics*, 14 (3), 43–9.

Morgan, K. O. (1984) *Labour In Power, 1945–51*, Oxford: Clarendon Press.

—— (1992) *The People's Peace: British History 1945–1990*, Oxford: Oxford University Press.

Mouffe, C. (ed.) *Gramsci and Marxist Theory*, London: Routledge.

Nairn, T. (1964) 'The British Political Elite', *New Left Review*, 23, 19–25.

—— (1976) 'The Twilight of the British State', *New Left Review*, 101 / 2, 3–61.

—— (1981) 'The Crisis of the British State', *New Left Review*, 130, 37–44.

—— (1993) 'The Sole Survivor', *New Left Review*, 200, 41–8.

Nelson, R. (1995) 'Recent Evolutionary Theorising about Economic Change', *Journal of Economic Literature*, 33 (1), 48–81.

Newton, S. (1991) 'The Keynesian Revolution Debate: Time for a New Approach?', in A. Gorst, L. Johnman and W. Scott Lucas (eds), *Contemporary British History, 1931–61*, London: Pinter.

Nield, K. (1980) 'A Symptomatic Dispute? Notes on the Relation Between Marxian Theory and Historical Practice in Britain', *Social Research*, 47 (3), 479–506.

Norton, P. (1991) *The British Polity*, 2nd edition, New York: Longman.

Nugent, N. (1992) 'Public Opinion', in S. George (ed.), *Britain and the European Community*, Oxford: Clarendon Press.

Ohmae, K. (1990) *The Borderless World*, London: Collins.

—— (1995) *The End of the Nation State: The Rise of Regional Economies*, New York: The Free Press.

O'Shea, A. (1984) 'Trusting the People: How Does Thatcherism Work?', in *Formations of Nations and People*, London: Routledge.

Overbeek, H. (1990) *Global Capitalism and National Decline: The Thatcher Decade in Perspective*, London: Unwin Hyman.

Panitch, L. (1996) 'Rethinking the Role of the State', in J. Mittelman (ed.), *Globalization: Critical Reflections*, London: Lynne Rienner.

Panitch, L. and Leys, C. (1997) *The End of Parliamentary Socialism: From New Left to New Labour*, London: Verso.

Peck, J. and Tickell, A. (1994) 'Searching for a New Institutional Fix: The After-Fordist Crisis and Global-Local Disorder', in A. Amin (ed.), *Post-Fordism: A Reader*, Oxford: Blackwell.

Pelling, H. (1984) *The Labour Government 1945–51*, London: Macmillan.

—— (1986) 'The Impact of the War on the Labour Party', in H. Smith (ed.), *War and Social Change*, Manchester: Manchester University Press.

Peters, G. (1997) 'Globalisation and Governance', paper presented at the conference, *Globalisation: Critical Perspectives*, University of Birmingham, 14–16 March.

Pierson, C. (1991) *Beyond the Welfare State? The New Political Economy of Welfare*, Cambridge: Polity.

—— (1996) 'The Post-War Consensus and the Transformation of the Welfare State', paper presented at the *Political Studies Association* Annual Conference, University of Glasgow, 10–12 April.

Pimlott, B. (1988) 'The Myth of Consensus', in L. M. Smith (ed.), *The Making of Britain: Echoes of Greatness*, London: Macmillan.

Piore, M. and Stabel, C. (1984) *The Second Industrial Divide*, New York: Basic Books.

Piven, F. F. (1995) 'Is It Global Economics or Neo-Laissez-Faire?', *New Left Review*, 213, 107–14.

Pollin, R. (1995) 'Financial Structures and Egalitarian Economic Policy', *New Left Review*, 214, 26–61.

Ponting, C. (1989) *Reforming Whitehall*, London: Unwin and Hyman.

Powell, E. (1971) *The Common Market: The Case Against*, Kingswood: Elliot Right Way / Paperfront.

Radice, G. (1992) *Offshore: Britain and the European Idea*, London: I. B. Tauris and Co.

Radice, H. (1995) 'Britain in the World Economy: National Decline, Capitalist Success?', in D. Coates and J. Hillard (eds), *UK Economic Decline: Key Texts*, Hemel Hempstead: Prentice Hall / Harvester Wheatsheaf.

Reich, R. (1992) *The Work of Nations*, New York: Vintage Books.

Richardson, R. (1991) 'Trade Unions and Industrial Rela
    tions', in N. Crafts and N. Woodward (eds), *The British Economy
    Since 1945*, Oxford: Oxford University Press.
Riddell, P. (1983) *The Thatcher Government*, Oxford: Martin Rogerson.
—— (1991) *The Thatcher Era and Its Legacy*, Oxford: Basil Black-
    well.
Ridley, N. (1992) *My Style of Government*, London: Fontana.
Ritschel, D. (1995) 'The Making of Consensus: The Nuffield College
    Conferences During the Second World War', *Twentieth Century
    British History*, 6 (3), 267–301.
Roll, E. (1985) *Crowded Hours*, London: Faber.
Rollings, N. (1988) 'British Budgetary Policy, 1945–52: A "Keynesian
    Revolution"?', *Economic History Review*, XLI, 283–98.
—— (1994) 'Poor Mr Butskell: A Short Life, Wrecked by Schizophre-
    nia?', *Twentieth Century British History*, 5 (2), 183–205.
Romer, P. (1993) 'Idea Gaps and Object Gaps in Economic Develop-
    ment', *Journal of Monetary Economics*, 32, 543–73.
Rose, R. (1991) 'Comparing Forms of Comparative Analysis', *Political
    Studies*, 39, 446–62.
Rose, R. and Peters, B. G. (1978) *Can Government Go Bankrupt?*
    London: Macmillan.
Rubinstein, W. D. (1990) 'Cultural Explanations for Britain's Economic
    Decline: How True?', in B. Collins and K. Robbins (eds), *British
    Culture and Economic Decline*, New York: St Martin's Press.
—— (1994) *Capitalism, Culture and Decline in Britain*, London: Rout-
    ledge.
Rueschemeyer, D. and Skocpol, T. (eds) (1996) *States, Social Know-
    ledge and the Origins of Modern Social Policies*, Princeton, NJ:
    Princeton University Press.
Russell, C. (1996) 'New Labour: Old Tory Writ Large?' *New Left
    Review*, 219, 78–88.
Sanders, D. (1990) *Losing An Empire, Finding a Role*, Basingstoke:
    Macmillan.
Saville, J. (1988) *The Labour Movement in Britain*, London: Faber and
    Faber.
Scharpf, F. W. (1987) *Crisis and Choice in European Social Democracy*,
    Ithaca, NY: Cornell University Press (trans. Ruth Crowley and Fred
    Thompson).
Schneer, J. (1987) 'The Labour Left and the General Election of 1945',
    in J. Bean (ed.), *The Political Culture of Modern Britain*, London:
    Hamish Hamilton.
Seldon, A. (1994a) 'Consensus: A Debate Too Long?', *Parliamentary
    Affairs*, 47 (4), 501–14.

—— (1994b) 'The Conservative Party', in D. Kavanagh and A. Seldon (eds), *The Major Effect*, London: Macmillan.

Semetko, H. A., Blumler, J. G., Gurevitch, M. and Weaver, D. (1991) *The Formation of Campaign Agendas*, London: Lawrence Erlbaum Associates.

Shanks, M. (1977) *Planning and Politics: The British Experience 1960–76*, London: Allen and Unwin / Political and Economic Planning.

Shaw, E. (1996) *The Labour Party Since 1945*, Oxford: Blackwell.

—— (1997) 'The Trajectory of New Labour: Some Preliminary Thoughts', paper presented at the 1997 annual meeting of the American Political Science Association, The Sheraton Washington Hotel, 28–31 August.

Singh, J. V. (1990) *Organisational Evolution: New Directions*, London: Sage.

Smith, D. (1987) *The Rise and Fall of Monetarism*, Harmondsworth: Penguin.

Smith, H. (ed.) (1986) *War and Social Change: British Society in the Second World War*, Manchester: Manchester University Press.

Smith, K. (1989) *The British Economic Crisis: Its Past and Future*, London: Penguin.

Strasser, H. and Randall, S. C. (1981) *An Introduction to Theories of Social Change*, London: Routledge and Kegan Paul.

Sztompka, P. (1993) *The Sociology of Social Change*, Oxford: Blackwell.

Taylor, I. (1991) 'Labour and the Impact of the War, 1939–45', in N. Tiratsoo (ed.), *The Attlee Years*, London: Pinter.

Taylor, P. J. (1989a) 'Britain's Changing Role in the World Economy', in J. Mohan (ed.), *The Political Geography of Contemporary Britain*, London: Macmillan.

—— (1989b) 'Britain's Century of Decline: a World-Systems Interpretation', in J. Anderson and A. Cochrane (eds), *A State of Crisis*, London: Hodder and Stoughton / Open University Press.

—— (1992) 'Changing Political Relations', in P. Cloke (ed.), *Policy and Change in Thatcher's Britain*, Oxford: Pergamon Press.

Taylor, R. (1996) 'The Heath Government and Industrial Relations: Myth and Reality', in S. Ball and A. Seldon (eds), *The Heath Government, 1970–74*, London: Longman.

Thatcher, M. (1993) *The Downing Street Years*, London: Harper Collins.

—— (1995) *The Path to Power*, London: Harper Collins.

Thompson, E. P. (1965) 'The Peculiarities of the English', *The Socialist Register*, 2, 311–62.

244 *Bibliography*

—— (1978) *The Poverty of Theory*, London: Merlin Press.

Thompson, G. (1984) 'Economic Intervention in the Postwar Economy', in G. McLennan, D. Held and S. Hall, *State and Society in Contemporary Britain: A Critical Introduction*, Oxford: Blackwell.

Tiratsoo, N. (ed.) (1991) *The Attlee Years*, London: Pinter.

Tiratsoo, N. and Tomlinson, J. (1993) *Industrial Efficiency and State Intervention, Labour 1939–51*, London: Routledge.

Titmuss, R. (1950) *Problems of Social Policy*, London: Allen and Unwin.

Tomlinson, J. (1981) 'Why Was There Never a "Keynesian Revolution" in Economic Policy?', *Economy and Society*, 10 (1), 72–87.

—— (1984) 'A "Keynesian Revolution" in Economic Policy-Making', *Economic History Review*, XXXVII, 258–62.

—— (1994) *Government and Enterprise Since 1900*, Oxford: Clarendon Press.

—— (1995) 'The Iron Quadrilateral: Political Obstacles to Economic Reform under the Attlee Government', *Journal of British Studies*, 34, 90–111.

—— (1997) *Democratic Socialism and Economic Policy: The Attlee Years 1945–51*, Cambridge: Cambridge University Press.

Turner, J. (1989) 'The Decline of Post-War Consensus: Commentary Three', in A. Gorst, L. Johnman and W. Scott Lucas (eds), *Post-War Britain 1945–64: Themes and Perspectives*, London: Pinter.

Wallace, H. (1995) 'Britain out on a Limb?', *Political Quarterly*, 66 (1), 46–58.

Wallace, W. (1986) 'What Price Independence? Sovereignty and Interdependence in British Politics', *International Affairs*, 62 (3), 367–89.

Ward, H. (1997) 'The Possibility of an Evolutionary Explanation of the State's Role in Modes of Regulation', in J. Stanyer and G. Stoker (eds), *Contemporary Political Studies 1997, Volume 1*, Belfast: PSA.

Watson, M. (1997) 'The Changing Face of Macroeconomic Stabilisation: From Growth Through Indigenous Investment to Growth Through Inward Investment?', in J. Stanyer and G. Stoker (eds), *Contemporary Political Studies, 1997, Volume 2*, Belfast: PSA.

—— (1999a) 'The New Malthusian Economics: Globalisation, Inward Investment and the Discursive Construction of the Competitive Imperative', in C. Hay and D. Marsh (eds), *Globalisation, Welfare Retrenchment and the State*, Basingstoke: Macmillan, forthcoming.

—— (1999b) 'Re-thinking Capital Mobility, Re-regulating Financial Markets', in C. Hay and D. Marsh (eds), *Putting the 'P' Back into IPE*, *New Political Economy*, Special Issue, 4 (1), forthcoming.

Watson, M. and Hay, C. (1998) 'In the Dedicated Pursuit of Dedicated

Capital: Restoring an Indigenous Investment Ethic to British Capitalism', *New Political Economy*, 3 (3), 407–26.

Weiner, M. J. (1981) *English Culture and the Decline of the Industrial Spirit, 1850–1980*, Cambridge: Cambridge University Press.

Wendt, A. (1987) 'The Agency / Structure Problem in International Relations', *International Organization*, 41 (3), 335–70.

Wickham-Jones, M. (1995) 'Anticipating Social Democracy, Preempting Anticipations: Economic Policy-Making in the British Labour Party, 1987–1992', *Politics and Society*, 23 (4), 465–94.

Wilks, S. (1996) 'Britain and Europe: An Awkward Partner or an Awkward State?', *Politics*, 16 (3), 159–65.

Winch, D. (1969) *Economics and Policy*, London: Fontana.

Wincott, D. (1999) 'Globalization and European Integration', in C. Hay and D. Marsh (eds), *Demystifying Globalization*, London: Macmillan, forthcoming.

Wolfe, J. (1991) 'State Power and Ideology in Britain: Mrs Thatcher's Privatisation Programme', *Political Studies*, 39, 237–52.

Young, H. (1989) *One of Us*, London: Pan.

—— (1994) 'The Prime Minster', in D. Kavanagh and A. Seldon (eds), *The Major Effect*, London: Macmillan.

Young, H. and Sloman, A. (1986) *The Thatcher Phenomenon*, London: BBC Books.

Young, M., Henn, M. and Hill, N. (1997) 'Labour Renewal Under Blair? A Local Membership Study in Middleham', in J. Stanyer and G. Stoker (eds), *Contemporary Political Studies, 1996, Volume 1*, Belfast: PSA.

Zysman, J. (1983) *Governments, Markets and Growth: Financial Systems and the Politics of Industrial Change*, Oxford: Robertson.

Index